# WHAT'S *RIGHT* WITH AMERICA

HONORABLE PAUL JOHNSON
& LARRY ALDRICH

# WHAT'S *RIGHT* WITH AMERICA

### ...AND HOW WE CAN KEEP IT THAT WAY!

A POST HILL PRESS BOOK
ISBN: 979-8-89565-055-4
ISBN (eBook): 979-8-89565-056-1

What's Right with America:
...And How We Can Keep It That Way!
© 2025 by Honorable Paul Johnson & Larry Aldrich
All Rights Reserved

Cover design by Conroy Accord

This book, as well as any other Post Hill Press publications, may be purchased in bulk quantities at a special discounted rate. Contact orders@posthillpress.com for more information.

This is a work of nonfiction. All people, locations, events, and situations are portrayed to the best of the author's memory.

No part of this book may be reproduced, stored in a retrieval system, or transmitted by any means without the written permission of the author and publisher.

Post Hill Press
New York • Nashville
posthillpress.com

Published in the United States of America
1 2 3 4 5 6 7 8 9 10

*Dedication by Paul Johnson:*

To General Wesley Clark, whose service as Supreme Allied Commander and candidate for President of the United States, are a profound source of inspiration. But your continual service to foster dialogue among diverse voices in defense of freedom inspired this work. And so we dedicate this book to you and the many veterans who continue to defend this nation—not just in battle, but against division and discord from tribalism and partisanship. You helped us understand that if you want to be patriotic quit insulting other Americans. More than anyone else you and those you represent are what's right with America.

*Dedication by Larry Aldrich:*

For James ("Jim") H. Click, Jr., a business and political leader endowed with the essence of what truly makes America great, a man with a heart of gold and a once-in-a-lifetime leader who left his marks all over Tucson, the State of Arizona, and America. Jim, I'm honored and lucky to know you...

# CONTENTS

*Introduction:* Why This Book, Now ..................................11

## PART I

### AMERICAN COURAGE:
### LAUNCHING "THE GREAT EXPERIMENT"

Chapter 1  Living the American Dream ........................35
Chapter 2  Birthing America and Securing Her Future....58
Chapter 3  Calling the Philosophers...............................71
Chapter 4  Innovating through the Lens of the
           Enlightenment ...............................................94

## PART II

### AMERICAN IMAGINATION:
### INSPIRING FREEDOM, COLLABORATION,
### AND CREATIVITY

Chapter 5  Embracing the Constitution and the
           Institutions It Created .................................111
Chapter 6  Supporting the Privilege of
           Self-Governance .........................................129
Chapter 7  Equal Protection of the Laws: America's
           "Second Founding" .....................................158
Chapter 8  Creating Opportunities for Prosperity ........170

## PART III

### AMERICAN GRIT: PROTECTING THE NATION

| | | |
|---|---|---|
| Chapter 9 | Entering the Era of International Tension | 199 |
| Chapter 10 | Protecting Americans at Home, as We Rediscover Our "Better Angels" | 221 |
| Chapter 11 | Honoring Our Individualism | 240 |
| Chapter 12 | Defending Democracy and the Rule of Law | 250 |

## PART IV

### AMERICAN GENEROSITY AND FORESIGHT: THE HORN OF PLENTY

| | | |
|---|---|---|
| Chapter 13 | Ensuring the Prosperity of America | 273 |
| Chapter 14 | Encouraging Entrepreneurial Opportunities | 294 |
| Chapter 15 | Ensuring an Abundant Future | 307 |

*Conclusion:* The Case for Optimism.................322
*Acknowledgments*..................329
*About the Authors*..................335

# INTRODUCTION
# WHY THIS BOOK, NOW

Rosa Parks sat on a bus next to Paul Johnson, the young mayor of Phoenix, on their way to speak to advance the Martin Luther King Jr. legacy. They thumbed through a book of the historical events when Parks was arrested for not surrendering her seat on a bus to a white woman. A photographer captured the visage of a young police officer, hair cut short, a leather strap across his chest, who fingerprinted her. Paul said, "That officer looks like the wall of oppression." Parks shot a disapproving glance at Paul and immediately scolded him, saying, "Now, Mayor, don't say bad things about that young man. He was a good person. Just like other Americans, he was doing his job to care for his family." Parks opined that he was not doing the wrong thing—"The law was doing the wrong thing."

Emotions overcame Paul. He was so used to hearing divisive issues described as good versus evil. Yet, here was this woman who lived through grave injustices in America. She refused to allow those injustices to become reasons to harm other Americans. She loved America, even with its many faults. And she loved other Americans. She was optimistic about our future. She inspired and embodied the best portraits of Americans.

This book is about what's right with America. We ask you to set aside, just for a while, all the negative information bombarding you. We will give you new (and renewed) ways to think about America. For some, it will re-awaken their faith in the US. For others who have not heard similar arguments, analyses, and critical facts, we will present an awakening about the many gifts our nation gives us.

Data drives our view of American optimism, about what's *right* with America. The historical evidence and prospects enlighten our optimism about and confidence in the US. But there is a spirit here that is much harder to capture, the spirit of those who came before us, the spirit of the wealthy and poor, heroes and hard hats, inventors and moms and dads, that we witnessed. Our inspiration comes from people all over America and the challenges they overcame (or tried to overcome). Their belief that the hard work and stress were worth it rang bells in our minds as we wrote this book. Their stories inspired us and made us proud to be Americans. We learned—and continue to learn—from many people who shaped our country, people who shaped us.

In this book, we share examples that support vital concepts. In most of these examples, only one of us was present. Yet, we use the word "we" throughout because, together and collectively, these people helped shape this book. From being mayor of the nation's sixth largest city (fifth largest today), publishing major newspapers, being engaged in political work around the world and presidential campaigns, being an entrepreneur, and prosecuting "white collar" criminals, we were blessed to meet many people from all walks of life who inspired us about what's right and best about America, and her and our unique advantages.

We did not write this book for those considered our leaders. We strongly believe in the role of leadership. Leaders should inspire us toward a more significant aim and thus encourage us to sacrifice some of our beliefs for what we call the collective ideal. Most importantly, we need to know where we are going—as individuals and as a country—and believe in our abilities to get there. Unfortunately, we are disappointed today that some of our so-called leaders provide little hope, optimism, and inspiration to drive that more significant, collective aim.

We wrote this book for ordinary people—those who don't see themselves as leaders, and those whose importance is often overlooked. What amazes us is how our American culture, based on individual rights and freedoms, frequently requires ordinary people to step into the role of leader.

★ ★ ★

The operations that publish a newspaper are like those found in many other mid- or large-sized businesses. Such businesses employ top managers, middle managers, and those who do the daily work to publish a newspaper. While top management—the suits, as they might be called—make decisions about the newspaper's long-term direction, the reporters, photographers, and first-level editors create the essence of the business.

Reporters work hard to write stories that achieve the ideal we call "truth." They find sources of information, try to create an interesting angle to the stories they craft, and sort and assemble facts in ways attractive to readers. If these reporters are exceptional, the facts tell stories themselves. Then, these stories allow the audiences to decide what to conclude.

Of course, a story based on facts and fairness is ideal. Not all reporters are talented enough to accomplish it. So, in the newspaper business, editors review the stories to look for factual errors and ensure that multiple sources of information are used. The standards are high for newspapers because, unlike their social media counterparts, they may be liable if a story is wrong.

Reporters and editors are often remarkable and talented, usually true skeptics of what they initially see and hear. The nature of their business to investigate wrongdoing frequently causes them to miss what is going right. But they provide an incredible service to readers and society. They work hard under increasingly challenging conditions and criticisms.

However, another group of people employed in businesses like newspapers is often overlooked. They are the people who clean the floors and bathrooms, run the printing presses (and their electronic equivalents), and load and unload the newspapers onto large trucks. Many of these people wake up at 3 a.m. to deliver a newspaper to someone's front step.

Reporters, editors, and delivery personnel are the people in the "middle" of America. They work hard while hoping their leaders will best represent them. These people write the stories, deliver the papers, secure our streets, and serve in our militaries. They are the people who do most of the work in this large country. Unfortunately, too many leaders overlook them, don't know them, and don't understand their hopes, dreams, and wishes.

★ ★ ★

Rosa Parks, a beacon of civil rights activism, is celebrated for her pivotal role in challenging racial segregation in the United States. On December 1, 1955, in Montgomery, Alabama, Parks took a courageous stand by refusing to give up her bus seat to a white passenger. This nonviolent protest ignited the Montgomery Bus Boycott. Her resolute stance against segregation laws helped galvanize the civil rights movement, leading to a US Supreme Court ruling that declared segregation on public buses unconstitutional.

Before that day, Parks had not been considered a leader on the Montgomery bus. She didn't lead a significant civil rights organization or head some large company. She wasn't even in elective office, nor did she ever try to be elected. She was a person going to work whose feet were tired, and she didn't want to walk to the back of the bus.

Parks was just one of those people from the middle. She had every right to be angry at being arrested. Yet she had the decency to see police officers as human beings, empathetic and caring for people other than herself. Her perspective was much broader than that of the leaders around her.

As the authors of this book, we are deeply concerned that the perspectives of some leaders are limited. They may overlook those individuals they work with, those who show us daily the value of their work. Instead of inspiring us, many leaders are preoccupied with following popular trends, often set by other leaders. They are so obsessed with what is going wrong—with the "darkness"—that they do not spend their valuable time believing in the "light"—cheerful, optimistic, what's going right. We strongly believe that it must be the job of those recognized as our leaders to provide the light, the optimism. If not, who will?

Where leadership is in the shortest supply is in our political system—not just those who are elected but those who report on those who are elected. Many of these political leaders frame what's wrong with America to advocate for a cause or a particular interest. However, only from an optimistic perspective can we truly represent the common interest among all of us.

The common interest cannot be understood without understanding those living and working in the middle. These people want their children to attend good schools with strong and positive learning. They understand and live the differences between right and wrong, lessons instilled in elementary school. They are the people who pay their bills, struggle to pay their taxes, and are worried about how they will pay to fix the carburetor on their car. Most importantly, these are the people whose only lobbyists for their hopes and wishes are the ones they elect.

★ ★ ★

At a private table long ago, we listened as former President Ronald Reagan and Speaker of the House of Representatives Tip O'Neill told terrific stories of one another. These two men learned to set aside political differences to enjoy the gifts the other had to offer. We sat at the table with these two masters, trying to learn lessons that might help guide our lives. We asked these two giants what the most important thing we could do was to represent our constituents' views properly.

O'Neill said not to forget that issues were less important than the relationships you built. Reagan said, "Mayor, sometimes when we advocate a cause, people hear what's wrong with America. It is easy to forget that we live in the greatest place the earth has ever witnessed. Ensure you always leave people hopeful and believing in who we are."

Co-author Larry Aldrich saw Reagan from a different perspective. He started working in the US Justice Department when Jimmy Carter was president and witnessed firsthand the federal government's leadership transition to Reagan. Despite the dramatically different policies, especially concerning how the behavior of large private companies should be regulated, there was a "peaceful transfer of power" from a Democratic administration to a Republican one. Inspired, we watched how both presidents allowed the Justice Department to work professionally and carefully without regard to partisan politics. Even though both presidents had quite different ideas, the "rule of law" was a constant force, with little, if any, political interference.

However, Reagan wasn't a unique president in our history. Pierre Salinger, the famous press secretary for President John F. Kennedy, said at a dinner Paul attended that he observed how much Kennedy and Reagan had in common. While they had different approaches, they were both highly optimistic about America. They had incredible faith in what Americans could accomplish.

We recognized similar enlightened leadership from the corporate side. Many of our nation's most significant leaders come from the private sector, which makes us so different from our authoritarian foes worldwide. The most considerable investor of our lifetime, Warren Buffett, told us, when we asked about all that was going wrong in our economy, that when he started investing, he heard apocalyptic views about the prospects for American businesses. But he said, "You live in the United States of America; this is a great country (with great businesses) to bet on...but just remember that you get to sit in the shade today because someone planted that tree a long time ago." In other words, we reap today the benefits from the hard work of other Americans before us.

★ ★ ★

We began our journey to create this book when Larry reached out to Paul to focus on this great cause of American optimism. Larry was inspired by Paul's podcast, *The Optimistic American*. The podcast promotes the idea that the brilliance of America came from our government empowering the individual over itself. A core value of the podcast is that as America promoted the power of the individual, we dramatically improved the human condition. It drives the story about what is right with America. The podcast is about the light in America, optimism.

Promoting that light, inspired by the giants on whose backs we stand, is the cause of both of our lives now.

We were inspired by leaders whose greatness became most evident when they lost key elections or other challenges. As we stood in the audience of Senator John McCain of Arizona as he closed his campaign for president, we could see the pain on his face that one feels after any significant loss. Yet he tipped his hat to Senator Barack Obama, the newly elected president, and those who supported the president-elect. He said Obama inspired millions of Americans who once wrongly believed that they had little at stake or little influence in the election of an American president. "This is an historic election, and I recognize the special significance it has for African Americans and for the special pride that must be theirs tonight."

McCain, as he neared death—a man who spent years in a Vietnam prison, where his captors broke his bones and convinced him that he had no chance to survive—told us that we would thrive in these challenging times. He told us that while Americans often argued and competed through raucous public debates, we are more similar than we thought. He said, "If only we remember that and benefit each other from the presumption that we all love our country, we will get through these challenging times. We will come through them stronger than before. We always do."

Most of all, the sentiments underlined in our book come from the stories of ordinary people, albeit those who sometimes do extraordinary things. Chuck Yeager, the man who broke the sound barrier as a test pilot, told us not to use safety as an excuse to stop those who drive toward the edge of the possible. When asked how to respond to our country's complex problems, he said, "The cockpit shakes the most right before you go through the sound barrier." In other words, the journey to the destination may be rough but well worth the ride.

Our lists include so many people who are not known to most Americans. Sophia Lopez-Espindola confronted us at her son's funeral after he died in a drive-by shooting; the angry mother demanded the Phoenix mayor do more. She jumped in and led the effort when we called her later to help start a Mothers Against Gangs chapter. She worked hard, lobbying for legislation that cut violent crimes in Phoenix among children by over 40 percent. Though her own life was hard, she worked diligently to make the lives of others better.

Medal of Honor recipient Herrera Silvestre advanced, alone, against heavy machine-gun fire ravaging his platoon. He would lose both feet after stepping on a mine, and yet he pinned the enemy with rifle fire until his platoon came to safety. When we called him a hero, he said, "I'm not a hero; I'm an American. I appreciate all the gifts America gave me."

There's also Lieutenant General Robert Johnston, who retired from a long service in the US Marine Corps. He was not native-born but heard the call of the America he adopted to protect our extraordinary freedoms. He served in many capacities in the Marines, but most notably as the chief of staff to General Norman Schwarzkopf during Operation Desert Storm to liberate Kuwait from the invaders from Iraq. A self-made and selfless man, he brought his leadership experience to continue serving the business community in Tucson, Arizona.

We find these people who inspired us in extraordinary roles and everyday life. We see them in the local firehouse, police stations, and teaching in our schools. Many serve on aircraft carriers, submarines, and in the air. We met them in intelligence and forward deployment positions. We met them in newsrooms and in the stories they wrote or edited. We met them in the hundreds of entrepreneurs who test the standard, challenge the status quo, and push thinking to cure cancer, extend human life, and create cars that drive themselves. But we also found them as seemingly "ordinary" people who struggle to pay their bills or make parole, who try to keep their kids in schools, and who work hard, yet who always find time to coach a local sports team, serve as part of a neighborhood block watch, or feed people experiencing homelessness.

Both of us are blessed to live extraordinary lives. It is not that there was anything special about either of us—we are just two guys who came from the lower and middle classes of America. Our lives were great because of our opportunities to see and work with people in America who are committed to success, people at all levels of society, and to witness and benefit from their significant contributions. We noticed it so many times; we heard so many stories, and it became clear that it was more than a coincidence. There was something special about the place they and we call home—America!—a country with significant assets and optimism.

★ ★ ★

Optimism, however, is a choice. Optimism focuses on the future, while pessimism dwells on the past. Realistic optimism grounds itself in believing that if we focus on innovation and allow people to own what they create, our history says we can overcome significant challenges. We found that optimism in America is often more abundant in ordinary people than those leading them. And as we make clear throughout this book, you can find great optimism in the data about American strengths. The data paints a vastly different picture of America than many leaders paint today.

In the data and opinions we share in the stories contained in this book, we do not ignore the darker sides, the complex challenges. Darker sides we witness and know exist. Like you, from our experiences, we gained keen insights regarding significant challenges in America and around the world over the last seventy-five years: Vietnam, the Cold War between the US and Russia, three impeachments of American presidents, 9/11, and many other events that left many wondering if the US was a declining power, a democracy sliding to oblivion like so many past superpowers. Like many of you, we listened as American critics argued at those times that the Soviet Union, Japan, the European Union, or China would overpower the US, leaving us somehow in the ash heap of history. In every instance, our nation grew stronger.

During those years, we heard how American capitalism would eventually fail. Yet America's guiding principles protected the rights of individuals, defended equal rights, human rights, and civil rights, developed free markets, protected private property rights, and led to a society based on free enterprise, dramatically improving the daily results for all Americans. Capitalism continually not only survived but created greater prosperity for more of its citizens than its socialist/authoritarian counterparts in other countries.

At a human level, we heard stories of people of every race, gender, and economic status overcoming incredible odds to succeed in America—stories of those who capitalized on the advantages of our educational system, worked hard, and built good lives and wealth. We watched the amazing ceremonies of immigrants becoming US citizens, listening to their hopes and joys. We watched people move repeatedly from the bottom quartile of income and net worth to the top or second quartile. We know the American dream is alive and well.

America's wealth and prosperity often drive leaders of authoritarian governments worldwide to anger and envy. With their state-controlled economies and state-controlled media, they watch the seeming chaos of American democracy (including free speech) and markets and cannot imagine how we survive. Not only do we endure, we thrive! We continue to grow ever stronger.

Authoritarian competitors believe they will surpass American democracy and capitalism because of the infighting among our democracy's political leaders. Yet, Americans intuitively understand that unchecked power and systems corrupt over time. Our opponents miss the checks and balances hardwired within our American government and how such systems, stressed at times, prevent consolidated power. Moreover, these systems continue to root out corruption, continually providing oversight on behalf of the best interests of the American people.

Critics may laugh at American confidence and hubris, but they miss the core ingredients of the American founding principles that allow us to address significant societal problems rationally. Despite shifting tides and political excesses, we live in a country that cherishes initiative and self-responsibility and defends our American Founders'[1] focus on freedom—gifts that enable us to benefit from our hard work. After nearly 250 years, this country still enjoys the unique status of a free nation envied by others worldwide, a nation road-tested repeatedly!

Fortunately, incredible abundance exists across the United States. This abundance is the fruit of the "truths" our nation held from its inception: that all individuals have fundamental rights. This was our moral foundation. When we rediscover these truths, we reconnect with our nation's power. Our Founders had no illusions that they were creating a flawless new homeland; they just wanted it to be better than the monarchy they had left behind, to create "a more perfect Union."

---

[1] We use the terms "Founders" and sometimes "Framers," but rarely "Founding Fathers." All the recognized Founders were men, but we note that many women at the time were freedom fighters.

We stand in awe of the insight of our Founders and the principles they chose that have survived the incredible test of time. When we take a refreshingly deep dive into the thinking behind the US Constitution and the Declaration of Independence (from England and its monarch), we uncover the reasons for the success of this country: these "moral-focused" documents based on spiritual components that are essential to understanding the rights of individual citizens.

We can only begin to appreciate America when we see how the Founders chose to prioritize the individual over the government, how they balanced powers and separated institutions that preserve our lives as Americans, and how they outlined a justice system that protects the rights of the individual over the political power of the majority. We see the role of educators that enable people of all ages to learn and tolerate each other's differences. With all the challenges of a free press, we see how the private sector check became a check on the government.

★ ★ ★

We refuse to mire this book in the divisiveness of the 2024 political race. Instead, we remind ourselves that America's strength transcends the success of any single leader or political figure. The past presidential election underscores a more profound truth: The United States remains an exceptional nation built on enduring principles enshrined in our Constitution, our beacon of stability in turbulent times. While every campaign brings lessons—victory always risks sowing the seeds of future defeat, and in every setback lies an opportunity for renewal—the foundation of our democracy ensures that the nation moves ever forward.

Moreover, the 2024 elections emphasize the robust engagement of the American electorate, demonstrating a thriving democracy where our citizens actively participate in shaping the future more to their desires. The diversity reflected, especially at the top of the election ticket, testifies to America's ongoing and strengthening commitment to inclusivity, a broader narrative about the nation's ability to embrace change while remaining anchored to its founding principles of liberty and justice for all.

For Democrats and other voters who feel disheartened by Donald Trump's re-election, it's crucial to remember that the strength of American democracy lies in its foundational principles and institutions, designed to endure beyond any single election or administration. We truly believe this election reaffirms the resilience of the American political system with the opportunity to regroup and advocate for change in the next cycle. The ability to voice dissent, organize, and influence policy remain cornerstones of the American republic.

American elections will continue, and how each side absorbs the lessons of 2024 matters. We began this reflection with Rosa Parks because her legacy encapsulates an abiding belief: The United States is expansive enough for all its people, but fulfilling this promise demands empathy—not only for the least among us but often from them. Her words resonate in this book's thesis: What is *right* with America begins with the Constitution, whose checks, balances, and protections anchor our freedoms and provide a framework for progress.

Unlike after the 2020 presidential election, this past election underscored America's commitment to the peaceful transition of power from a Democratic administration to a soon-to-be Republican one, reinforcing the strength and stability of our country's political framework. These elements paint the picture of a nation that, despite its many challenges, continues to embody its founding principles.

The 2024 election highlighted two key divisions: education and gender. Gender played a notable role in candidate preferences. Among men, Donald Trump led by an 18 point margin (58 percent to 40 percent), whereas Kamala Harris garnered a 16 point advantage among women (57 percent to 41 percent).[2] This reflects a continuation of gender-based voting trends observed in prior elections, where men have leaned Republican while women tended to support Democratic candidates. Regarding education, Harris performed better than Trump for Americans with college post-secondary degrees, while Trump did better with voters with less formal education.[3]

Many young men, particularly new voters, rallied behind Trump, inspired by figures in alternative media—podcasters and streamers who spoke directly to their frustrations and ambitions. Conversely, women, energized by issues like abortion rights, mostly backed Harris, though her support fell short of President Joe Biden's 2020 winning margins. These shifts reflect deeper undercurrents of dissatisfaction rooted in the nation's complex social and political landscape.

---

[2] Pew Research Center, "How Voters See the Harris-Trump Matchup, and How Engaged They Are in the 2024 Election," *Pew Research Center*, published October 2024, accessed November 29, 2024, https://www.pewresearch.org.

[3] Associated Press, "AP VoteCast: How America voted in 2024," *Associated Press, https://apnews.com/projects/election-results-2024/votecast/ (accessed December 3, 2024).*

A liberal society, by design, fosters progress. The civil rights movement, economic liberalism, and global trade have expanded freedoms and opportunities, while immigration and technological innovation have fueled growth. Yet, this progress has not come without cost. The 2024 campaign brought renewed attention to the "lost," often white men—a demographic burdened by the unintended consequences of globalization and liberal ideals.

Lower-income men, regardless of race, often feel abandoned by the very systems that claim to offer equality and opportunity. Suppressing their voices bred anger and alienation, particularly among younger men who see no place for themselves in a rapidly evolving society. Politics, inevitably, found them—and gave their frustration a megaphone.

This dynamic highlights a core theme of this book: the resilience of American institutions. While the nation faces polarization and tribalism, points we discuss in the chapters ahead—America's enduring structures, founded on principles of liberty and balance of power, offer stability. The 2024 election revealed this tension. Traditional liberals and conservatives share more in common than the progressive left and MAGA[4] loyalists, yet both groups struggle to confront the extremes within their ranks. We'll discuss these issues in the chapters ahead.

Traditional conservatives and liberals prioritize maximizing individual liberty and safeguarding institutions. Their disagreements revolve mainly around the size of government and how to distribute the revenues (i.e., taxes) that run govern-

---

[4] "Make America Great Again," the slogan popularized during Trump's 2016 presidential campaign, a political movement centered around populism, economic revitalization, and a focus on American interests.

ment. In contrast, progressive left and MAGA factions focus more on identity politics, framing individuals by group affiliation. These extremes, from cries of "white genocide" on the right to "white privilege" on the left, often reject the individualistic ideals at the heart of the American experiment.

Instead of uniting against these excesses, traditionalists often tolerate them, wary of fracturing their coalitions. This form of tribalism fosters moral relativism and deepens divides. The situation's urgency is apparent, though, and we believe it's time to unite against these extremes. The real threat to American values lies within the views of these extremes—forces that view institutional checks as impediments to their ambitions, seeking to undermine the structures that ensure a fair and just society.

The 2024 presidential campaign revealed much about America's challenges and its resilience. As we argue in this book, our nation's greatest strength lies in its capacity to learn, adapt, and renew. Our institutions, from the judicial system to the electoral process itself, remain the backbone of our democracy. Through its interpretation and application of the Constitution, the judiciary ensures that the rule of law prevails. The electoral process, through its fairness and transparency, upholds the principle of democratic representation. Even amid heated divisions, the Constitution continues to protect the nation from both demagoguery and tyranny, enabling a uniquely American promise: that every generation can strive for a freer, fairer, and more prosperous society.

# WHAT'S RIGHT WITH AMERICA

★ ★ ★

Liberal democracy—America's democracy—endures and strengthens over time. As noted by Martin Luther King Jr., "The arc of the moral universe is long, but it bends towards justice."[5] We believe humanity's moral arc and democratic institutions bend toward freedom, justice, and liberty. The 2022 war in Ukraine powerfully underscores the necessity of the battle between freedom/democracy and dictators. These are battles worth investing our talents, treasures, and even our lives to triumph over those seeking to wrest them away.

This book honors the wisdom and grace that gave birth to America. America today is better and stronger than you know! Indeed, it is much better than the current power center leaders (politicians, media, other loud voices) want you to believe. American optimism grows when we are reminded of those strengths.

This is the time for this book. We welcome you along for the ride. It is time for Americans to have this awakening, or what will be, for many, a reawakening. We know people are losing faith in what America has always stood for, but it is time to remind ourselves about who we are, what we have accomplished, and how that happened. It is time to look hard at the alternatives to recognize why we succeeded in the past while the government systems in other countries failed. And it is time to look hard at the foundations of this place we call America, to remember the common narrative that holds us

---

[5] Martin Luther King, Jr., "I Have a Dream," *American Rhetoric*, https://www.americanrhetoric.com/speeches/mlkihaveadream.htm (accessed May 30, 2024).

together, that designs and protects the rights of the individual over collective interests and, for that matter, over the limited rights of government. And to know that if we stay the course, our future will be even more spectacular.

Finally, we author this book because we still believe in the visions and executions that our Founders designed almost 250 years ago.

## ABOUT THE AUTHORS

Meet Paul Johnson and Larry Aldrich, two Americans from different backgrounds who joined forces at a critical moment in this country's history. It was crystal clear to them both that America was under attack—not just by foreign actors, but from within its borders. A possibly existential question facing Americans today is: Do we want to focus on tearing America down or building it up? After many years of diving back into American history to determine how we arrived at where we are today, both Larry and Paul came to the same conclusion: It is time to recognize America for what it truly represents—the best, the brightest, and the most powerful force in the world. The title says it all: This book is about American optimism, about what's *right* with America!

Our belief in what's right with America comes from firsthand experience. Larry operated two of our nation's newspapers; Paul led one of America's biggest cities. Larry worked in the US Justice Department; Paul founded several tech companies. Larry came from the middle class; Paul came from something less. They have the views of someone who made the law and someone who enforced it; someone who held truth to power and someone who was elected to power; someone who founded tech companies and someone whose job was in the older economy world. They come from the views of someone who started in the middle class and someone whose family dreamed of becoming a part of it.

Larry was born in 1952 to an upper middle class-income family living on Long Island, a family that valued education and reading. He benefited from New York's strong educational system during the 1950s and 1960s. He decided to become an engineer and build spaceships (following the landing of the Apollo mission on the Moon in 1969), entering Georgia Tech in 1970. But America's essence as a "land of many new opportunities" arrived before his graduation, encouraging a move to law school.

Larry's professional journey took him into the Justice Department as an antitrust lawyer. He served as the president and chief executive for the two daily newspapers in Tucson, Arizona, for eight years. He gained a deep appreciation of the media's oversight role across America to prevent government corruption and retain the power of the free marketplace of ideas. Larry learned firsthand about the conflicts of using news content to sell advertising, the challenges of newspapers being displaced by the internet, and the problem of negative news dominating positive news. Yet it was here, leading the presses that provided daily news to Americans, that Larry realized the incredible opportunities available to Americans today.

His work as the president and CEO of the newspapers, seeing the power of media voices and the protections placed in their care by the US Constitution, underscored how the Founders of America envisioned a "more perfect" United States. It was there—in American newsrooms that focused on bringing truth to power—that Larry became a patriot for the principles established by America's Founders.

Meanwhile, Paul became the mayor of the city of Phoenix, Arizona. He was a grateful beneficiary of the American dream. His parents came to Arizona from the Appalachian Mountains, and his mother's first job in their new state was picking cabbage, and his father's was shining shoes. They started their family in the second highest poverty pocket of Arizona. Paul witnessed firsthand how even a kid from the wrong side of the tracks could become part of the political system in America.

When he entered politics, Paul found new doors opening for him, and the US State Department asked him to study the oil cartel in Saudia Arabia, leading to a better understanding of the political issues of the Middle East. After the fall of the Soviet Union, the State Department selected him to go to Poland to help advise that country's new local governments as they moved to democracy. He studied and visited almost every major genocide site, including Cambodia, Rwanda, and Bosnia, as well as those genocides that came from the Great Leap Forward in China and the "central planning" in the Soviet Union.

Thanks to his travels on behalf of the US government, Paul gained a unique understanding of the differences between authoritarian governments and Western liberal democracies.

# PART I

## AMERICAN COURAGE: LAUNCHING "THE GREAT EXPERIMENT"

# CHAPTER 1

# LIVING THE AMERICAN DREAM

The Sunday heat was almost unbearable. The three boys pedaled in a panic, with only their ballcaps shielding them from the hot Arizona sun. Baseball cards flapped against the spokes. The boys leaned hard to get just a little more speed. Only one of the boys had a television at home, so they sped as fast as they could down the dusty dirt road from the local church. When they got to the small white picket fence around the front yard, the three boys jumped off the moving bikes and busted through the screen door.

The black-and-white TV set blared. The old man in overalls adjusted the rabbit ears antenna for a clearer picture. The hot and dusty boys threw themselves on the concrete floor that felt cool and damp. Long before air conditioning and in a home with only a fan, the boys dripped sweat on the floor as they jockeyed for the best viewing position. The old woman brought sandwiches, which they grabbed ravenously. She laughed and clasped her hands in joy, then turned toward the TV with a grave look of concern. The old man and old woman in this story were Paul's grandparents.

Across the US continent, another group of boys played Little League baseball at a field on Long Island, New York, a long stone's throw from Huntington Harbor, which opened to the Long Island Sound. Their young coach, almost seventeen, watched the baseball action while he listened to AM radio. Occasionally, the younger players fought for his attention, distracted as he was by the real-time lunar communications and stupendous success (or failure) to come. This was Larry, a few years older than Paul. Both boys in different places, at different ages, watched and listened along with almost the rest of the world. It was 1:05 p.m. Arizona time and 4:05 p.m. New York time; all over the world, young and old, stopped to watch or listen to this historic event.

On the television broadcast and over the radio, one could hear: "Three, two, one, zero, ignition, 10 percent." The boys' attention pierced the TV screen, trying to make out the picture of the American Eagle lunar landing module as it descended to the Moon, the first time humans ever landed on another celestial body. The boys could see flames coming out of the engine designed to slow its descent; they thought, "Is this a real picture or simulation?" The announcer noted that Eagle's engine might interrupt transmissions. One of the boys commented that they couldn't land unless the module communicated properly with Mission Control in Houston, but the machine doing most of the communication was a computer.

About 239,000 miles away from Earth, on board the Eagle module, a computer called Program 63 communicated with the Apollo Guidance Computer (AGC) at Mission Control. That communication commanded a rocket firing sequence to slow and guide the Eagle module to a safe landing on the Moon. Without the communication of that data, landing safely would be problematic. Piloting the module was like flying a small tin can with an antenna in many respects. Over and over, as its orientation toward Earth spun and wobbled,

Mission Control would lose the connection. The connection was essential to keep data going to the Eagle.

Those listening heard Mission Control say, "Columbia, Houston, we lost them." Mission Control could talk to the pilot, astronaut Michael Collins, who remained in the Columbia capsule but had lost transmission to the Eagle module. Edwin "Buzz" Aldrin and Neil Armstrong in the Eagle adjusted the antenna by hand to improve signal strength.

Aldrin piloted the module. Armstrong looked out the window and compared what he saw to his notes on the surface before the trip to the Moon. His notes showed that the module might land short of the optimal landing site. When the module radar locked on the lunar surface, Aldrin asked why the landing radar altitude differed from that reported by the module's Primary Guidance and Navigation System (PGNS). Armstrong asked that again in a few moments, but the astronauts were startled by another alarm during his readout. The calm in their voice belied the terror that this could spell:

Armstrong: "Program Alarm."

Mission Control: "It's looking good to us."

Armstrong: "It's a 1202."

Aldrin: "1202?"

Aldrin to Armstrong: "Let's incorporate the landing radar."

Neither Aldrin nor Armstrong knew what a 1202 alarm meant. They both felt immense stress. The alarm occurred because the processing system, the best system in the world, was overloaded with tons of incoming data.

Armstrong to Mission Control: "Give us a reading on the 1202 program alarm."

Mission Control: "Roger, we got you. We are a go on that alarm."

These two men, packed into this tiny module, moved furiously yet calmly, trying to understand what was happening. Some hiccups they trained on; for others, they were in the dark. Then, as one alarm silenced, a new one rang out. Aldrin noticed several monitors turning off. Four 1202 and one 1201 alarm would sound after Mission Control said the landing was a "Go."

Over the television screen and across the radio airwaves, the Arizona and New York boys heard Aldrin tell Mission Control how close they were to the surface. They listened to the alarms go off. Aldrin called out a 5 percent figure, giving Mission Control the fuel left for the landing. When the fuel reached that level, Mission Control set a timer to help them make a "Bingo" call to determine their distance from the Moon and whether to land or abort.

The boys in America (and boys and girls and adults worldwide) heard Aldrin say he saw the Eagle's shadow on the Moon's surface. Those watching worldwide could see the images of the shadow and dust kicking up. Those listening to the radio needed words to convey what was happening. Then, everyone heard the now-famous words: "Houston, Tranquility Base here. The Eagle has landed." The date? July 20, 1969.

The Arizona boys leaped to their feet, jumping and screaming. The New York baseball coach screamed in delight. The old woman clasped her hands at her heart, grabbing her cross and saying a prayer. The old man smiled and wiped away tears. Baseball was suspended. In Arizona, enormous pride settled over the living room, as well as in millions of other living rooms across the world. This was not merely an American achievement; it was an enormous achievement for all the people of the world, just a few decades following the first television and radio transmissions. But a miracle it seemed by itself, that here in the living room of their home—and across other television sets and radios—all heard the transmissions from the Moon in nearly real-time.

It was an American success moment!

★ ★ ★

The enormous risks associated with the first lunar landing are downplayed today. Yet, the outcome that day was not assured. In a letter to President Richard Nixon's Chief of Staff, H.R. Haldeman, White House staffer (and later newspaper columnist) Bill Safire wrote on July 18, 1969, just a few days before the Eagle's landing, a memo in the event of a Moon disaster. The letter stated:

> FATE HAS ORDAINED that the men who went to the moon to explore in peace will stay on the moon to rest in peace.
>
> These brave men, Neil Armstrong and Edwin Aldrin, know that there is no hope for their recovery. But they also know that there is hope for mankind in their sacrifice.
>
> These two men are laying down their lives in mankind's most noble goal: the search for truth and understanding.

They will be mourned by their families and friends; they will be mourned by their nation; they will be mourned by the people of the world; they will be mourned by a Mother Earth that dared send two of her sons into the unknown.

In their exploration, they stirred the people of the world to feel as one; in their sacrifice, they bind more tightly the brotherhood of man.

In ancient days, men looked at stars and saw their heroes in the constellations. In modern times, we do much the same, but our heroes are epic men of flesh and blood.

Others will follow, and surely find their way home. Man's search will not be denied. But these men were the first, and they will remain foremost in our hearts.

For every human being who looks up at the moon in the nights to come will know that there is some corner of another world that is forever mankind.

And then the words to the President to assure the right process would follow:

PRIOR TO THE PRESIDENT'S STATEMENT:

The President should telephone each of the widows-to-be.

AFTER THE PRESIDENT'S STATEMENT, at the point when NASA ends communications with the men:

# WHAT'S RIGHT WITH AMERICA

> A clergyman should adopt the same procedure as a burial at sea, commending their souls to the deepest of the deep, concluding with the Lord's Prayer.[1]

★ ★ ★

Was our landing on the Moon America's peak? Some argue that America can't afford this type of financial commitment to explore new frontiers. We will tell you something very different. In this book, we will explain why achieving this type of spectacular change, albeit overlooked too frequently, is a regular occurrence today.

Changes happen so fast that we can't keep up with them. Changes in robotics, nanotechnology, genetics, driverless technology, and even extending human life. They are overlooked because they happen regularly, because of the complexity of the changes, and because maybe it has become more "profitable" in the near term to focus on what's wrong with America than what is right. Perhaps these incredible acts, leaps of faith successfully landed, are overlooked because most of the significant changes that improve the human condition are funded by private money instead of government money. Nowhere is that more evident than in what has happened in outer space.

Fifty-two years after that July day in 1969, another event—for some, certainly as big as the early Apollo missions to the Moon—began to take shape. On September 16, 2021, four private citizens sat on the Inspiration4 mission, waiting for launch. The flight reached an altitude of approximately 364 miles above the Earth, higher than the Hubble Space

---

[1] William Safire, "In Event of Moon Disaster," Memo to President Richard Nixon, July 18, 1969.

Telescope. And at a speed of 17,500 mph, they launched into space atop a Falcon 9 rocket built by Elon Musk's SpaceX. What made this epic was that the private sector, not the federal government, commanded this flight. Private sector leadership and innovation, supported by the government but fueled with private funds, make modern space flight more affordable and democratic.

This was the last of three billionaires to lead flights from the US into space. Richard Branson sent a suborbital flight skyward, the Virgin Galactic Unity 22, on July 11, 2021. Jeff Bezos, the owner of Amazon, led a successful suborbital flight on Blue Origin NS-16 on July 20, 2021.

This race started fifteen years before with commercial groups responding to the Ansari X Prize, a $10 million prize offered to the first non-governmental organization to launch a reusable crewed spacecraft into space twice within two weeks. Microsoft co-founder Paul Allen and aerospace designer Burt Rutan earned the prize in 2004 with SpaceShipOne, and a new and less expensive market was launched. Then, in 2008, SpaceX Falcon One achieved the first privately developed mission to orbit.

We often overlook that the history of space flight is filled with errors and tragedy. In 1967, the entire flight crew on NASA's Apollo 1 mission died on the launchpad in a fire. In 1986, Americans watched in horror as the space shuttle Challenger ended in spectacular disaster. Then, the shuttle Columbia broke apart during re-entry in 2003. We should ponder that some limits of our technology and courage will clash again in some fiery disaster that threatens our possibilities to explore the universe.

# WHAT'S RIGHT WITH AMERICA

Recently, you were able to witness a moment that speaks to the boundless potential of human ingenuity, a moment that may echo into the future as profoundly as our first steps upon the moon. But this time, that moment did not rest upon the shoulders of a nation-state nor under the banner of a government program. On October 15, 2024, SpaceX, a private endeavor born of bold vision, accomplished what many thought impossible: A rocket launched into the heavens and returned to Earth, delicately captured by mechanical "chopsticks" called "Mechazilla" by the company's founder, Musk.

This achievement is not merely an engineering triumph. It is a declaration—a testament to the daring spirit that defines the American experiment. It reminds us that, with courage and determination, there are no limits to what free individuals, unbound by convention, can achieve. With this act, Musk and his colleagues brought us closer to the stars and to the promise of a future where humanity is not bound by one planet but reaches out to inhabit many.

This milestone does more than make the journey to Mars seem possible. It assures us that the audacity of a single visionary can inspire nations, ignite the world's imagination, and reaffirm the truth that there is no force like the ingenuity of a free people. America has always been a land of pioneers; today, we have taken one more step into the great unknown.

The intrigue of failure, the courage of the participants, and the massive amounts of private money racing to the next frontier should lead to massive media coverage of these events. Just as in 1969, when every newsgroup in the world covered the inspirational Moon landing and seemingly every human was listening, this was a moment to behold. But something has changed since 1969.

Any young person watching the news in 2021 would, instead, see "wall-to-wall" coverage of either former President Donald Trump and an alleged threat to democracy or, if you watched another channel, wall-to-wall coverage of immigrants at the border. Coverage was almost nonexistent for privately-led monumental space events, which gave hope to millions and helped all see what was going right in America. There was no countdown or coverage of the people who would enter space. While the news about Trump, the US Capitol insurrection, and immigration was important, we believe the coverage was out of perspective, given all the good things happening in America at the same time. In our view, media and social news failed to tell the truth about the continuing American success story.

What hadn't changed since 1969 was America's leadership position in technology. What hadn't changed was our country's bold belief in our possibilities. We still had men and women willing to challenge the unknown to take on new frontiers. What was new was the attitude of the leaders who made these news coverage decisions, people who somehow gained great cynicism toward the views of everyday Americans. It was as if the smoke from the rockets was so thick you couldn't see all this optimism, covered up by much of the media and other actors who long ago decided that the only profit in the news came from bad news.

Every day, the average American's sense of individual power (or agency) and potential weakens, intentionally or not, due to our darkening political narratives and pessimistic mes-

## WHAT'S RIGHT WITH AMERICA

saging. Attacking the core of the American brand has become the norm. The soul of our country is sacrificed for votes and viewership, leaving no room for celebration, only criticism. Our screens incessantly bombard us with pessimism, pushing us toward submission, partisanship, and savior worship.

Today, there isn't a single media platform where one can find solace in a brighter tomorrow. No political party celebrates the wonder of America, and few, if any, political candidates dare to proclaim that "It Is Morning in America"[2] or take pride in who we are today. Any glimmer of optimistic news is buried under the overwhelming deluge of pessimism.

We embark on a mission to alter this trajectory, a new trajectory that needs you and fellow Americans. We passionately believe there has never been a greater need to rekindle optimism. This country's past, present, and future brim with promise, upheld by courageous individuals and organizations dedicated to technology, improving the human condition, free markets, civil rights, human rights, individualism, and a belief in the American identity.

As Americans, we embrace the right of skeptics to express their points of view. However, the people who will solve America's problems are the ones who believe you can. You are born with hope, with optimism. We learn life's challenges only as we age, heading more toward realism, possibly even pessimism. Optimism is our natural state of being; pessimism, however, is a learned behavior.

---

2   Ronald Reagan 1984 Presidential Campaign, "Morning in America," 1984.

One could argue that the Apollo 11 landing on the Moon in 1969 changed nothing. And yet, it changed everything. Indeed, it was an enormous feat. We can see it as breaking into the next frontier or ask if spending these resources on other social programs would have been better. We can exalt it or ignore it—the joys (and burdens) of our free will.

Some Americans chose to let the Moon landing change how we saw ourselves. Larry, the Little League baseball coach living in a middle-class family on Long Island, decided to go to engineering college a year later and build spaceships. While he later changed the arc of his education and career, the miracle that was the Moon landing gave him the energy and interest to explore the many possibilities for his professional life. He would choose law. He worked for the Justice Department and later ran the daily newspaper business in Tucson, Arizona. But that July day in 1969 helped him set a life course. He built that life around a desire for justice, with an understanding of the intersections among the US Constitution, the Rule of Law, information/free speech, and business.

Paul was one of the three boys in the Arizona story. His parents came from the poorest parts of the United States, coming to Arizona looking for a better life. Paul grew up in Phoenix's second-highest poverty pocket with nine other brothers and a sister. He was inspired by the newsreel clips of President John F. Kennedy saying we go to the Moon because it is hard. Even at eight years old, he yearned to run for office, and at thirty, he became the mayor of Phoenix.

What is right with America? Amidst all the darkness, sometimes it is hard to see the light. However, this does not mean the light is not there. We choose to see what we want to see. It is undoubtedly harder in some ways for Americans today because it has become so profitable for others to tell you everything that is going wrong. And how *only they* can fix our problems!

We understand that when one is living on a meager wage, inflation isn't merely an economic statistic; it's a daily hurdle. Rising gas prices, housing costs, and medical costs create incredible stresses that can consume you. We know this because we, too, have faced those challenges. And while you struggle with this, our leaders seem unable to work with one another, our television screens are filled with daily dread, and the doomers, the people who frame everything as an existential threat, seem to be the only voices available.

*The Optimist American* podcast discussed Viktor Frankl, a holocaust survivor of Auschwitz and the author of *Man's Search for Meaning*, noting that he wrote, "The one thing you can't take away from me is the way I choose to respond to what you do to me. The last of one's freedoms is to choose one's attitude in any given circumstance.... Happiness cannot be pursued; it must ensue.... Life is never made unbearable by circumstances, but only by lack of meaning and purpose."[3]

Life can be challenging. A great many people face significant struggles, such as struggles with the cost of living or unfair disabilities or illnesses. Things happen to us. Sometimes, bad things happen to us and the people we love. Yet, we have often met people in direst circumstances who can tell you why life is fantastic, face each day with vigor, and believe they can control their destiny.

---

[3] Victor Frankl, *Man's Search for Meaning* (Boston: Beacon Press, 2006). See Paul Johnson, "Reclaiming Your Authentic Self by Letting Go of Addictive Ideologies and Negative Perspectives: With Dr. Emily Bashah," July 16, 2022, in *The Optimistic American*, podcast, 1:11:09, https://youtu.be/B-HVVUgfkJs.

We are a product of the spirit that fills us. If we are fully capable of all the benefits one can gain in life yet filled with a spirit of bitterness and envy and brood over our lot, we will live a life of darkness. On the other hand, so many people who have had almost everything taken from them still find ways to think about, plan for, and work toward the possible, remain optimistic about what the day will bring, and live lives full of light.

Paul served on the Phoenix City Council with a man, Howard Adams, who became a quadriplegic from an accident. Howard was confined to a chair, strapped to keep him upright. His only working hand barely worked to push the small stick that would drive him around city hall. In every bodily function, he needed help. Yet, he came to work happy, singing, and joyful. One day, Paul said to him how much he admired him. Howard asked, "Why?" Paul said, "Howard, you have had some hard knocks, and yet I never see you unhappy; you address life with joy. If this happened to me, I just don't know that I could do what you do." To this, Howard responded, "Oh Johnson, if all you think about is your arms and your legs, you are much more handicapped than I am."

Howard made his life joyful by helping other people accomplish their goals. He loved the private sector, innovators, and creators. He wanted to empower them to create great things. He used the benefits he had left to create a fantastic life.

★ ★ ★

We are a nation of dreamers, a launching pad for those with the audacity to dream, a place that rewards ingenuity and innovation. More than any other nation, the US has thrived by unleashing the human spirit. While that spirit sometimes faces suppression, we aim to help others remember what brought us this far and what will propel us into the future. We aim to show our readers that their daily struggles to live and thrive will be rewarded best in America.

What's right about America is based on our belief that it wasn't an accident. What's right about America is by design, the Founders' design,[4] that empowered citizens who individually and collectively created America's great abundance.

The proof of American results and future potential is abundant. Yale historian Paul Kennedy elucidated America's historical position as a global superpower.[5] Despite comprising less than 5 percent of the world's population, the US holds 30 percent of global wealth (according to Credit Suisse, in a report titled *Global Wealth Report, 2021*),[6] 40 percent of global military spending (per Statista),[7] and boasts one-third of the world's 2000 most profitable companies (as reported by Forbes).[8]

Income disparity persists undoubtedly, but progress continues to be made. In his book *The Myth of American*

---

[4] However, George Washington referred to the establishment of the United States as "The Great Experiment," based on its founding democratic principles. George Washington, "Letter to the Philadelphia Convention," 1787.

[5] Paul Kennedy, *The Rise and Fall of Great Powers: Economic Change and Military Conflict from 1500 to 2000* (New York: Random House, 1987).

[6] Credit Suisse, *Global Wealth Report, 2021* (Zurich: Credit Suisse Research Institute, 2021).

[7] Einar H. Dyvik, "Countries with the Highest Military Spending Worldwide in 2023," *Statista*, July 4, 2024, https://ww.statista.com/statistics/262742/countries-with-the-highest-military-spending/ (accessed July 24, 2024).

[8] Andrea Murphy and Matt Schifrin, eds., "The Global 2000 (2024)," *Forbes*, June 6, 2024, https://www.forbes.com/lists/global2000/#7c8fa1d-f5ac0 (accessed July 24, 2024).

*Inequality*,⁹ co-author Phil Gramm points out that in the next decade, almost all children will earn more than their parents. He demonstrates how the lowest-income households have benefited the most from upward mobility over the last fifty years. Today, most people enjoy economic prosperity comparable to the top 20 percent of earners from half a century ago, adjusted for inflation.

Further, more Americans attain higher education levels, and the value of education has grown. Women enter the labor force in 60 percent of households, and the trend of highly educated individuals forming households together has substantially increased household income in the last five decades. We have employed new workers in the workforce and improved the quality of life for families.

Undoubtedly, things will improve in the US. According to the federal Bureau of Labor Statistics, we are poised to add nearly five million jobs by 2032, with slowing job growth (compared with early projections) based partly on lower population growth.¹⁰ This book illuminates the reasons for the renaissance in American re-industrialization, with companies reshoring jobs domestically, undoubtedly continuing the trends that make America's job market the best in the world by far!

We will remain the major superpower of the twenty-first century, continuing to trade more deeply with countries that accept the "rules-based order" that America led following

---

9   Phil Gramm, Robert Ekelund, and John Early, *The Myth of American Inequality: How Government Biases Policy Debate* (Maryland: Rowman & Littlefield, 2022).

10  US Bureau of Labor Statistics, "Employment Projections: 2022–2032 Summary," August 29, 2024, https://www.bls.gov/news.release/ecopro.nr0.htm (accessed July 24, 2024).

World War II and the rebuilding of Europe and Asia. Those who follow their own rules will find themselves poorer and more at risk of governmental disruption. While the American education system faces ongoing and new challenges, fifty of the world's top one hundred universities are located here, continuing to educate for jobs in America and worldwide. Michael Beckley of Tufts University writes[11] that the US workforce is not only the most educated in terms of years of schooling but also the most productive among major powers. It is the only large workforce that will continue to grow throughout this century.

Throughout our lifetimes, we have repeatedly heard that our competitors would overtake the United States. We heard it compared with the Soviet Union post-World War II, with Japan in the 1980s and 1990s, and today compared with China. However, the US maintains significant (sometimes overlooked) demographic and geographic advantages. We retain dozens of formal alliances worldwide, over 500 military bases across over forty countries, and eleven aircraft carrier groups maintaining maritime supremacy worldwide.[12]

We live in an era of abundance, improving the quality of life within the United States and globally. Our expenditures as a percentage of income on housing, transportation, communication, appliances, food, and other goods are significantly lower than they were fifty years ago, a fact often overlooked in discussions of economic disparity. American technology has

---

11  Michael Beckley, *Unrivaled: Why America Will Remain the World's Sole Superpower* (New York: Cornell University Press, 2018).
12  Beckley, 2018; see Peter Zeihan, *The Accidental Superpower: The Next Generation of American Preeminence and the Coming Global Disorder* (New York: Twelve, 2014).

undeniably enhanced the quality of life both domestically and worldwide.

With Apollo 11, technology gave the US the edge over the Soviet Union. But more important than that advantage in the space race was how related technology improved the lives of all Americans, technology that was primarily responsible for Americans having the highest quality of life in the world.

During the 1960s, the AGC computer system used by NASA was the most advanced computer of its time. Mission Control desperately tried to maintain the connection with Eagle by having Aldrin move the antenna so the computers could guide a successful landing. The onboard computer had four kilobytes of brainpower and thirty-two kilobytes of hard disk memory. It measured approximately two feet by one foot by six inches high, weighing almost sixty-six pounds. A cell phone today is two million times more powerful with six million times more storage, weighing just a few ounces.[13]

While pessimists claim the free-market system is destined to fail, one undeniable fact remains: Our free-market system has done more to advance the human condition than any other system in history. Electric vehicles, autonomous driving, 3D printing, robotics, quantum computing, nanotechnology, artificial intelligence, vertical farming, desalinization, green nuclear energy, gene editing, space travel, and even life extension are all remarkable achievements. The pace of change is set to become even more exponential.

Larry Summers, economist and former US Treasury Secretary (and newly appointed Board member at OpenAI,

---

[13] Peter H. Diamandis and Steven Kotler, *Abundance: The Future is Better Than You Think* (New York: Free Press, 2012), 23.

the leading artificial intelligence company in America), stated on *The Optimistic American* podcast, "Am I worried about [our country's] finances? Yes. Am I worried about our investment in technology leadership? Yes. But this is not the first time we've faced significant challenges. We have a more solvable set of problems and a more dynamic society than our competitors for solving them. People from around the world still want to come to the US and invest their money here."[14]

Let's underscore that one fact: Millions of people continue to risk their lives to come to America to experience the American dream. Millions come here bringing their assets to invest in American success. The desire to immigrate to America and invest in the US remains strong. We continue to solve big societal problems, sometimes contentiously but always successfully, eventually. Many will continue to hear the clarion call toward America and our democratic system.

As authors who witnessed the resilience of American society, we remember the turmoil of the Vietnam War, a period of division at least as significant as today's challenges. American history is replete with challenges, from the Revolutionary War to the Civil War and even more recent divisions during the twentieth century. Yet, we have consistently overcome adversity. An important question for you to ponder is, whose "hand" would you rather be playing today? China's, India's, Asia's, Russia's, or Europe's? There is no better hand to play than the one we hold here and now. And it's all yours *simply by being born or naturalized here.*

---

14   Paul Johnson, "Leading Economist Counters the Changing World Order Narrative: With Larry Summers," June 19, 2022, in *The Optimistic American*, podcast, 35:53, https://youtu.be/Wvpzq_o5ysU.

Our advantages far outweigh our problems, yet our potentially greatest threat is the loss of faith in who we are and our founding ideals. Countries, individual geographic states, money, and our monetary system are all based on faith. We must never lose that faith in what has made America great for centuries.

★ ★ ★

We should take careful stock of why we have all this prosperity. The title of this book reflects what is *right* with America. We believe there is so much right that it is evident to anyone looking. But a critical question is, where did all this prosperity come from? We believe that while our government has accomplished many things, the single greatest thing our government ever did was to empower the individual over itself. And this was done by the powers defined in the US Constitution, written by our Founders in the late eighteenth century. They built an idea that would withstand the test of time. And, by golly, how right they were!

While our geography is a giant strategic advantage, our strong demographics (America, in many ways, continues to be the best place to raise families) are hugely important, and our technological development propelled us past our competitors. Moreover, these factors add to America's advantages. Our most significant advantage has come from over 200 years of the "rule of law" with a written constitution that placed the rights of individuals on the altar we worship, protecting the rights of individuals to speak freely, practice whatever religion they choose (or none), vote, petition their government for changes, work in businesses they choose, among so many other rights and freedoms.

The Constitution captured the limited rights of government and how we would govern ourselves. Then, the Bill of Rights, the first ten amendments to the Constitution, defined the rights of individuals, rights superior to the government and superior to the rights of collective interests. Those rights allowed all Americans to own what they created and mostly retain the economic benefits of that creation.

In this book, we will argue that our institutions are designed to protect the individual. This has undoubtedly resulted in benefits to the collective interests of all Americans. In our country, we protect the individual and limit government powers, with collective actions determined following free elections.

Western liberal democracies (such as America's democracy), through free markets, free enterprise, property rights, and human rights, have dramatically higher qualities of life than their authoritarian counterparts.[15] Our strong property rights come from our country's focus on individual rights under the moral doctrine captured by the Declaration of Independence. Our "Creator" gave each of us inalienable rights that led to free markets, property rights, the end of slavery, civil rights, human rights, and equal rights, the founding principles of the United States of America.

Those rights, defended repeatedly, led to the most robust economy in the world. In America, we can more easily spend our dollars on things we desire and often do so with unknown

---

15    Daron Acemoglu et al., "Democracy Does Cause Growth," *Journal of Political Economy* 127, no. 1 (2019): 47–100.

companies and other individuals because we know the rules when we buy and sell. We can count on our rights being protected. This, among other American advantages, led to great abundance.

The idea of abundance is that we continue to enter new eras where there are no shortages but surpluses that improve our quality of life. With abundance, all the rules change for our betterment.

We have faith that an abundant future will improve our lives, as evidenced by what it has done in the last twenty years, fifty years, and 250 years. This is the story of that greatness, the philosophy behind it, the philosophy of those who would undermine it, and the importance of the institutions that serve it and all Americans.

★ ★ ★

We hope to drive forward this factual narrative of abundance, the promise we have in our future based upon the ideals of our history. We need to make it consumable for everyday Americans. How do we pivot our conversations toward the positive? Our greatest wish is to make today's doom and gloom begin to play a minor part at our dining tables, to help our mornings start with promise and faith rather than fear and despair.

As authors, our gain from this is to help others navigate past the dread, the doomers, and the nightly news. We hope to create the sexton that gives all Americans better ways to see where we have been and where we are going, to help them see how American institutions and philosophy resulted in so much good, give us such great promise, and are designed to protect us. We hope a newer generation can use our experience to chart a path forward.

We remain inspired, in awe, by those who charted a path when there was none to be found. Those who sailed out bravely into the unknown, charging forward without concern for how they would ever make it back. And those with the vision to imagine and manifest what could be rather than accepting what was. These men and women were carried by faith, faith in human potential, faith in the power of togetherness, and faith in a better tomorrow because they were willing to play their parts in making that a reality.

The infinite string that bound them, the force that propelled them, and the faint light that guided them was the same as it is for us and the generations to come: *optimism*. And a belief in what is *right* about America.

## CHAPTER 2

# BIRTHING AMERICA AND SECURING HER FUTURE

AMERICA'S BEST IDEA SHINES THROUGH the preamble to the US Constitution:

> We the People of the United States, in Order to form a more perfect Union, establish Justice, insure domestic Tranquility, provide for the common defence, promote the general Welfare, and secure the Blessings of Liberty to ourselves and our Posterity, do ordain and establish this Constitution for the United States of America.

The preamble exudes confidence in America's future and breath-stealing humility in the phrase "to form a more perfect Union." The Founders stated their grand visions in both the Declaration and the Constitution based on the views of many past philosophers, but they understood the journey ahead. They knew America must always strive toward a more perfect union, a destination never to be reached.

The aura of slavery that drove much of our country's economic success in its early years constrained both the vision and the reality. Even today, America reckons with this challenging history and strives to advance everyone. When successes are uneven, optimism is challenged, but many can now see a more explicit definition of success for all Americans and others who live and work here.

Many people think we are forever divided in our views, especially politically. This book discusses why Americans are less divided than they seem. Others suggest Americans no longer move toward that "more perfect Union."

They're wrong.

Some think America's successes are mainly in the rearview mirror, and countries like China, India, and even Russia seem to be rising as America falters.

That, too, is false.

Others worry that our standard of living is falling and that future generations will do less well than past ones have or will.

Wrong!

The writing of this book allowed us to discuss why the future will be a great place to work, that jobs will not be taken over by technology, and that better communication and understanding are possible. As we see it, future jobs in America will be enabled by additional education. America is the country that mostly perfected public education, and it will use its educational prowess to create well-trained, self-responsible people to be employees who can attain better, more sustainable lives because of their ability to make good use of satisfactory, and even enhanced, incomes. Better educational opportunities likely will drive better equality for all Americans.

We deeply understand that the ideas we have brought to these pages are our views, based on our perspectives, and they are from the standpoint of what is known as "the privileged white male syndrome." We admit to that, but we also hope and believe that our many years of service to other people of all genders, races, cultures, and economic classes provide us with robust and balanced perspectives. Ultimately, you, dear reader, will determine that truth we hold to be self-evident. We invite and welcome your comments.

As you read our views, we assume you will disagree with many of them. That's great! Civil discourse is made possible through rational argumentation. Another wonderful thing about America is that we can disagree and argue as we choose, although we should also argue respectfully. At the fundamental level, we believe that the clashing of ideas, coupled with productive conversations, ends up welcoming and embracing compromise and leading to a better America.

And, for incredibly insightful readers, please understand that our views are simply ours. We don't pretend to have the answers. The topics covered in this book always have more questions than answers. Fortunately, so much scholarship exists around most of the issues addressed in this book. We believe in our optimistic views because they are based on historical data and grand visions. Even as our Founders wondered what this new country could become and how its governance could support a country with limitless potential, they also focused on optimism in emerging ideas. Our world cannot advance without better arguments amid democratic institutions that value debate and dissent and ultimately implement solutions most fellow American citizens respect.

Please note that it took many thoughtful people to work on the founding of America and make it the greatest country the world has ever seen. Indeed, today, we are still the greatest country. Yup, we said it again, so you can get used to feeling it. Come and rediscover some of those important voices, then add your own.

Here's a message for our friends interested in political philosophy (and in the twenty-first century, we're all political philosophers to some degree): This book is not meant to be a work of the highest academic distinction. Many books and authors spend much time describing views with academic rigor. Still, our focus is mainly on the visions our Founders implemented under the Declaration and the Constitution and the sources and opinions of key philosophers, economists, and other thinkers on whom they relied. Thus, we concluded that summary treatment was the best approach. You might believe philosophers like Socrates, Plato, John Locke, and economists like Adam Smith had different views than we have brought to this book. Our views are what they are, but please know our opinions were crafted with modesty. We are being as humble as possible because we are in awe of what prior thinkers thought and created.

We greatly admire the Founders of America; however, those leading men were far from flawless. They came from an aristocratic society, enslaved people, ran large farms, and battled for their vision of American freedom. And they began with a conviction that only men, primarily landowning men, could lead this new country. Earlier, they created a failed American government institution under the Articles of Confederation. Fortunately, that prior work and mistakes led to the Constitution, following a declaration of independence from English tyranny.

Slavery remained in America after we became independent of England, despite inconsistent core elements against it embedded in the Constitution ("all men are created equal"). It took almost seventy-five additional years and a civil war to dissolve those founding flaws. The Founders favored only men and primarily white Christian men. Like most of the rest of the world, women and enslaved people were considered possessions. Native American tribal members were treated similarly, if not as enemies, despite their ancestors living on American soil first. It took even longer for tribal populations to achieve formal American recognition.

In this book, you will read what we believe are the two major flaws in America's founding: the failure to determine and define who the "People" are as referenced by the Constitution and, thus, who could vote for the government sought; and the failure to create national requirements or standards for educating Americans[1] and other residents, specifically on the ideals of American democracy and capitalism. The Founders punted on these big issues, deferring voting rights and educational systems to state governments. How different might twenty-first-century America look if we had national standardized systems of voting and education?

Commentators have noted that America's federal system created the fifty states as "laboratories of democracy" to test systems enabling American citizens to build better democratic solutions. We disagree. The most crucial balance was between the individual and government, not states and the federal government, and many of the most egregious actions that have damaged individual freedoms arose under state governments. The Constitution's Framers had few choices in the late eighteenth century; all came together from state systems and constitutions, which, at the time, were more potent than

---

[1] Founder Thomas Jefferson deeply believed in the need for public education: "Above all things I hope education of the common people will be attended to; convinced that on their good sense we may rely with the most security for the preservation of a due degree of liberty." Thomas Jefferson, "To James Madison from Thomas Jefferson," December 20, 1797, https://founders.archives.gov/documents/Madison/01-10-02-0210.

the emerging federal system. Much of the Constitution's language works to limit the power of the new federal government, deferring first to the power of the "People" and next to the state governments. But those facts don't wash away the problematic choices in our experiences today.

In no place was this choice more punitive than the continuing endorsement of slavery and discrimination against formerly enslaved people. Even after passage of the Thirteenth, Fourteenth, and Fifteenth Amendments following the Civil War (which eliminated direct support of slavery in the Constitution), it took more than one hundred years to eliminate those vestiges in various states. This is powerful history; some relics continue into today's realities.

Although you might pine for a more unified, visionary federal system, you shouldn't overlook that even where the federal government had power, legislation often passed in Congress that attacked various activities and freedoms that those in charge wanted to end. One of the most egregious examples began in 1798 under the new federal government and President John Adams with passage of the Alien and Sedition Acts.[2]

The Alien Act gave the president unilateral authority to deport non-citizens where the claim was that they were subject to the authority of foreign enemies. The Sedition Act attacked core elements of a free press and free speech—the right to criticize the government. Only the election of Thomas Jefferson as president led to those acts expiring and Jefferson pardoning those convicted under them.

Even in its infancy, the federal government couldn't resist passing laws to support behavior it liked and discourage what

---

[2] *Alien and Sedition Acts*, 1798, 1 Stat. 570–597.

it didn't like. Federal, state, or local governments can't help themselves. And even the "People," the citizens who are governed, can't resist pushing for attacks on individual freedoms of others and demanding that governments support what most of those people desire. Unfortunately, there are too many examples of laws passed over America's first 200 years that bear indications of the failure to support minority rights. One example is how lawmakers condoned actions like the internment of Japanese American citizens during World War II under the guise of national security.

Another example is the Patriot Act, passed following the attacks of September 2001 (9/11), which bears indicia of reduced civil rights of some to balance against the supposed greater rights (namely, security) of the majority. America's founding as a liberal democracy paved a trail for bad behavior at the federal level for decades.

We live in an America where many view the overall institutions, especially the independent court systems, including the Supreme Court, as bastions that protect minority rights from the hordes of the majority. That belief overlooks or ignores history, both past and present. For many years, the Supreme Court (and numerous lower courts) undercut many individual freedoms. The tripartite system of federal governance—Congress, the President, and the Supreme Court—colluded for many decades to enable most Southern states to continue discriminating against formerly enslaved African Americans, especially regarding equality on many levels and especially regarding the right to vote.

While the Bill of Rights (the first ten amendments to the Constitution, ratified in 1791) embraces individual rights, freedoms, and liberties, the Supreme Court waited until the twentieth century before it rejected specific government actions restricting those freedoms. Today, as a conservative Supreme Court addresses other liberties, there is a risk that decisions will withdraw certain individual rights and protections. The necessity of independence of the American judiciary should be admired for its role in checks and balances. Still, one should never believe that that institution is the ultimate source of protection for American rights and freedoms.

Suffice it to say that America, in the twenty-first century, is much farther down the path of forming a "more perfect" union than it was at its birth. The formation of America began with only men, mostly property-owning men, protecting the rights of others who (in their minds) were subordinate to them. We evolved as a society, eliminating slavery by law (and much later, in fact), bringing women and younger adults the right to vote, breathing new life into all elements of the First Amendment's protections for religious freedom, free speech, free press, and the right to gather and lobby the government for change peaceably. America today is a shadow of its agrarian, aristocratic, Caucasian founding systems, and its citizens certainly have been extraordinarily lucky in so many ways.

The United States is the greatest superpower of all time. That is not a throwaway line. Most historians agree: Nothing exists like what we have in the US, based on principal ideals that brought us from the early days of a more perfect union to the greatness of where we are today. If we boil this down to the most fundamental truth, it was not state rights nor a dominant federal government that provided this greatness. The most powerful truths that brought us here were based on the rights and freedoms of individuals.

Our reasons for optimism are based on the significant advantages present in American society and the foundations of liberty and freedom that allow Americans to choose opportunities and begin anew as they wish. No other place in the world has more advantages and opportunities than America, and those advantages and opportunities only accelerate from here.

★ ★ ★

Borrowing from the Bible and John Winthrop's sermon in the seventeenth century, President Reagan described America as a "shining city on a hill," a country whose vision of success beckoned the rest of the world, an aspiration for all those who sought freedom, liberty, and prosperity.[3] President George H.W. Bush spoke about America having a "thousand points of light," a country that was generous, noble, and welcoming. He noted that America's "[ideas] are timeless: duty, sacrifice, commitment, and a patriotism that finds expression in taking part and pitching in."[4]

For four centuries, America beckoned almost everyone motivated by hard work to succeed and by the freedom to believe what a person wanted to believe and to act upon such beliefs consistent with society's obligations. Over the years, many people on foreign soil observed America's special and unique role in the world. To them, we became a lighthouse to guide them to a new home as they yearned for additional freedoms.

---

[3] President Ronald Reagan, "Farewell Address to the Nation," January 11, 1989, https://www.reaganlibrary.gov/research/speeches/011189i (accessed July 26, 2024).

[4] George H.W. Bush, "Inaugural Address," January 20, 1989, https://www.presidency.ucsb.edu/documents/inaugural-address-0 (accessed July 26, 2024).

Immigrants have always viewed America as a land of opportunity that allows beginnings, restarts, and do-overs, a country that enables its citizens to work on almost anything and keep most of the benefits of that work. American society works better than most due to our extensive legal systems, including laws, courts, adjudicators, and those who argue before them, fostering a sense of underlying fairness. America's reputation was that of a country that mostly welcomed new immigrants to share in liberal democracy. After World War II, the United States stood stoic as a symbol and protector of democracy.

We Americans are lucky; indeed, we are. We live in the twenty-first century, where various technologies at our fingertips make life easier. Most of us work in jobs that require as much brain as brawn, and those who work with their hands do so in jobs that are much safer today. We care about safety and keeping ourselves (and our families) as healthy as we/they can be. Despite the recent challenges across America due to COVID-19 and the opioid drug crisis, most Americans are living longer and healthier and mostly with enough resources to remain optimistic.

We have worked with numerous founders and entrepreneurs. One entrepreneur in Tucson, when asked about his success (he had started a technology company in his garage decades ago and sold it for more than $2 billion), noted that he "always positioned my company to be lucky" and, when luck arrived (as it does for everyone), to take advantage. We call that micro-luck, or the individual opportunities America presents us throughout our lives. But there is also the aspect of America's overall macro-luck from which each American gains merely by living here.

We live in an era marked by extreme perspectives: one side denies the atrocities of slavery, while the other claims that racism continues as pervasively today. Both views are fundamentally flawed. Denying our historical misdeeds undermines our progress, and overstating current woes detracts from our collective resolve to improve, rendering past efforts insignificant. It is crucial to acknowledge that while slavery was a global blight persisting for millennia, the principle that "all men are created equal" initiated a significant paradigm shift, positioning America at the forefront of a worldwide movement toward equality and justice. This foundational ideal has, more than anything, cemented America's role as a force for good in the world.

There is much to be thankful for in America, especially the vision and execution of our Founders who created America's liberal democracy. We stand on the backs of these giants. What makes them extraordinary is not that they were perfect men or women. It's that despite their imperfections, they created something unique in world history. We are the beneficiaries of that creation.

Be thankful for the work of everyday Americans who put food on our tables, build our homes and vehicles, roads, bridges, and dams, and toil long hours to make a better life for all. The culmination of this work by those who came before us created America's strengths upon which we can build successful lives. America's emphasis on individual rights and freedoms enabled the most innovative entrepreneurs to develop their very cool, transformative companies that today provide our suite of great gadgets, with their companies themselves enabled by our infrastructure of financial institutions that gather American and other riches to lend.

In addition, thank the wisdom of prior American leaders who cleaned up our air, waters, and lands and created the systems to keep them clean. In June of 1969, the Cuyahoga River in Ohio caught fire and was the focus of intense news coverage. It had caught fire roughly a dozen times before due to oil and other pollutants floating on the river's surface. But what should stand out is that it was the last time it caught fire because the US government passed the Clean Water Act.

The good news is that the Act was largely successful. Since its implementation in 1972, government and industry have invested over a trillion dollars to abate water pollution. Studies found that water pollutants dropped substantially based on over fifty million pollution readings from 240,000 monitoring sites.[5]

We also live in cities where citizens live healthier and longer lives because of the Clean Air Act. Since 1970, we have seen enormous reductions in carbon monoxide, ozone, and particulates, with over a 50 percent decrease in the latter. Today, Americans are exposed to particulate pollution at a rate of only 35.1 percent of what it was in 1970. This has benefited both big and small cities and towns.[6]

We give thanks, appreciate, and value those serving in the military and public safety. In this book, we discuss how amaz-

---

[5] See David A. Kaiser and Joseph S. Shapiro, "Consequences of the Clean Water Act and the Demand for Water Quality," *The Quarterly Journal of Economics* 134, no. 1 (February 2019): 349–396.

[6] See US Environmental Protection Agency (EPA), *Our Nation's Air: Status and Trends through 2020* (Washington, DC: EPA, 2020); EPA, *The Benefits and Costs of the Clean Air Act 1990 to 2020* (Washington, DC: EPA, 2021). See also American Lung Association, *State of the Air 2022* (Chicago: American Lung Association, 2022); AQLI Air Quality Life Index, *United States: Clean Air Act (1970)*, https://aqli.epic.uchicago.edu/policy-impacts/united-states-clean-air-act ("With 64.9 percent less pollution, Americans are living healthier, longer lives. Reductions in particulate air pollution alone, thanks in large part to the Clean Air Act, have added 1.4 years to the life expectancy of the average American since 1970.") (accessed August 22, 2024).

ing the American military is. But we should not forget the first responders' role in our communities. For example, firefighters populate public safety departments that do much more than fight fires. Their impact on lives saved from strokes, heart attacks, and other emergencies cannot be overstated.

Public opinion, significantly influenced by the nightly news and social media, believes the crime rate is increasing. However, numerous studies make it clear that the crime rate today, including violent crimes, is half of what it was in the 1990s.[7] Let us state that, again, the crime rate, including violent crimes, is half of what it was in the 1990s! Don't let the doomers make you believe our cities are falling apart. Public safety needs to be a priority, and in a free society, we must comply with the rules we agree on.

But the data is clear: It is getting better. America truly is a great place to live today. But to better understand how and why, we must return to the founding principles of the United States of America.

---

[7] See, for example, Ames Grawert, Matthew Friedman, and James Cullen, "Crime Trends: 1990–2016," *The Brennan Center for Justice*, April 18, 2017, https://www.brennancenter.org/our-work/research-reports/crime-trends-1990-2016 (accessed August 22, 2024); Federal Bureau of Investigation, *Crime in the Nation, 2022* (Washington, DC: Department of Justice, 2023), October 16, 2023; Federal Bureau of Investigation, "FBI Releases 2022 Crime in the Nation Statistics," *FBI*, October 16, 2023, https://www.fbi.gov/news/press-releases/fbi-releases-2022-crime-in-the-nation-statistics (accessed August 22, 2024).

# CHAPTER 3

# CALLING THE PHILOSOPHERS

THE FOUNDERS OF AMERICA STUDIED Western philosophical thought.[1] It's worth reflecting on how philosophy, often defined as the study of wisdom or love of wisdom, drove political thought. From the days of Socrates, and even for those wisdom seekers pre-Socrates, much of the focus was on the power of wisdom. To the ancient philosophers, wisdom was not about facts or other information. It was more, much more, and it often required many life experiences to realize—that thoughts along life's way lead to truths about how people should best live their lives.

In this book, we focus exclusively on Western democracy. We rely on how our Founders used Western philosophy (from the Greeks) instead of Eastern (from the Asians). While Eastern wisdom shows no clear distinction between philosophy and religious thought, Western philosophy closely aligned with theology from medieval times until the nineteenth century. America's Founders and their assumptions often reflected that integration. Not until French philosopher René Descartes in the early to mid-seventeenth century (who said, "I think,

---

[1] For a wonderful, comprehensive review of philosophy over the centuries, we recommend reading A.C. Grayling, *The History of Philosophy* (New York: Penguin Random House, 2019).

therefore I am") described people as thinkers who reason, was there a distinct separation between philosophy and religion.

Understanding these historical facts and thoughts matters. They are reflected in our founding documents, the Declaration and the Constitution.

Pre-Socratic philosophy focused mostly on questions about nature and the origins of the world. Socrates moved that dialogue toward ethics and away from what many philosophers of his time believed, which often was how to argue more forcefully using rhetoric and oratory techniques. Socrates leveraged Greek thinking from mere argument to deeper thinking and questioning. He illuminated ideas like human virtue and humanity's search for truth.

In a simplified view, Socrates, Plato, and Aristotle are three cornerstones of the early Greek philosophical thoughts. Plato was a student of Socrates and a teacher of Aristotle. Socrates was not a writer but a talker who didn't lecture or teach.[2] He fostered discussion, inquired, and engaged in dialogue to reach consensus. Plato and Aristotle were writers and teachers.

Plato's philosophy dove into issues beyond basic humanity. He espoused that the wisest life was best seen as the ordinary life of an average person. He drove thoughts about how a just person would or should act and what justice requires. He described the ethics of individual actions, discussed how individuals should live their lives in relation to others, and described ideas about the best way for anyone to live. Arguably, he was the first to espouse the view that humans have immortal souls.

---

[2] Three of history's greatest thinkers—Socrates, Buddha, and Jesus—did not write books about their philosophies. They just lived the questions, found their answers, and allowed others to witness them and write the books.

Plato's *The Republic*[3] is a work of justice. It draws comparisons and distinctions between persons and their governments to illustrate the balance or harmony in the justice that should exist between them. The main thesis in his work is that a specific class of rulers, whom he called philosophers-kings, should rule over an ideal society. The philosopher-kings were individuals selected early in life and educated to manage society for all properly. They were expected to be wise, just, and virtuous rulers. Plato believed that governments are best served by an aristocracy, led by the best persons in society, those educated to lead, persons who had attained those positions not by inheritance but via merit and education.

Aristotle also became a teacher of philosophy. He was a scientist dedicated to bringing more of its theory to bear on human experience. Politics was a core element of his discussions—the study of the state, the government, and its intersection with the people. He even wrote a theory of how the state should conduct itself, its ethics, moral qualities, and overall character. Aristotle argued that a state emerges to allow people to live safely, work fairly, and be free from physical attacks. He said that the state should evolve to allow men (most of the recognized earliest philosophers were men who wrote about and for other men) to live better lives because, ultimately, the evolved state allowed them to develop their intelligence and related interests.

Those early philosophers also believed in idealism, that the "thinking" mind is more important than the "feeling" mind. Empiricism—perception of truth through the senses—

---

3    Plato, *The Republic* (2nd ed.), trans. Allan Bloom (New York: Basic Books, 1991).

is based on feeling. Idealism and, to a lesser extent, empiricism, played roles in developing the Declaration and the Constitution.

Beyond the Greek philosophers, America's Founders turned to other, more recent wisdom seekers and truth tellers. Here's a sampling of them and their impact on American democracy.

## JOHN LOCKE

John Locke (1632–1704) and his writings were central to America's founding ideas. He was an empiricist, one who embraced the theory that all knowledge is based on experience derived from the five senses. He was a celebrated English philosopher, government official, and theologian. Many believe that without Locke's perspectives, we might not have the America we have today. Many US presidents have given Locke most, if not all, of the credit for the wisdom instilled by the Framers in the Declaration and the Constitution.

Best known for his *Two Treatises of Government*,[4] Locke asserted in other writings that human wisdom and divine inspiration were entirely compatible and that the laws of human life came from God. Yet, he argued forcefully (and often at the time anonymously) that the monarchy in England and religion should be separate. During his life, the Church of England—the Anglican Church—was the state's official church. It was established and run by the government, and attendance was required of all citizens of England.

---

[4] John Locke, *Two Treatises of Government*, ed. Peter Laslett (England: Cambridge University Press, 1988).

Locke also focused on the education of youth. He believed that the success of who they would become was a function of their education and training.

Like an earlier philosopher, Thomas Hobbes (1588–1679), Locke argued for a "state of nature" that existed before civil societies began, a place not of strife but where individuals enjoyed natural freedoms. He believed there was a basic human tendency to band together to protect the individual members of such groups. He argued that individuals often gave up much of their freedoms to get the benefits of a civil society. And he described "natural rights," such as life, liberty, and property, arguing that these things could and should not be traded away. Here are samples of his thinking, according to the *Second Treatise*:

> To understand political power right, and derive it from its original, we must consider, what state all men are naturally in, and that is, a state of perfect freedom to order their actions, and dispose of their possessions and persons, as they think fit, within the bounds of the law of nature, without asking leave, or depending upon the will of any other man. A state also of equality, wherein all the power and jurisdiction is reciprocal, no one having more than another.... [5]

Many of Locke's writings directly influenced America's founding principles, including government and the role of religion in civic life. Here is his "theory of social contract":

> Men...join and unite into a community for their comfortable, safe, and peaceable living one amongst

---

5   Ibid., II.4.

another, in a secure enjoyment of their properties, and a greater security against any, that are not of it.[6]

Such a social compact reflected his thoughts about how citizens could unite to defend themselves against challenges from outside their community or country and from within. You can find evidence of Locke's compact in the Declaration, which notes that valid governments "derive their just powers from the Consent of the Governed."

Locke also opined that a just government must be erected on the consent of the governed to protect certain fundamental rights such as "life, liberty, and property," which cannot be given or contracted away. The Declaration picked up that idea:

> We hold these Truths to be self-evident, that all Men are created equal, that they are endowed by their Creator with certain unalienable Rights, that among these are Life, Liberty and the Pursuit of Happiness—That to secure these Rights, Governments are instituted among Men, deriving their just Powers from the Consent of the Governed, that whenever any Form of Government becomes destructive of these Ends, it is the Right of the People to alter or to abolish it, and to institute new Government, laying its Foundation on such Principles, and organizing its Powers in such Form, as to them shall seem the most likely to effect their Safety and Happiness.

These key phrases reflect the depth to which the Founders borrowed Locke's thoughts. They embedded the idea that America's fundamental freedoms were endowed by a Creator

---

6  Ibid., II.95.

and protected by a government-granted power by citizens who were also free (even obligated) to abolish laws, rules, or entire governments that didn't align with expected outcomes.

## JEAN-JACQUES ROUSSEAU

While Locke, to many (and to history), was the primary source of philosophical thought undergirding the American democratic experiment, other philosophers influenced the Founders' thinking. Philosopher Jean-Jacques Rousseau (1712–1778) wrote extensively about governments while reflecting the common understanding that a monarchy was a superior form of government. Even a flourishing monarchy required the consent of the governed, a core concept in the Declaration. In Rousseau's work titled *The Social Contract*, he noted:

> Each of us puts his person and all his power in common under the supreme direction of the general will, and, in our corporate capacity, we receive each member as an indivisible part of the whole.... The problem is to find a form of association which will defend and protect with the whole common force the person and goods of each associate.... This is the fundamental problem of which the Social Contract provides the solution.[7]

In *The Social Contract*, Rosseau also wrote about the contradiction and conflicts between man's natural freedoms and civil freedoms, which they delegate collectively to governments to better manage the "general will" under which

---

[7] Jean-Jacques Rousseau, *The Social Contract*, trans. G.D. H. Cole (London: J.M. Dent and Sons, 1913), Book I, Chapter 6.

they live and are protected. He questioned how man could be deemed free and still be bound by laws (or "wills") that were not his own. The Framers addressed that challenge by putting into the framework of the Constitution language denoting that while citizens did not consent specifically to certain outcomes, they consent to the rules by which such outcomes are determined with a tacit agreement to be bound accordingly under the rules of a free, liberal, democratic society.

Rousseau's important philosophical contributions to America's founding included the notion that general will or free will of the people is the basis for viable state or federal government power. One of Rousseau's other important ideas is that just laws arise from the intersection of self-interest and impartiality.

## CHARLES LOUIS DE SECONDAT (MONTESQUIEU), THOMAS HOBBES, AND ADAM SMITH

Another influencing philosopher was a French judge, Charles Louis de Secondat, Baron de La Brède et de Montesquieu (1689–1755). He described how separating powers among a government's legislative, executive, and judicial branches promotes justice and liberty. Montesquieu believed in civil liberties for the governed.

Thomas Hobbes also wrote about the social contract between the government and those governed and argued that one needed to be part of a political society to guarantee personal safety. He believed in human equality—equality established via natural laws, not governments. He was concerned that in the absence of some central authority, an environment of anarchy would destroy a free, open, and otherwise equal society.

Adam Smith (1723–1790), often described as the father of capitalism, influenced America's founding with his thoughts about how economic self-interest and freedoms could successfully build a free society. He felt the mere fact of freedom of choice would create conditions for all individuals to live better.

## JEREMY BENTHAM

Jeremy Bentham (1748–1832) was a philosopher who deeply influenced Locke. Bentham's expertise included thoughts on laws, governments, economics, political reforms, and ethics. He mainly appealed to experts in those fields, but his philosophy was seen as a radical attack on the English establishment of the time. He communicated with the Founders, especially on government and laws, including judicial power. He is best known for founding the utilitarian concept of philosophy, arguing that governments should be limited to driving overall happiness in society, that outcomes rather than intentions should determine moral values.

Bentham articulated the view that governments and laws are negative or reductive. He believed that laws impose restrictions on individual liberties and should thus be approached cautiously and in as limited a manner as possible. He particularly believed in religious liberties, irrespective of government-oriented religious doctrines.

## WHAT IS LIBERAL DEMOCRACY?

Philosophy's impact on American democracy resulted in what is called liberal democracy. It is a system of governance where key individual freedoms are protected, but in some cases, their protection happens in tension with majority decision-making. The theoretical basis of democracy requires that most of its citizens be empowered to make all decisions. If that is true, then technically, America's governance system is not a democracy—it is a constitutional or democratic republic. Citizens can't and don't make every decision; those they elect to represent them are empowered to act on their behalf. This elected class of citizens should operate wisely and beneficially. If not, the electorate can replace those representatives via free and fair elections.

As many philosophers have opined, the social contract is our Constitution's basis. The Constitution, in seven articles, outlines the rights of government and, thus, the obligations of the people. Those seven articles also acted as limits on the government itself. Later, the Framers added the Bill of Rights (the first ten amendments) to provide strong, articulated guarantees that the new government would not trample upon freedoms of speech, press, and religion, or institute warrantless searches and seizures, among other restrictions. This fulfilled, in a unique way, a social contract between the new federal government and its citizens, a contract between the individual and the collective outlining the rights and obligations of each.

Under America's Constitution, individual rights are protected against the majority's wishes. The Constitution protects the basic rights of individuals—free speech, freedom to practice any religion, freedom to own personal firearms, and so on—even when a majority might try to limit or restrict those freedoms.

Probably the most significant advantage of a representative government is that our constitutional republic sets up a system of laws—not a system based on the power of humans. No one is above the law in America. Our constitutional republic is quite different from England's monarchical rule from which America emerged after the American Revolution. In a monarchy, the king or queen, as ruler, is considered the supreme law of the land. While the Declaration expressed the philosophical ideas that undergirded American independence, the Constitution contained the details of how the federal government would run and defined the sanctity of individual freedoms.

These founding documents underscored that every individual was equal. Each shares and possesses all the rights of every other individual in America. The origin of those rights was Creator-given, the natural rights of mankind, not granted by any monarch or government. Since the government did not create those rights, it can never take them away. The government must protect those rights and allow its citizens to enjoy the fruits of those rights.

In most ways, democracy should be defined generally as a method of collective decision-making, considering all individuals in the collective as equal at any key stage of a decision-making process. By this definition, collective decisions bind all individuals who are part of the collective, namely all Americans.

Under this definition, democracy means that individuals directly vote on certain matters or elect representatives to make such decisions on their behalf. Using this definition, America is defined as a democracy that protects individual rights against possible tyranny of the majority. In some states, like Arizona, a referendum process enables citizens to make some direct decisions. However, we mostly elect people we believe to be wise enough to make many decisions on our behalf.

By now, you should sense the concerns of the Founders regarding the possible tyranny by one group over another. James Madison observed, in Article 51 of *The Federalist Papers*:

> [I]f men were angels, no government would be necessary.... In framing a government which is to be administered by men over men, the great difficulty lies in this: you must first enable the government to control the governed and in the next place oblige it to control itself.[8]

The Constitution establishes how overall rules across federal America are determined and outlines how the US government works, including how its powers are separated across the three branches: legislative, executive, and judicial. Much of the constitutional text discusses how the federal government is limited, that there are many things it can't and shouldn't do. In particular, the Tenth Amendment (a part of the Bill of Rights) notes that the federal government is limited: "The powers not delegated to the United States by the Constitution, nor prohibited by it to the States, are reserved to the States respectively, or to the people." The people are the ultimate source of power in America, the "consent of the Governed."

---

8   James Madison, *The Federalist Papers*, Article 51 (1788). National Constitutional Center (see https://constitutioncenter.org/the-constitution/historic-document-library/detail/james-madison-federalist-no-51-1788). Note, we now will use the framework of *The Federalist Papers*, Article 51, for example, for future references to this source.

No one should suggest that the Founders were always wise and made all the right choices. But for the times, they made some of the most enlightened choices for freedom and individual rights. They also recognized that America was a work in progress and would be forever. As the Preamble to the Constitution notes, in part: "We the People of the United States, in Order to form a more perfect Union...."

Some suggest there is no magic in the founding documents. They point out that many of these individuals crafted an earlier constitution, the Articles of Confederation, that failed to create an economic and freedom-based society across America. Clearly, the Declaration and Constitution injected key rules for how this new country governed itself, but other factors were also in play. Starting with the thirteen original states, finding ways to integrate their work across one combined federal system was quite powerful. Even at its birth, America's advantages, due to its geography, the grit of its early immigrants and settlers, and the fact that the land offered many natural resources and a lot of room to grow, were huge factors that allowed democracy to flourish.

Were the Framers divinely inspired when they wrote the Constitution? That question will always be open to debate. Suffice it to say that a document that protected the rights and liberties of its people, defined limits on the role of the new federal government, and articulated why the American people should give up some freedoms and agree to a collective process—and to do it in writing at a time when the mother country, England, mostly relied on case law (not laws written down)—was foundational to the success America has seen for almost 250 years.

There are examples of other societies that faced factors similar to America's but chose different paths—often destructive paths—in part due to factors such as demography, geography, governance gone wrong, and so on. The example of Germany in the latter decades of the nineteenth century comes to mind. Germany's choices led to various iterations of instability and ultimately into both the Great War (World War I) and World War II. Other European civilizations, such as the Nordic countries, appeared to have moved more toward socialism and central government control, yet they never lost sight of the primacy of individual rights. Denmark, Iceland, Greenland, Finland, and Norway have societies that differ from today's America, but few can argue convincingly that they are not democratic nations.

Some commentators suggest societies have few choices to create predictable outcomes that co-manage society and its norms. For example, under a system where a government guarantees certain property rights of its members, its people look to the government to deliver on its promises. They try to hold that government accountable as needed, often by rising into a revolution. When one system of governance replaces another, the daunting challenge of establishing a workable society remains.

Similar to the Framers adopted for the United States, other systems focus less on outcomes and more on inputs. The rules are set to enable individual freedoms and collective behavior. Under this system, the government promises not to deliver substantive results; rather, it helps the governed agree on a set of rules to manage society and then serves to referee disputes under such rules. Those rules are easier to change over time by democratic initiatives than by revolt or by overturning an underperforming government.

Under a founding constitution, it is easier to ensure that a majority's collective wisdom and interests will not undercut fundamental individual rights, creating societies that can coalesce over time. When a democracy centers itself around individuals, where individuals, not society in general, are primary, there is less risk of those individuals believing the social order fails them.

The central players in America's system—citizens—gain from their individual work and division of labor toward higher economic and other values. Thus, they theoretically have much less concern for corruption, graft, and insider dealing to achieve otherwise impossible outcomes. By contrast, in socialistic or communistic countries that manage society through government, individuals have much less self-interest in succeeding. They are often merely pawns, not powerful agents for self-benefit and societal success.

This self-interest can, should, and does lead to a more liberal society and democracy. It may not be the only way to get there, but history suggests it's the best way. Liberal democracies evolve and grow. A constitution creates the methodology for determining rules of societal behavior. It creates flexibility through the power of politics and political engagement around the voting booth. However, this structure can't compel the right decisions. It enables its citizens to make poor or wrong decisions but also lets them amend or change systems and institutions to address past mistakes.

Liberal democracies are not rigid; they are not set in stone. They remain works in progress. Liberal democracies help their citizens understand where to create binding agreements—the rules—that determine societal norms without challenging the primacy of individual liberty.

Using author Nassim Nicholas Taleb's book *Antifragile*[9] as a point of reference, liberal democracies are durable. Anti-fragile systems are not the opposite of fragile systems or merely resilient. Anti-fragile systems grow stronger when stressed. In the case of American democracy, as the challenges of the eighteenth and nineteenth centuries moved into the mega-challenges of the twentieth century, our society's pillars were stressed. In our view, democracy is strengthened as a result.

As society and culture in America continue to diversify, evolution and growth follow. Diversification sometimes sets up tensions between groups that support the American system, but a liberal democracy is flexible enough to accommodate changes.

★ ★ ★

The Declaration of Independence declares that "all men are created equal." When it was written in the eighteenth century, the Founders meant "men," mostly Caucasian landowning males. Thus, these "equal men" created our initial republican system of who could serve as the president, vice president, senators, and representatives and decided how they were to be elected. It took until early in the twentieth century—and the passage of the Nineteenth Amendment—to establish the federal right for women to vote.

The failure of the Founders to allow all men (and women) of all races to be equal in America is worthy of additional discussion. There was only a superficial treatment of slav-

---

[9]  Nassim Nicholas Taleb, *Antifragile* (New York: Random House, 2012).

ery by the Founders, even though they knew it had been imposed mostly on unwilling natives of Africa, who were violently removed from their homelands, shipped to America, and made to work and serve without compensation for many years. The Founders came from several states, including those where the economy was mostly supported by slavery. While some Founders saw the sin of slavery and hoped to eliminate its practice in America, others refused.

This conflict, among others, threatened to derail America before it began. The framework for power by individual states, such as determining the number of representatives from each state and how federal taxes would be allocated, was based on a state's total population. Even though enslaved people were denied the right to vote, some Founders wanted their populations to count toward representation (if not necessarily toward relative tax burdens). They wanted those freed from slavery and those indentured to others to be counted as full persons.

The three-fifths compromise agreement was reached during the 1787 constitutional convention:

> Representatives and direct Taxes shall be apportioned among the several States which may be included within this Union, according to their respective Numbers, which shall be determined by adding to the whole Number of free Persons, including those bound to Service for a Term of Years [i.e., indentured individuals], and excluding Indians not taxed, three fifths of all other Persons.[10]

By including this provision to determine legislative apportionment, this compromise provided additional represen-

---

10   US Constitution, Article 1, Section 2, Clause 3.

tation of slave states compared with free states. Moreover, a major blot on the Constitution is found in the so-called (but not so named in the Constitution itself) Fugitive Slave Clause (Article 4, Section 2), which provided:

> No Person held to Service or Labour in one State, under the Laws thereof, escaping into another, shall, in Consequence of any Law or Regulation therein, be discharged from such Service or Labour, but shall be delivered up on Claim of the Party to whom such Service of Labour may be due.

The Founders also wrote and included another provision in the Constitution that allowed twenty years of protection for slave importation to America (Article 1, Section 9).

There is little doubt that the Constitution continued to endorse the American conditions of slavery, even after independence and despite the utopian views expressed in the founding documents. But an important point to note is that not once is the word "slave" or "slavery" used in either the Declaration or the original Constitution (before passage of the Thirteenth Amendment). Instead, those founding documents called those individuals (relating to those enslaved at the time) "persons," not property. The absence was deliberate. There were many Founders who saw slavery for what it was.

We underscore our view that it was not an oversight when the Founders avoided naming slavery as a right nor used the words "slave" or "slavery." This was a choice, not an oversight or diversion. At the time of their drafting, there was a division among those Founders who attended the Continental Congress, and it was resolved when the "better angels" of the Founders prevailed. Collectively, they aspired to equality for all. Most of them understood slavery was inconsistent with all their other founding principles.

Many of these statesmen—Thomas Paine, John Adams, Benjamin Franklin, Alexander Hamilton—opposed slavery outright and worked to end slavery in America. Others, like George Washington, who was a slave owner, wrote his thoughts in 1786 in a letter to Robert Morris, "There is not a man living who wishes more sincerely than I do, to see a plan adopted for the abolition of [slavery]."[11]

In 1781, Thomas Jefferson (a slave owner) published *Notes on the State of Virginia*. In it, he wrote:

> And can the liberties of a nation be thought secure when we have removed their only firm basis, a conviction in the minds of the people that these liberties are of the gift of God? That they are not to be violated but with his wrath? Indeed, I tremble for my country when I reflect that God is just: that his justice cannot sleep [forever]....[12]

Madison observed in his three-volume work, *The Records of the Federal Convention of 1787*: "We have seen the mere distinction of [color] made in the most enlightened period of time, a ground of the most oppressive dominion ever exercised by man over man."[13]

---

[11] George Washington, "Letter to Robert Morris," April 12, 1786, *The Papers of George Washington: April 1786–January 1787 (Volume 4) (Confederation Series)*, ed. W.W. Abbot (Virginia: University Press of Virginia, 1995).

[12] Thomas Jefferson, *Notes on the State of Virginia*, ed. William Peden (North Carolina: University of North Carolina Press, 1955).

[13] James Madison, *Notes of Debates in the Federal Convention of 1787*, ed. Adrienne Koch (Ohio: Ohio University Press, 1966).

The debate against slavery continued into the nineteenth century, with many concluding that the Constitution was a pro-slavery document. Others disagreed. For example, abolitionist and former enslaved person Frederick Douglass noted in 1860, on the eve of the Civil War:

> [The Three-fifths Compromise]...is a downright disability laid upon the slave-holding States, one which deprives those States of two-fifths of their natural basis of representation. Instead of encouraging slavery, the Constitution encourages freedom, by giving an increase of two-fifths of political power to free over slave States.[14]

Douglass encouraged the free states to use the powers in the Constitution to end the institution of slavery in America. He argued that the Constitution did not support slavery in its text. Instead, it had a "very opposite meaning."[15] Douglass, a noteworthy intellectual and civil rights advocate, understood that wrapping the foundations of the Constitution around the cause of racial equality was much smarter than arguing that our Founders and the Constitution approved slavery.

Douglass was not alone in advancing what he believed was the Founders' intent to base the new country on equality for all. Abraham Lincoln also supported that view. He issued an

---

14 Frederick Douglass, *Life and Times of Frederick Douglass: His Early Life as a Slave, His Escape from Bondage, and His Complete History* (California: CreateSpace Independent Publishing Platform, 2017).

15 Frederick Douglass, "The Constitution of the United States: Is It Pro-Slavery or Anti-Slavery?" Speech, Glasgow, Scotland, March 26, 1860, in *The Frederick Douglass Papers, Series 1, Vol. 3: Speeches, Debates, and Interviews*, ed. John W. Blassingame (Connecticut: Yale University Press, 1985).

Executive Order, the "Emancipation Proclamation," effective as of New Year's Day in 1863:

> And by virtue of the power, and for the purpose aforesaid, I do order and declare that all persons held as slaves within said designated States, and parts of States, are, and henceforward shall be free; and that the Executive government of the United States, including the military and naval authorities thereof, will recognize and maintain the freedom of said persons.
>
> And I hereby enjoin upon the people so declared to be free to abstain from all violence, unless in necessary self-defence; and I recommend to them that, in all cases when allowed, they labor faithfully for reasonable wages.[16]

Also importantly, in our view, supporters of continuing slavery in America could not use the Constitution as a defense. Senator John Calhoun of South Carolina, one of the most adamant voices defending slavery in the mid-nineteenth century, could not draw support from the founding documents. Instead, he challenged the overall concept of equality.

I, Paul Johnson, am the former mayor of a major American city, and I, Larry Aldrich, am a former chief executive of a local newspaper. We both believe that Americans still have significant work to do regarding racial equality. Our leaders must

---

16   Abraham Lincoln, *The Emancipation Proclamation*, January 1, 1863, National Archives, https://www.archives.gov/milestone-documents/emancipation-proclamation.

continue to modify laws and regulations on police authority, drug abuse policies, and criminal sentencing standards and bend them toward even more fair and equal justice.

However, for those who believe in promoting equality, it is a grave mistake to ignore, much less to reject, the idea that this nation was founded on that ideal. Many early leaders fought to move the ideal forward so that all are created equal, trying not to cede this ground to those who rejected that ideal.

Nowhere else can this be done more effectively, fairly, and equally than in America. As our American culture and society continue to evolve, as the moral arc of justice in America bends, we must respect and protect the civil liberties granted to every citizen.

We must continue to use the tools provided in the language of the Declaration and the Constitution and the many laws passed under them to resolve our differences better and remedy past failures. The Founders, despite accepting what history suggests was a horrific compromise, might have seen elements of the journey still ahead. We're blinkered if we do not recognize that our democracy continually needs improvement. And we're myopic if we don't recognize America's progress, especially over the past fifty to seventy-five years. We should not condemn America's vision and future by our past racism and other exclusions. America and other diverse liberal democracies are vastly more inclusive today than in the past.

The Declaration's concept of "all men are created equal" was not just a statement but a transformative idea that the statesmen embedded in our founding documents. This concept has empowered future generations to use the language to insist that all men and all women are equal in America. Instead of a moment of failure, the Founders could foresee much of how the future would unfold in America, and they ensured its correction by embedding a powerful tool in the Constitution.

Slavery was a stain on the US, just as it was a stain on the entire world. We abhor discrimination. We support civil rights, equal rights, and human rights. These concepts, including the eventual abolition of slavery, are derived from America's founding documents that eloquently stated that every person was created equal. Our founding was established by imperfect people who sacrificed greatly to reach a perfect ideal.

## CHAPTER 4

# INNOVATING THROUGH THE LENS OF THE ENLIGHTENMENT

THROUGHOUT HISTORY, MAINLY SINCE THE Industrial Revolution, the strides made in human progress can be linked to the principles of the Enlightenment.[1] The pillars of this era—reason, science, individualism, and the establishment of a government restrained by the rights of its citizens—elevated human progress to unprecedented heights. These tenets, embodying the essence of freedom and liberty, consistently fostered environments where innovation thrives, with individual potential realized. The Enlightenment championed reason, empirical evidence, and the intrinsic worth of the individual. It laid the philosophical groundwork for the Declaration of Independence, which boldly asserted the equality of all people.

Conversely, the human condition experienced regression or stagnation as countries strayed from these Enlightenment ideals. Adopting philosophies antithetical to those principles—such as collectivism, tribalism, dialectical materialism, and unrestrained government authority that usurps personal property, ideas, and even lives for the so-called greater good—

---

1   The Industrial Revolution began in the mid-seventeenth century; the Enlightenment, often called the Age of Reason, also began in that century.

repeatedly led societies into periods of decline and darkness. Such ideologies, frequently advanced under the guise of equity, damaged the collective well-being and the advancement of human societies.

The Enlightenment ideals of reason, individual freedom, and limited governance guided humanity toward progress. In contrast, the opposing ideologies, emphasizing collective authority and suppression of individual rights, cast shadows, impeding human progress and dimming the light of advancement.

★ ★ ★

Today, in America, we battle against authoritarian forces abroad and against authoritarian uprisings and pressures within our own country. These battles reflect clashes between the ideals of the Enlightenment on the one hand and collectivism, tribalism, dialectical materialism, and unrestrained government authority on the other. The threats from authoritarianism jeopardize the rights and dignity of individuals and challenge the very concepts upon which our nation was founded, eroding the unifying ideals of Western liberal democracy.

In contemporary America, we observe a troubling divergence from the Enlightenment principles of rationality, science, and individualism at both ends of the political spectrum. In our view, today's political extremes often betray America's foundational ideals, captured in the Declaration of Independence.

On the left side of the political spectrum, there is an increasing tendency to view individuals primarily through the lens of their group identity, often defined by race or gender.

While seeking to address historical injustices, this perspective risks overshadowing an individual's unique experiences, thoughts, and contributions, reducing them to mere representatives of their demographic categories. Such a view undermines the Enlightenment's emphasis on individual merit and agency and contradicts the Declaration's proclamation of inherent equality.

On the right side, we observe similar deviations from Enlightenment values. Here, the ideal of rationality is often compromised by an embrace of populism that prioritizes emotional appeal and group loyalty. This can manifest in skepticism toward scientific consensus, a phenomenon that undercuts the Enlightenment's veneration of empirical inquiry. Moreover, a segment of the right occasionally veers into collectivist territory, championing national or cultural identity in a manner that diminishes the importance of the individual, approaches contrary to the Enlightenment ideals of personal liberty and reason and the Declaration's vision of a society where individuals are judged on their merits rather than their membership in particular groups.

The polarized nature of contemporary American politics, with its inclination toward group identity, whether based on demographics, culture, or ideology, poses profound challenges to the Enlightenment principles that have long guided our nation. Both extremes, in different ways, risk undermining the commitment to reason, individual dignity, and the pursuit of knowledge.

Americans must recommit to these Enlightenment values—celebrations of reason, individualism, and a shared human dignity transcending group identities.

## TRUTHS AND IDEALS

Even before their independence from England, Americans fervently held certain truths and ideals. America flourished on a bedrock of unifying ideals, where equality transcends gender and race, and everyone is intrinsically endowed with inalienable rights, not as grants from government but as gifts from their Creator. These tenets are the pillars of America's identity, the universal truths that most Founding Fathers firmly upheld.

The words "truth" and "ideal" share similar concepts. Both embody the aspiration to fulfill a greater purpose. Truth entails understanding the past and improving the present, whereas ideal pertains to the future. Plato's writings vividly capture the essence of the word "ideal." He and his Platonic idealism[2] offer valuable insights into the significance of ideals for human progress. Ideals may appear elusive, yet Plato argued that they possess more reality than physical entities.

The Founders' conviction in the self-evident nature of certain truths drew its philosophical lineage from Plato. In an age where Plato's contemporaries, the Sophists, championed the notion that truth was an entirely subjective and relative concept, he stood as a steadfast advocate for the existence of objective truths, truths that soared above individual perceptions and societal constructs.

Central to Plato's philosophical crusade against relativism was his seminal Theory of Forms, which posited the existence of a transcendent realm, far removed from the tangibility of the physical world, where abstract, perfect "forms" resided. These forms represented self-evident truths and encompassed uni-

---

2   Plato, *The Republic*, trans. G.M.A. Grube, revised by C.D.C. Reeve (Indianapolis: Hackett Publishing Company, 1992), 117.

versal ideals such as goodness, beauty, and equality. In Plato's mind, these forms created the cornerstones of all knowledge.

The genesis of Plato's recognition of these self-evident truths was twofold: a rigorous intellectual battle with the Sophists over the nature of truth and the profound impact of his mentor's death, Socrates. Plato sought to illuminate a transcendent justice, a universal ideal that starkly contrasts the flawed human execution typically seen. Plato's philosophical journey became a beacon for the Founders, guiding their belief in the self-evident truths that would form the bedrock of a new nation.

The death of Socrates (as determined by the citizens of Athens) deeply depressed Plato. In his novel *Apology of Socrates*,[3] Plato delved into the accusations against Socrates for his philosophical pursuits, the related trial and guilty verdict, and his subsequent sentencing to death. A jury of Greek citizens convened to pass judgment on the accusations, and they were incensed by Socrates's condescension. Although many Greeks served on the jury, only a slim majority convicted him. After Socrates further provoked their anger, even more people sentenced the great philosopher to death. The jury's failure to achieve justice stunned Plato. Justice embodied an ideal, and Plato sought to impart the importance of ideals, which America's Founders might have referred to as truths.

Plato's opus, *The Republic*,[4] features a well-known essay, "The Allegory of the Cave." This cave was adorned with magnificent paintings, yet only the individuals positioned at the mouth of the cave, near natural light, could truly grasp their beauty. Those dwelling in the darkness at the rear of the cave

---

[3]  Plato, *Apology of Socrates*, trans. G.M.A. Grube (Indianapolis: Hackett Publishing Company, 1981).

[4]  Plato, *The Republic*, trans. Allan Bloom (New York: Basic Books, 1968).

remained oblivious to such splendor. This allegory serves as a metaphor for enlightenment, with the enlightened individuals being those closest to the light.

Plato employed the idea of a triangle to further illustrate the concept of ideals in the context of perfection. A perfect triangle only exists in the mind—an ideal shape of three lines with three corners. However, a perfect triangle cannot be drawn by hand onto a surface. Why? Because the triangle drawing is a facsimile of the shape's idea. Only the idea is perfect; the facsimile is imperfect.

Plato referred to the ideal triangle, or any ideal fashioned by a human mind, as a "form." A form could manifest in numerous representations in the real world, yet it represents the epitome of perfection. Countless forms exist, and each represents a specific ideal. The culmination of these forms is "logos," or the comprehensive embodiment of all forms, symbolizing the rational force permeating the universe.

Plato intended not to discuss triangles but to demonstrate the higher ideals of forms to elucidate human characteristics. Although traits such as honesty, truth, courage, and faithfulness cannot be physically drawn, they exist in life as forms. Justice embodies a form, and the perfect ideal of justice only resides in our minds. Plato employed the death of his mentor and friend Socrates to discuss the creation of an ideal. Even though they had not initially regarded him as guilty, those who voted for Socrates to be executed were driven by anger rather than a profound sense of the greater ideal of justice.

Justice, in its most exalted form, exists as an archetype of a higher ideal, a conceptual perfection that, while it may reside solely in the realm of thought, inspires our aspirations in the tangible world. By focusing on this more perfected form of justice, one deeply rooted in the foundational ideal that all humans are born equal, bestowed with inalienable rights by their Creator, our Founders endeavored to bring a more significant measure of justice into reality, a formidable challenge in 1776. Yet, through the wisdom gleaned from Plato's writings, they comprehended the possibility of manifesting a higher ideal, a beacon of justice that, while perhaps unattainable in its purest form, could guide the nascent nation towards a more just and equitable society.

When our Founders met, wrote, and worked to create the United States, they were leaving behind another union, another system, one led by the English monarchy. They knew they could not create a perfect union overnight, nor did they say they would. Instead, they said, "We the People of the United States, in Order to form a more perfect Union...." It was not a perfect union then, but a pathway ahead to a more perfect one than the one they left. They thought about the ideal, and the ideal was a nation conceived in liberty and freedom. These men had the audacity to believe they could overthrow the most powerful nation on the planet and create the foundations for a more perfect country. They exuded idealism.

Our Declaration and Constitution expressed these unifying ideals. Like all ideals, their meaning expanded over time. These ideals have united our people for almost 250 years. From its inception, America emphasized individual freedoms. From the beginning of their new world, Americans naturally rejected authority and control over themselves as individuals. They greatly valued privacy, free speech, religious freedom, gun ownership, the right to assemble peaceably, property ownership, and other rights, and they expected no government to restrict them.

The Protestant religions practiced by many new Americans around 1776 certainly drove this self-interested focus. Martin Luther, the father of the Protestant Reformation during the early sixteenth century, significantly influenced thinking about the rights of individuals endowed by their Creator. Luther's central doctrine, "justification by faith alone," transformed the mindset of Western society. In his mind, people did not need a church to justify who they were. He believed each individual enjoyed the grace and favor of God. Luther courageously stood up against the power of the Catholic Church in 1521, risking his life.

Luther's belief that each soul had a personal relationship with God meant that everyone was worthy of respect and dignity, that each individual alone could decide to accept or deny his faith, not as part of the blessings of a church or by the grace of a king. This revolutionary concept denied the collective powers of the church or state to control an individual through salvation. Each person had dignity and made their faith choices as an individual.

★ ★ ★

America was founded on the ideals of some great philosophers, such as Locke and his natural rights theory. Locke argued that the government had obligations to its people, that the government should have limited power over its citizens, and that citizens should be able to overthrow the government under certain circumstances.

Rousseau's writings articulated the notion of a social contract. He wrote that the progress of mankind started long before governments or hierarchies, and mankind was free and independent. But once agriculture began, and farms were established, along with the first stages of property ownership, inevitably, one man tried to triumph over another. Yet Rousseau saw a final stage where men would seek a government that gave dignity to each individual. Through a social contract between a government and its people, humans would be free but have obligations to the greater good in exchange.

Rousseau's construct, including the social contract, was secular. If all individuals were worthy of dignity in the eyes of God, and if God saw all beings as equal when they were made to stand before him at the end of life and the time of reckoning, then government owed that same sense of equality. The justification that humans are "saved by faith alone," and that the choice to accept or reject God was an individual choice, expanded into the entire construct surrounding the rights of individuals.

In addition, Adam Smith's philosophy influenced the young nation as it helped citizens understand the values of an economy based on freedom, a democratic economy where moral decisions to buy or not buy, to build or not build, were based on individual choices. The idea of a free market created a system where individuals could better work together, divide their labor to achieve based on their talents, and collectively accomplish more in the marketplace.

Early in American history, Alexis de Tocqueville recorded how American individuals differed from their European counterparts. During his tour of America, he claimed that no one cared about making money in Europe. The upper class found this crass; they were guaranteed wealth. The poor had no hope of gaining wealth. But in America, he saw a trait in Americans that valued hard work.

He saw that Americans could and did build better lives through hard work. He observed that, unlike his European countrymen, Americans did not despise the elite individuals in their society, and they did not defer power to them, either. The United States eradicated the old-world aristocracy when it cut its colonial ties to England. The voices of ordinary Americans sang loudly. In fact, they sang so strongly as a collective in the public square that the power of elites significantly diminished compared to the power controlled by the elites of Europe.

★ ★ ★

In the evolving landscape of modern society, the foundational values of democracy and the Enlightenment are being reexamined and challenged. Individual liberty, a cornerstone of Enlightenment thought, is central to this introspection, now juxtaposed against collective security needs, such as public health initiatives and the complexities of digital privacy. The ideal of equality, intrinsic to democratic ethos, faces rigorous scrutiny in the face of persistent disparities in income, race, gender, and access to opportunities. Once considered self-evident, these ideals are now subjects of intense debate, reflecting the changing societal fabric.

Moreover, the Enlightenment's steadfast advocacy for reason and rationality encounters contemporary challenges, as the authority of science and expertise is weighed against populist currents and the politicization of fact-based discourse. Secularism, once a revolutionary principle separating church and state, continues to stir debate over religion's role in public policy. Representative democracy grapples with the rise of populism, authoritarian inclinations, and issues like campaign finance and electoral integrity. Freedom of speech, a once unassailable right, is now scrutinized in the context of hate speech, misinformation, and cancel culture. At the core of these debates lies the Enlightenment's legacy of critical inquiry and the scientific method, which finds itself at times in conflict with modern movements questioning established scientific consensus.

Proponents of the individualism theory hold that the interests of all are best served by allowing individuals maximum freedom balanced with responsibility for choosing their objectives and finding the means for obtaining them without interfering with the rights of other individuals. What followed from those principles in America was a government system that kept its interference in the lives of individuals to a minimum.

The opposition to individualism today pushes the idea that a Creator granted such rights. Opponents claim this is a religious myth, not moral certainty or truth. If a Creator did not grant these rights but they sprang instead from a moral construct of the mind, can alternative thoughts not focused on the individual be equally moral?

While many believe certain human rights are from a source greater than the human construct, it is a mistake to think that freedom is a universal value. Regardless of it being a truth, it is not a universal value. Religion is a more important value than a governing system in many places on Earth. And one value, much more universal than freedom, is the value of power. Power, as it is concentrated in leaders, is seen in how they benefit the collective. Power is almost always concentrated in an individual or a small group—a monarch, oligarch, or religious leader(s)—who establish their power by relying on tradition or by arguing they must have the authority to serve the collective's interests.

The evidence of this is abundant. From the fall of the Roman Republic until 1776, when Americans broke from a monarch and established the Constitution, no democracy or republic existed anywhere else. Western liberal democracy evolved from the Greeks into the Middle Ages, greatly influencing the Framers of the Constitution. They defined American liberal democracy as a representative democracy that protects individual liberties and properties by the rule of law. They also built a system for checks and balances of power.

The American Revolution revived something that had disappeared for almost 1,700 years after the time of Greek city-states and government by the people. However, America's initial steps failed to support key rights and liberties of all individuals. The outgrowth of that failure resulted in the Civil War, the Civil Rights movement, suffrage (voting rights), equal rights for women, free elections, and human rights extended to ensure dignity for all individuals.

★ ★ ★

When the Framers of the Declaration wrote, "We hold these truths to be self-evident, that all men are created equal," they did not mean that each of us is identical to one another. The theory of universal human nature—that humans are endowed with certain inalienable rights—is a commitment against discriminatory thought and segmentation, which evolved and expanded as our nation grew and matured to include rights afforded to different races, to women, and to those with different sexual orientations, regardless of any existing genetic differences. One significant distinction between the views of the Founders and revolutionaries in other countries was that in creating a system that empowered the individual, individuals were also expected to be responsible for their actions.

The true believer is attracted to an enticing pitch in authoritarian movements. The state creates the ideal of the model citizen, protects individuals from villainous groups, outlines their roles, and ensures safety and prosperity. There is little discussion about the need to build an expensive and all-powerful government or surrender political, individual, and economic rights. Individuals gain the pride of being part of something bigger, and the authoritarian leader and government unwittingly persuade individuals to give up these rights in exchange for guarantees.

The Constitution does not make such guarantees. Our social contract, the Constitution itself, defines the government's role and citizens' rights without guaranteeing outcomes. The only guarantee it provides is a limited federal government that treats individuals with dignity and equal opportunities. The Framers and their successors—all who benefited from their wisdom and vision—have built something unparalleled in human history.

Preserving individualism requires struggle. You, we, and all Americans must regain our sense of personal agency and responsibility. As Americans, we must regain collective agency. We must believe that our actions determine our destiny. We must embrace optimism about who we are. We must also trust in our ability to find creative solutions to problems. Recovering our sense of agency requires the traditional political right, the political left, and the center of the political spectrum to recognize how the philosophies of individualism, rationalism, modernism, and universal truths unite rather than divide us. We must reject extremist, alternative views from both the left and right and vigorously defend individualism and the principles of Enlightenment.

Consider what made the United States the mightiest nation in world history. Ask why America is wealthier and more prosperous than any other country. While we discuss many reasons elsewhere in this book, we cannot overlook individualism's crucial role. Empowering the individual over the collective allowed for incredible innovation, discoveries, and advancements in the human condition that surpassed any other era in history. We prioritize the rights of individuals above the government's rights, and we have prospered because of these rights and liberties.

★ ★ ★

By prioritizing the genius of individuals above all else, we enrich the collective without ever prioritizing the collective over the individual. Yet, many individuals can be found who prioritize collective interests over their own interests. These individuals are the ones we call heroes. Everyday heroes can be found in firehouses, police stations, and schools. They can be found on military bases, aircraft carriers, submarines, and fighter jets, working in intelligence agencies, and even operating in hostile countries, all to ensure the safety and security of all Americans. Some heroes are ordinary people who work hard but struggle to pay their bills, put food on the table for their families, and educate their children. Indeed, some answer the call to be elected and serve in government as representatives, establishing laws and safeguarding America's enduring liberties.

We also believe that entrepreneurs are heroes. They challenge the "ways things are always done," test and disrupt the status quo, push scientific endeavors to find cures for diseases, improve education delivery systems, and create marvels like self-driving cars, three-dimensional printers, and energy-saving devices.

In America, one can find evidence of these heroes in cemeteries across the country.

Revolutionary and Civil War soldiers risked their fortunes and lives in battles like Charlestown, Saratoga, and Bunker Hill. About 50,000 soldiers died in Gettysburg during the war to end slavery. Heroes perished in the jungles of Vietnam, the deserts of Afghanistan, the island caves of the South Pacific, the freezing forests of Europe, and the beaches of Normandy. These heroes came from beach towns in California, the heartland in Texas, and the skyscrapers of New York. They did not define their life experiences as red or blue voters but as Americans.

Humankind, and America specifically, owe a debt to those who sacrificed their lives to protect individual rights above all else. Regardless of your identity or the sacrifices you have made for the privilege of living as an American, you are responsible for relentlessly defending your freedoms, your self-determination, your duty, and your accountability. It is upon these cornerstones—the unwavering support for the ideals of the Enlightenment—that America was founded. And upon these enduring principles, America will continue to stand as the most formidable and exemplary democracy the world has ever witnessed.

# PART II

## AMERICAN IMAGINATION: INSPIRING FREEDOM, COLLABORATION, AND CREATIVITY

## CHAPTER 5
# EMBRACING THE CONSTITUTION AND THE INSTITUTIONS IT CREATED

WHILE AMERICA IS NEARLY 250 years of age today, the country experienced an existential threat to its democracy before it reached the age of one hundred, a sibling-versus-sibling, hand-to-hand, grand-scale insurrection—the Civil War. In addition, our country has faced other challenges over its history, including a most recent "lesser" insurrection—the one regarding the post-election transfer of leadership following the presidential election of 2020. That led to a different type of Civil War—an ideological, mind-to-mind combat.

Echoes from that challenge remain today. However, we believe that America will make it through this crisis even better and stronger than before. We always have.

Throughout American history, there have been several periods of profound instability that threatened the nation's very fabric. The most profound stress, of course, was the Civil War (1861 to 1865). This devastating conflict tore the country apart over issues of slavery and states' rights, bringing America to the brink of dissolution. Another critical challenge was the Great Depression (1929 to 1939), coupled with the Dust Bowl, which caused unprecedented economic hardship and social unrest, challenging the government's ability to maintain order and provide for its citizens. The 1960s—marked by the Vietnam War, the Civil Rights Movement, and the assassinations of key figures like Martin Luther King Jr. and John F. Kennedy—witnessed deep social and political divisions, bringing widespread protests and civil disorder. The early 2000s, especially following the September 11 attacks in 2001, saw heightened tensions and fear as the nation grappled with issues of terrorism, war, and the erosion of civil liberties.

The period leading up to and following the 2020 presidential election unveiled deep political and social divides, amplified by misinformation and the COVID-19 pandemic, threatening the core principles of democracy and civic unity in the United States. The divisions continue, with some Americans demanding significant changes in managing the country and questioning the authority of many institutions developed over the centuries since our founding.

Some of the changes that come from this division will strengthen America. But we must be careful before dramatically reshaping vital American institutions. We believe that evolutionary rather than revolutionary approaches make more sense as we assess the roles such institutions play while recognizing how the current instability threatens the bedrock of institutions designed to balance power across the three branches of the American government.

Prior difficult periods and Americans pulling back together exemplify the resilience of the American spirit and the continual efforts necessary to uphold the principles upon which the nation was founded.[1]

---

[1] Yuval Levin, in his excellent book, *American Covenant: How the Constitution Unified Our Nation—and Could Again* (New York: Hachette Book Group, Inc., 2024), makes this key point: "The Constitution not only gives form to the governing institutions, laws, and political practices of our society, it also shapes the American people." See, especially, Chapter 3.

## AN ALTERNATIVE VISION: AN AMERICAN INSURRECTION

On January 6, 2021, following the defeat of the then-president of the United States, Donald Trump, in the 2020 presidential election, a mob of his supporters attacked the US Capitol in Washington, DC. The mob sought to keep Trump in power by preventing Congress from formalizing President-elect Joseph Biden's victory.

Called to Washington by Trump, thousands of his supporters gathered near the Capitol to defend the soon-to-be former President's claim that the 2020 election was "stolen" by forces unknown, leading to the improper election of Biden. Trump and his supporters demanded that Vice President Mike Pence reject Biden's victory by not certifying the electoral ballot totals, possibly delaying the constitutionally mandated presidential inauguration on January 20, 2021.

Five people present at the insurrection died either during or following the attack. Many more were injured, including dozens of police officers. For several hours, as the rage and violence escalated, the record shows Trump refusing to send federal officials to defend the Capitol, including members of the local National Guard. Even so, the Capitol's police force and others were able to clear the building of rioters. The counting of the electoral votes resumed and was completed after midnight on the early morning of January 7th. Pence declared President-elect Biden victorious. Trump later committed to an orderly transition of power to the new administration, and Biden took the oath of office on January 20th.

For many citizens across America, the scenes of January 6th chilled both spines and resolve. Even after the inauguration, threats continued across America, followed by numerous and ongoing investigations and prosecutions. We remember and underscore these events—not to condemn them, although condemnation may be natural—but to remind ourselves that without the various institutions of democracy established by the Constitution and various state constitutions, as well as the public servants who staff those institutions, anarchy (and worse) would have a chance to rule across America. The institutions of democracy and its traditions, challenged as they were, withstood the stress thrown at them after the November 2020 election. Many elected and appointed officials in both major parties—Republican and Democrat—stepped up to support the ultimate power in America, namely each vote cast by every American citizen.

But we must ask ourselves:

- What would have happened if the insurrection had succeeded?
- What if, by brute force, the counting of delegates had stopped?
- What if the vice president declared a different winner?
- What if numerous state and federal judges declared the ballots from several states invalid?
- What if the states' governors or legislatures declared the votes invalid?

Would both sides have edged toward broader violence? Would the federal government have failed? Would citizens have been subjected to martial law when there was no declaration of an attack by an external enemy? Would the world have lost faith in the United States and its democratic foundations?

Looking at the possible answers to these questions objectively, it is a shock that democracy didn't wobble more, that no governor or state legislature waffled. Republican secretaries of state, under extreme pressure from the most popular Republican in the country, said a collective "No." More than sixty cases, supervised by judges (many appointed by Trump himself), held firm on preserving the Constitution, the rule of law, and free elections. Vice President Pence did his job as required by the law.

Why did these attempts at insurrection against democracy fail? We offer one conclusion: Because almost everyone, citizen and representative alike, believed (and still believes) in the power of the Constitution and the great value it stands for, that defending our foundations of liberty—defending America—still matters to most Americans. Most of us still believe in the values of American democracy.

We ask that you and other readers join us in seeing this recent sad chapter as ringing proof of the soundness of democracy, that regardless of which candidate you support, you will be protected from the excesses of any person by the strength of the Constitution, the authority of innumerable elected and appointed persons simply doing their jobs, and our collective faith in all our democracy represents.

Yet, Trump's re-election in 2024, following the events of January 6, 2021, underscores complex facets of American politics and society. That election reflected deep political divisions, where most of the electorate remained steadfast in supporting Trump's vision and policies, viewing his leadership as aligned with their values and concerns. Trump's victory can be interpreted as an expression of the American electorate's views regarding traditional norms and institutions, and his re-election might suggest a push against the established political order, resonating with voters who feel disillusioned or left behind by mainstream politics.

Moreover, Trump's return to the presidency could be interpreted as a testament to the enduring strength of popularism in American politics, where the appeal to the interests of the "common people" against so-called elite interests remains powerful. The intensity surrounding the 2024 election demonstrates the dynamic nature of American democracy, a system capable of swinging between different political spectrums, reflecting its citizens' diverse aspirations and concerns.

Overall, we believe the election exemplified the potency of American democracy, a system that must always adjust to the wishes of American citizens.

★ ★ ★

We see little evidence that faith in our Constitution is supported by anything less than an overwhelming number of Americans. Yet, we understand that good people across the American political spectrum question this. Restoring faith in the principles that support the success of America is a good way for all to bolster continuing belief in the greatness of our homeland.

We must always recall that the Founders created America as a democratic republic based on the rule of law rather than the rule of man (for example, a monarch or autocrat). In particular, we can never forget that our public servants (federal, state, and local) took an oath of office, swearing to support and defend the Constitution.

The threat of authoritarianism hearkens back to the darkest days of the Civil War. After the Civil War began,

Congress amended the oath of office for Senators and Representatives from:

> "I, [name of person swearing the oath] do solemnly swear or affirm (as the case may be) that I will support the Constitution of the United States."

to:

> "I solemnly swear (or affirm) that I will support and defend the Constitution of the United States against all enemies, foreign and domestic; that I will bear true faith and allegiance to the same; that I take this obligation freely, without any mental reservation or purpose of evasion; and that I will well and faithfully discharge the duties of the office on which I am about to enter. So help me God."

The change to the oath of office, making it more explicit about defending the Constitution against all enemies, both foreign and domestic, directly responded to the circumstances surrounding the Civil War. The war posed a profound threat to the very existence of the United States. It highlighted the need for a clear and strong commitment from government officials to the Constitution and the nation's founding principles.

By including the phrase "against all enemies, foreign and domestic," the oath recognizes that preserving the constitutional order may require vigilance and defense against threats that may emerge within the United States, not just from outside it.

We underscore the Declaration's and the Constitution's first focus on the rights and freedoms of all Americans—the ultimate source of power to create collective successes—that drives America's democracy, a system that provides for individuals collectively what they cannot do for themselves. The Constitution created discrete systems: elected officials, separation of powers, and institutions to support its framework of limited government to guide citizens towards reaching a consensus regarding the societal rules we follow and "referee" or "umpire" the resolution of disagreements.

At its core, democracy is the design of the Constitution, which enables citizens of every state to operate across a broader federal society.

It may be challenging to understand the task undertaken by the Founders. They obviously were chastened by the burdens of a centralized government, namely England, through its monarchy, and the language of the Constitution embedded these sensitivities. Still, the states and their citizens had concerns. Before the Constitution was ratified, enacted, and implemented, the states, on behalf of their citizens, demanded passage of the Bill of Rights, the first ten amendments to the Constitution.

While the terms of the Constitution reflected a limited role for the new federal government, the Bill of Rights specifically limited its powers. The Ninth Amendment provides: "The enumeration in the Constitution of certain rights shall not be construed to deny or disparage others retained by the people." The Tenth Amendment underscores: "The powers not delegated to the United States by the Constitution, nor prohibited by it to the States, are reserved to the States respectively, or the people."

The Founders and those who voted in the states to ratify the Constitution required this balance, this limited grant of powers, to create a more powerful union that could protect

America's future and individual freedoms and fundamentally protect the Constitution itself.

Remember, the separation of powers framework in the Constitution ensures that power is disbursed to avoid tyranny. Under the Constitution, the citizens, as voters, elect federal officials, with the direct election of congressional representatives and senators, and the indirect election of the president and vice president (via Electoral College electors chosen by majority vote in the states). Thus, citizens are *the* source of all power under the American Constitution.

Our Constitution, the foundational social contract of the United States, outlines the framework of governance through its seven articles while concurrently describing individual rights via the Bill of Rights. However, the significance of the seven articles extends beyond merely delineating the scope of governmental authority. By establishing a sophisticated system of checks and balances, these articles not only enumerate governmental powers but also implicitly restrict them, restrictions reinforced by the Tenth Amendment. Thus, the Constitution serves a dual purpose: It empowers the federal government while also curbing its reach, striking a balance between national authority, state autonomy, and the ultimate power of American citizens via elections.

The Constitution sets in place this limited federal government system. It is managed by individuals who themselves manage the institutions the government created. The Constitution lists specific institutions, beginning with Congress (Article 1: House of Representatives and Senate), the president and vice president (Article 2), and the judiciary (Article 3). That order matters. It starts with the people's representatives (chosen by popular vote), followed by the Executive Branch (president and vice president) to implement laws passed by Congress, and the Judicial Branch (the Supreme Court, and the hierarchy of state and federal courts) to assess the validity of laws passed by Congress and signed into law by the president.

In other words, and as supported by contemporaneous statements from the Founders, the Article 1–established Congress, directly elected by the people, was deemed the most important branch of government, with the judiciary the least important.

The Constitution also, either directly or by implication, creates many other institutions. The document details some management of the ways Congress conducts its work (and some of the rules it follows); it determines the minimum requirements (such as the minimum age) of those who can serve; it lists the specific powers of each legislative house (such as that laws to raise revenues via taxation must begin in the House); and, it lists the overall powers that Congress itself has (for example, to borrow, regulate international commerce between and among the States, establish immigration rules, "coin Money," allow for patent and other intellectual property rights, and declare war).[2]

Article 2 vests all executive power in the president of the United States. The president supervises all executive departments of government, and the Constitution states directly (or via implication) what those departments are: Treasury, State (manages international affairs), Defense (war), Justice (law enforcement), a department to gather the decennial census information, a system to manage where the federal government resides (the District of Columbia), and other departments as determined and funded by Congress and the president.

---

[2] US Constitution, Article 1, Section 8.

Article 3 is where the Constitution created the third federal government branch—the Judiciary. This article contemplates and allows for creating courts inferior to the Supreme Court, which was established directly in the text. Congress created the inferior courts under the Judiciary Act of 1779,[3] and created additional inferior courts over the years, including certain administrative courts (for example, to manage immigration and tax controversies). Judges on federal courts, including Supreme Court Justices, hold their positions for life, if they choose.

The overall structure and breadth of the federal government today likely is much broader and bigger than even the most visionary Founders imagined. Beyond specific departments that are headed by members of the president's cabinet who must be confirmed by the Senate, many numerous administrative agencies or departments (like the Food and Drug Administration [FDA], the Federal Trade Commission [FTC], and the Environmental Protection Agency [EPA]) were created, some by Congress (where specific funding was required) and some by presidential fiat (where funding is embedded in the overall budget provided by Congress to the president to manage the Office of the Presidency).

It is beyond the scope of this book to analyze the powers of the various administrative departments. Some people believe those departments usurp the authority of Congress; some in Congress and some in the courts have pushed back on the authority of such departments. An example of administrative departments potentially usurping the power of Congress can

---

[3] *An Act to Establish the Judicial Courts of the United States,* Chapter 20, 1 Stat. 73 (1789).

be seen in the use of "regulatory rulemaking." For instance, the Clean Air Act, passed by Congress, sets broad goals and standards for air quality. However, the EPA writes the rules and regulations for achieving these goals. Some critics argue that this practice gives unelected officials in administrative agencies too much power to create rules that can have significant economic and social impacts, a power that constitutionally belongs to Congress.

Tensions between authority and delegated powers continue to vex people and the media, but this is a normal part of a complex constitutional democracy—one where the people's rights have been delegated to the government to manage the agreed-upon rules properly and to referee disputes.

In the modern era, some areas of our society are strongly regulated by our democratic government. You may agree that our society may be able to restore some freedoms by reducing the tasks adopted by federal agencies. For example, during the Reagan Administration in the 1980s, certain agency powers were reduced—removing the federal government from setting the prices for airline fares or restricting the telecommunications industry, for example. This led to explosive growth and, in most cases, lower consumer costs.

Which agency powers could further be limited? This is a discussion worth having. A new balance may lie ahead,[4] but it will be an evolution rather than a revolution, one that continues to assure the people that its government is there to serve the wishes of a majority and protect various individual rights, regardless of majority view.

---

4  See, for example, *Loper Bright Enterprises v. Raimondo*, slip opinion (US 2023), which limited the power of federal agencies to interpret congressional laws, overruling an earlier opinion (*Chevron*, 1984).

★ ★ ★

Authoritarian leaders (where one leader has all the power) make decisions (whether positive, negative, or neutral) unilaterally, which generally guarantees that decisions are of lower quality. In our view, without support from the governed, an autocratic leader's decisions most often lead to lower-quality decisions with limited public support. However, the extent of corruption across democracies and authoritarian systems demonstrates even clearer differences.

## CORRUPTION AND GOVERNMENT SYSTEMS

Corruption within governmental systems significantly undermines economic efficiency and market effectiveness. This inefficiency in the marketplace leads to reduced economic output, consequently diminishing citizens' overall quality of life. Notably, corruption erodes trust in public institutions and compromises the integrity of economic and political systems. According to Transparency International, a global coalition against corruption, there is a strong correlation between high levels of corruption and reduced economic growth.[5] This degradation of economic performance is particularly detrimental as it directly impacts individual prosperity and societal well-being. Moreover, corruption fundamentally undermines the power of the individual by skewing opportunities and resources in favor of those engaged in corrupt practices,

---

5   Marie Chêne, "The Impact of Corruption on Growth and Inequality," *Transparency International*, March 15, 2014, https://knowledgehub.transparency.org/helpdesk/the-impact-of-corruption-on-growth-and-inequality (accessed January 10, 2024).

thereby violating the principles of fairness and equality essential for a thriving society.

Corruption is the abuse of power or position for personal gain (as opposed to institutional gain)—corrupt people who exploit their government positions or offices for private gain. Corruption can take many forms, including taking bribes, embezzling from the government, or requiring that a private company hire a public employee's relative (nepotism). It occurs at all levels of government, from local government organizations, including public school districts, and regional or state governments to national governments.

Over time, corruption shifts some economic activity from societal to private gain. It damages governmental institutions, especially those developed under democracies, and leaves severe consequences for citizens. It undermines the rule of law, erodes trust in leaders and institutions, and can discourage foreign investment and economic growth. It can also lead to inequality and injustice, as those with wealth and power may be able to use their influence to receive favorable treatment. It is human nature to want to live in a society where a person does not have to navigate a black market of handouts and bribes to access services you have already paid for through taxes and fees. Most people worldwide live in regions where widespread corruption is embedded in their countries' cultures.

Yet, by most measures,[6] America and other democracies are better off than most other countries. Numerous analyses track measures of corruption. One of the best-followed is Transparency International's Corruption Perceptions Index.[7]

---

[6] See Ray Fisman and Miriam Golden, *Corruption: What Everyone Needs to Know* (England: Oxford University Press, 2017).

[7] Transparency International, "Corruption Perceptions Index," https://transparency.org/en/cpi (accessed July 25, 2024).

For 2021, the Index highlighted democracies in America, Europe, and Asia, with Scandinavian countries highest on the list of lower corruption-embedded countries. Only Mexico, a democracy, truly stands out as a democratic country with endemic corruption, in major part due to its embedded gangs dealing in the drug trade.

To address corruption, governments adopt laws and regulations to disclose conduct and prevent and punish corrupt activities. They may also establish independent agencies to investigate and prosecute corruption. Civil society organizations and the media also play a role in exposing and combating corruption. However, effectively addressing corruption is challenging. It often involves powerful actors who may be resistant to change.

In modern times, corrupt activities by public officials have been made illegal in virtually all democracies and even in some autocracies. America organized rigorous approaches to stamping out corruption, which is cause for optimism. We could have followed the views of the Greek philosophers, especially Plato, who argued in *The Republic* that society should select specific individuals at a young age and prepare and educate them to serve the public. But the Founders did not adopt Plato's views, and without that "philosopher-king" class, America and many other democracies must work hard to uncover and enjoin corruption by public officials. Moreover, our Founding Fathers, keenly aware of human imperfections, ingeniously crafted a system of checks and balances.

Are democracies truly bastions of corruption-free behavior? Certainly not, but the good news is that data suggests democracies have moved much further down the path to corruption-free governments than authoritarian governments. Authors Ray Fisman and Miriam Golden suggest in their book *Corruption: What Everyone Needs to Know*[8] that rather than government structures, overall gross domestic product (GDP, the overall measure of an economic system) is a better measure of the presence of corruption. For example, lower-income countries generally have higher incidences of corruption than higher-income countries. Since many of the world's democracies are also countries of higher income, GDP, rather than government structures, might be more relevant.

Under the auspices of Western liberal democracy, individual rights are powerful, and such power creates more prosperity. As they became more prosperous, citizens required less corruption to ensure equal access to government officials.

## REDUCING CORRUPTION

America, as the oldest continually operating democracy, has substantial advantages in the battles against corruption. We have laws that condemn governmental corruption, judicial and executive institutions to investigate and prosecute other types of corruption, and independent organizations like traditional and social media to investigate and expose corrupt behaviors.

Combating corruption in the quest to establish incorruptible democracies is a daunting yet crucial task. The inherent nature of democratic systems, characterized by regular elections and the marketplace of diverse ideas, offers a unique shield against corruption, a shield less robust in authoritarian regimes. However, lessening and eliminating corruption requires ongoing work by a country's citizens.

A comprehensive and multifaceted strategy is essential to address this issue effectively. Strengthening the legal frame-

---

8   Fisman and Golden, 2017.

work is paramount, as robust laws and regulations prevent and penalize corrupt activities. This includes enforcing laws against bribery, embezzlement, and other forms of corruption and promoting accountability through legislation.

Enhancing transparency is another critical step. By making government decision-making and financial transactions more transparent, the opportunities for corruption can be significantly reduced. This might involve making information about government contracts, budgets, and other financial dealings publicly available and requiring public officials to disclose their assets and economic interests.

Institutional strength is crucial in maintaining a check on public officials and enforcing anti-corruption laws. Independent institutions such as the judiciary, law enforcement agencies, and ombudsmen play a vital role. Similarly, civil society organizations, including non-governmental organizations and advocacy groups, are instrumental in exposing corruption and promoting transparency and accountability.

Media freedom is also crucial in the fight against corruption. A free and independent media can expose corrupt practices and hold public officials accountable. Lastly, fostering a culture of integrity is essential. Building a culture that values transparency, accountability, and ethical behavior requires sustained effort in educating citizens about the importance of these values.

Tackling corruption and building more transparent and accountable democratic systems requires a sustained and comprehensive approach. It demands persistence, vigilance, and a collective commitment to integrity and good governance, factors more easily implemented in America and other democracies.

In America and other democracies, citizens determine (often via their elected representatives) how the rules are set and enforced, who we choose to elect, and how our economies benefit from rules applied equally. Autocratic nations and emerging democracies have always struggled to reign in corruption. We believe democracies have, and will continue to have, the better "hands" to play.

★ ★ ★

America's framework isn't the only system that supports a free people. Many other countries have installed their versions of democracies using parliamentary systems. Still, ours continues to shine the bright lights of freedom that beckon many non-Americans to come to America.

The Constitution and the American institutions it creates enable its citizens to collaborate where they can operate successfully. Society's values and individual values strengthen when individuals come together for the greater good—for their protection against aggressors, to improve societal safety, and to enable individuals to divide their labors that increase efficiency while creating wealth and reducing poverty—in ways that centralized systems like monarchies and dictatorships can't do as well.

America's institutions and democratic system remain flexible, adjusting over the years to embrace the needs of American society. As freely elected leaders respond to the people's demands, they are often re-elected to continue to serve. When leaders fail, the people replace them. Nothing is stuck in neutral. America's democracy, partly due to the systems established to support its citizens, remains flexible yet firm enough to respond to our changing conditions and environments.

## CHAPTER 6

# SUPPORTING THE PRIVILEGE OF SELF-GOVERNANCE

IN MID-YEAR 1787, DELEGATES FROM all the thirteen original colonies met in Philadelphia. They threw out the existent Articles of Confederation and launched the greatest experiment in democratic self-governance by agreeing to the language in the Constitution of the United States. But the Founders weren't yet finished with it. Each of those colonies needed to ratify the Constitution, with at least nine states minimum necessary to launch America.

Alexander Hamilton and James Madison articulated what the Constitution wrought, as described in *The Federalist Papers*, Article 51, arguing, "Justice is the end of government. It is the end of civil society. It ever has been and ever will be pursued until it be obtained, or until liberty be lost in the pursuit."[1] That is quite the bold statement of what these key Founders felt was core to American democracy! They also observed:

> If men were angels, no government would be necessary. If angels were to govern men, neither external nor internal controls on government would be nec-

---

1   *The Federalist Papers*, Article 51.

> essary. In framing a government to be administered by men over men, the great difficulty lies in this: you must first enable the government to control the governed; and in the next place oblige it to control itself.
>
> ...
>
> In the compound republic of America, the power surrendered by the people is first divided between two distinct governments, and then the portion allotted to each subdivided among distinct and separate departments. Hence a double security arises to the rights of the people. The different governments will control each other, at the same time that each will be controlled by itself.[2]

No angels are we—true. However, most people will agree that justice is a great destination for democracies.

Article 51 is important for another reason. Here, Hamilton and Madison argue further for their vision for America:

> It is of great importance in a republic not only to guard the society against the oppression of its rulers, but to guard one part of the society against the injustice in the other part. Different interests necessarily exist in different classes of citizens. If a majority be united by a common interest, the rights of the minority will be insecure.
>
> There are but two methods of providing against this evil: the one creating a will in the community independent of the majority that is, of the society itself; the other, by comprehending in the society so many

---

2   Ibid.

separate descriptions of citizens as will render an unjust combination of a majority of the whole very improbable, if not impracticable.

The first method prevails in all governments possessing an hereditary or self-appointed authority. This, at best, is but a precarious security; because a power independent of the society may as well espouse the unjust views of the major, as the rightful interests of the minor party, and may possibly be turned against both parties.

The second method will be exemplified in the federal republic of the United States. Whilst all authority in it will be derived from and dependent on the society, the society itself will be broken into so many parts, interests, and classes of citizens, that the rights of individuals, or of the minority, will be in little danger from interested combinations of the majority.[3]

The Constitution specified the primacy of the individual rights and freedoms of the people of America, followed next by the primacy of state governments. America was to be governed in a limited way by the soon-to-be-created federal government. The Constitution articulated the powers of Congress, the powers of the presidency, and, to a degree, the powers of the federal judiciary. Thus, it specified what the federal government could do—with limited powers—but it was mostly silent on what it could not do toward individual freedoms. The Constitution was flawed in other ways, too, mainly including its continuing recognition of slavery and

---

[3] Ibid.

that individual powers and rights (and powers from the "consent of the governed") applied only to white men, especially those who owned land.

The Framers pondered the question of which of the "People" could vote on federal matters, but the final text of the Constitution mainly remained silent. It's hard to imagine a more critical unanswered question than who should be allowed to vote and for what offices and positions. History suggests that many Founders, including Madison, Hamilton, and Adams, believed only property-owning men could be trusted to vote intelligently, freely, and in support of true liberty. Jefferson felt the opposite; he believed universal suffrage (at least "universal" for adult white men) mattered toward liberty's ends.

If the Constitution and Declaration reflected the "consent of the governed," it seemed fundamental to ask, "Who were the governed?" Indeed, at that time, women, enslaved people, Native Americans, and convicts were excluded, but who else? Would every white man be allowed to vote? Would every white man be allowed to serve? How could America remain united when the principal action that held the country together—the right to vote—was limited to only a few citizens?

The Founders wanted every voter to be informed and to vote freely. Literacy mattered to them, and so did some form of financial wherewithal. Madison and Hamilton wrote, in Article 52 of *The Federalist Papers*, about who could be elected to serve as a member of the House of Representatives:

> The definition of suffrage [or the right to vote] is very justly regarded as a fundamental article of republican government. It was incumbent on the [constitutional] convention, therefore, to define and establish this

right in the Constitution. Under these reasonable limitations [e.g., the age, citizen requirements, inhabitant of the State "he" is to represent], the door of this part of the federal government is open to merit of every description, whether native or adoptive, whether young or old, and without regard to poverty or wealth, or to any particular profession of religious faith.[4]

The Constitution's language was clear on which white men could hold office in the House, Senate, or as president. But the Founders failed to establish who the voters could be in the Constitution. Ultimately, they ducked this key issue, leaving voting rights to the legislative determination of individual states.

★ ★ ★

Limiting the right to vote to some adult white men was one big flaw in the Constitution. but another was the lack of a Bill of Rights to protect individual freedoms. Hamilton disagreed. He argued in Article 84 of *The Federalist Papers*:

> The truth is, after all the declamations we have heard [regarding the absence of a Bill of Rights], that the Constitution is itself, in every rational sense, and to every useful purpose, a Bill of Rights…. And the proposed Constitution, if adopted, will be the bill of rights of the Union.

The people who agreed with Hamilton were concerned that specifying specific rights could overlook or exclude other rights.

---

[4]  *The Federalist Papers*, Article 52.

Regardless, the absence of a Bill of Rights stood in the way of getting enough states to ratify the Constitution. Jefferson argued that "a bill of rights is what people are entitled to against every government on earth, general or particular, and what no just government should refuse, or rest on inference."[5]

The pressures resolved as Madison drafted the first ten amendments to the Constitution—the Bill of Rights—ratified in 1791. The amended Constitution laid a firmer foundation and struck the American balance for liberal democracy, where one pillar stood for the will of the majority of voters while the other protected the liberty of American individuals to maintain their rights, irrespective of majority opinion.

New protections were extended during and after the Civil War with the passage of the Thirteenth, Fourteenth, and Fifteenth Amendments. However, this chapter concentrates only on the first rights written into the Bill of Rights, the key individual freedoms to be protected by the First Amendment, with a straightforward but simple statement:

> Congress shall make no law respecting an establishment of religion, or prohibiting the free exercise thereof; or abridging the freedom of speech, or of the press, or the right of people to peaceably assemble, and to petition the Government for a redress of grievances.

We have labeled these rights America's Fab Five freedoms: religion, speech, press, assembly, and redress of grievances.

Observe that the language of this amendment is phrased in the negative: "Congress shall make no law...." This artic-

---

[5] Thomas Jefferson, in a letter to James Madison, December 20, 1787, as cited in Julian P. Boyd, ed., *The Papers of Thomas Jefferson* Vol. 12 (New Jersey: Princeton University Press, 1955), 440.

ulation aligns with the Founders' philosophy that individual liberties and freedoms are of such paramount importance that they necessitate a government with clearly defined boundaries, thereby ensuring that the collective powers of a majority do not unduly compromise these individual rights.

Historians have noted that while the Bill of Rights established those freedoms and protections, the various early Supreme Court justices created little relevant case law. Then, in the early twentieth century, Justices Oliver Wendell Holmes and Louis Brandeis issued a series of opinions on constitutional rights (and also expressed concerns about how some of those freedoms impacted others, such as one's right to privacy).

The First Amendment was not interpreted to apply to the states until 1925, and no federal statute was declared unconstitutional under it until 1965. Thus, much of our belief concerning how the First Amendment protects Americans is of recent vintage.

## FREEDOM OF RELIGION

George Washington, our first president, played a pivotal role in ensuring that the United States was a nation open to people of different faiths, founded on the principle of natural rights. In his response to a letter from an early Jewish community, he firmly rejected the notion that the US merely tolerated any group because of their religion, instead advocating for a society free from bigotry and persecution.

One of the first Jewish citizens in America may have been Solomon Franco, a Sephardic Jew from Holland. Franco is believed to have settled in Boston in the Massachusetts Bay Colony in 1649. By 1677, Jewish families had acquired land for a burial ground. In 1759, they purchased land for a synagogue completed in 1763. Many of these families left during the British occupation of Newport but began returning after the war.[6]

In 1790, as the new president, Washington visited the recovering Jewish community in Newport. This significant visit symbolized the new nation's commitment to religious freedom and inclusion.

On August 17, 1790, Moses Seixas, the warden of the Congregation Yeshuat Israel of Newport, addressed Washington and presented his letter on August 18, 1790, simultaneously with letters from the town and Christian clergy of Newport.[7] When Washington read the letters, he responded with profound conviction about the purpose of the new nation. Washington firmly believed that all individuals, regardless of their faith or lack thereof, were entitled to natural rights. He emphasized that it was not a matter of one group tolerating another but that every individual had the right to enjoy these freedoms irrespective of others' opinions.

Washington's response underscored that no individual required the permission of others to exist and thrive:

> All [Citizens of the United States] possess alike liberty of conscience and immunities of citizenship. It is now no more that toleration is spoken of as if it were by the indulgence of one class of people that another

---

[6] Morris Adam Gutstein, *The Story of the Jews of Newport: Two and a Half Centuries of Judaism, 1658–1908* (New York: Bloch Publishing Company, 1936).

[7] Thomas Jefferson, *The Papers of Thomas Jefferson Volume 19: November 1790–January 1791*, ed. Julian P. Boyd (New Jersey: Princeton University Press, 1950), 610, n. 8.

enjoyed the exercise of their natural rights. For happily the Government of the United States, which gives to bigotry no sanction, to persecution no assistance, requires only that they who live under its protection should demean themselves as good citizens, in giving it on all occasions their effectual support.[8]

His words articulated a vision of a nation where acceptance and belonging were fundamental rights, not privileges granted by the majority.

The role that religion should play in America was debated from the beginning. That was partly due to the country's founding under the sovereignty of the King of England, who was also head of its Anglican Church. Although philosophers Bentham and Locke opposed it, the King required citizens of England to belong to that church.

Bentham and Locke supported religious liberty. Bentham expressed concern that non-members of the Church of England were excluded from much of society, keeping those who refused to practice out of universities, schools, government, and military offices. Locke and others argued for a separation between religion and government.

Locke, Bentham, and the Founders possibly saw no options for religion in society. But why did the Founders select their phrasing of the First Amendment? Indeed, they meant to preclude the federal establishment of any religion, but at the time of the Constitution's passage, many of the states had established churches and continued to support them well into the nineteenth century.

---

[8] George Washington, "Letter to the Hebrew Congregation in Newport, Rhode Island," August 18, 1790, *Founder Online*, National Archives, https://founders.archives.gov/documents/Washington/05-06-02-0135.

Some historians suggest that the states were not building walls between government and religion; rather, they assured that the new federal government wouldn't interfere with their existing governance frameworks. However, here we reference a famous 1802 letter from Jefferson to a Baptist organization in Connecticut:

> Believing with you that religion is a matter which lies solely between Man & his God, that he owes account to none other for his faith or his worship, that the legitimate powers of government reach actions only, & not opinions, I contemplated with sovereign reverence that act of the whole American people which declared that their legislature should 'make no law respecting an establishment of religion, or prohibiting the free exercise thereof,' thus building a wall of separation between Church & State.[9]

Was Jefferson talking about the state as a government, meaning that the Constitution precluded only the federal government from making laws regarding the establishment of religion? Nothing is clear, and scholars and courts have battled these issues since our founding.

Additional evidence that supports our view that the Founders believed that the First Amendment prevented the federal government from endorsing a national religion (for example, the Anglican Church) is found in the Treaty of Tripoli. The treaty was a diplomatic agreement signed in 1796 between the US and Tripoli, one of the Barbary States in the

---

[9] Thomas Jefferson, "Letter to the Danbury Baptist Association," January 1, 1802, in *The Papers of Thomas Jefferson, Retirement Series Volume 36*, ed. Barbara B. Oberg (New Jersey: Princeton University Press, 2009), 278-279.

Middle East. The treaty ended hostilities between the US and Barbary pirates and protected American ships from attacks by those pirates. The US Senate, including several Founders, unanimously ratified the treaty, and Founder and second president John Adams signed the treaty on behalf of the US. One of the most notable sections was the statement in Article 11, which said, in part, "As the Government of the United States of America is not, in any sense, founded on the Christian religion...."[10]

Yet, it is difficult to argue that America did not have a religious (and mostly Christian) foundation because it was at the center of much of life in the colonies. Most of the Founders recognized that while Americans were religious by nature, America could not become a successor to the governmental strictures imposed by England. They believed the newly created federal government and religion must be appropriately separated, but likely not in an absolute fashion.

Madison was the principal drafter of the Bill of Rights. He adapted much of it from the existing constitutions of the states, especially from his home state of Virginia. In the years before the 1787 Constitutional Convention in Philadelphia, Virginia maintained its version of a state-organized Anglican Church but had considered disestablishing that Church, something unprecedented in history worldwide.

Many Virginia leaders were Anglican Church members and struggled with disestablishment proposals. But in 1786, Virginia passed a bill proposed by Jefferson, the Virginia

---

[10] "Treaty of Peace and Friendship between the United States of America and the Bey and Subjects of Tripoli of Barbary," signed November 4, 1796, ratified on June 7, 1797, and proclaimed by President John Adams on June 10, 1797. See Article 11.

Act for Establishing Religious Freedom. Its preamble read: "Whereas Almighty God hath created the mind free...." The Act provided:

> Be it enacted by the General Assembly, that no man shall be compelled to frequent or support any religious worship, place, or ministry whatsoever, nor shall be enforced, restrained, molested, or burthened in his body or goods, nor shall otherwise suffer on account of his religious opinions or beliefs; but that all men shall be free to profess, and by argument to maintain, their opinions in matters of religion, and that the same shall in no wise diminish, enlarge, or affect their civil capacities.[11]

Madison agreed with Jefferson's views on religious separation. He noted at that time, "The religion then of every man must be left to the conviction and conscience of every man; and it is the right of every man to exercise it as these may dictate."[12] After passage of the Virginia Act and approval of the Constitution, Madison considered language for the Bill of Rights. He proposed (in a speech in June 1979) amendments to the Constitution to include: "The civil rights of none shall be abridged on account of religious belief or worship, nor shall any national religion be established, nor shall the full and equal rights of conscience be in any manner, or on any pretext, infringed."[13] Virtually every other state lobbied Congress

---

[11] Virginia General Assembly, *An Act for Establishing Religious Freedom*, Richmond 1786.

[12] James Madison, "Speech in the Virginia Convention to Ratify the Federal Constitution" (June 12, 1788), in *The Writings of James Madison* Volume 5, ed. Gaillard Hunt (New York: G.P. Putnam's Sons, 1904), 437–438.

[13] Ibid.

similarly to create this separation between the federal government and religion. And it seems this is how religious freedom and other provisions entered the First Amendment.

Today, some commentators suggest that America was founded as a Christian nation. Some support for this view is found in Article 2 of *The Federalist Papers*, where John Jay, Founder and first chief justice of the US Supreme Court, wrote:

> I have often taken notice that Providence has been pleased to give this one connected country to a united people—a people descended from the same ancestors, speaking the same language, professing the same religion, attached to the same principles of government, very similar in their manner and customs, and who, by their joint counsels, arms, and efforts, fighting side by side throughout a long and bloody war, have nobly established general liberty and independence.[14]

Jay accurately reflected what he saw across America then, including that most of the founding leadership shared much of the same religion. However, the First Amendment and contemporaneous comments demonstrate how intensely the Founders believed that all Americans (at least, all white male Americans) were free to exercise the religions of their choice.

We cannot help but see that the Founders tied their belief in God to the concept of separation of church and government. If the Creator gave each of us the dignity to choose or reject him, why wouldn't the government be required to do the same? If each of us was endowed with inalienable rights by our Creator, this suggests we should accept and respect people

---

14   *The Federalist Papers*, Article 2.

of different faiths or no faith at all. By doing so, we respect their choices as their natural rights.

## FREEDOM OF SPEECH

Intriguing is the language of the First Amendment that provides for free speech protections. It's worth pondering how the specifics of this provision were included. First Amendment guru and litigator Floyd Abrams, in his short, elegant book *The Soul of the First Amendment*,[15] notes how America's robust First Amendment protections for free speech (and freedom of the press) stand taller than in other democracies, with profound implications.

There is much chatter these days about the social media companies and how they block free speech rights of other Americans, especially politicians. But all must understand that the First Amendment and its protections apply solely to the federal government's actions (and after the Fourteenth Amendment, extended to state and local governments and officials). The First Amendment has never and will never apply to the sole actions of individuals or private companies. One might argue that the protections should be extended to any companies deeply regulated by governments, but any such regulation itself would likely fail a First Amendment test.

Some readers bemoan that conclusion, but it is what it is. Private individuals and private companies in America can never violate the free speech protections of other individuals when they're acting privately. That's not to suggest that, for example, actions by a private security company hired by a gov-

---

15    Floyd Abrams, *The Soul of the First Amendment* (Connecticut: Yale University Press, 2017).

ernment don't violate the First Amendment, but that's because they exercise government power, not private power. It's critical to understand the distinctions.

During Madison's June 1789 speech to the newly elected House of Representatives, he proposed key language and provisions, and many were drawn from amendments submitted by the states during the Constitution ratification process. In that speech, he focused mainly on those amendments related to the "great rights of mankind," and noted regarding free speech and free press, "The people shall not be deprived or abridged in their right to speak, to write, or publish their sentiments; and the freedom of the press, as one of the great bulwarks of liberty, shall be inviolable."[16]

Weeks later, the House of Representatives approved certain amendments, including: "The Freedom of Speech... shall not be infringed." Later, that was amended to read: "Congress shall make no law...abridging the freedom of speech...." After formal reconciliation of the language, the current First Amendment language passed Congress, and President Washington sent it to the states for ratification, which occurred in 1791.

The scope of First Amendment protections was first raised during the Sedition Act, which was enacted late in the eighteenth century but mostly cabined until the twentieth century. During those years, numerous justices on the US Supreme Court noted how First Amendment freedoms, especially the right of free speech, needed "breathing space" to roam protec-

---

16   "Proposed Amendments to the Constitution by the House of Representatives, August 24, 1789," Annals of Congress 434 (1789), 1st Congress, 1st Session, 760.

tively and that Americans could speak or write as they chose, mostly without government interference.

But free speech has never been absolutely free in America.

Specific speech is not protected, such as yelling "Fire!" in a crowded theater, as Justice Holmes formulated early in the twentieth century,[17] or slandering another person. Exceptions aside, even loathsome, hateful speech is protected chiefly in America. The Supreme Court even ruled that desecrating the American flag is protected speech, an opinion[18] that likely continues to divide average Americans today.

However, other rights, like copyrights and trademarks, are also protected, so the American justice system must weigh and balance often conflicting rights. Nevertheless, the weights never favor collective speech rights over individual rights; the First Amendment mainly protects individual speakers' rights.

In addition, the Supreme Court determined that "content-based" or "viewpoints-based" limitations are presumed invalid and subjected to strict scrutiny. Although certain content-neutral "time, place, and manner" restrictions[19] can apply to speech, the burden is on the party trying to regulate speech (often the federal or state government) to demonstrate that the restrictions were tailored narrowly to advance a significant government interest and that alternatives for expression remain.

Thus, the courts sometimes try to balance free speech rights against other interests like privacy, defamation, crowd control, and national security. American courts often weigh the rights of free speech higher than other interests unless

---

17   *Schenk v. United States*, 249 US 47 (1919).
18   *Texas v. Johnson*, 491 US 397 (1989).
19   *Ward v. Rock Against Racism*, 491 US 781 (1989).

those interests are compelling and narrowly tailored, and it's seen as the least restrictive approach. Per Abrams, this is a uniquely American protection.

Hate speech is more severely regulated in other democracies than in America. Here, politicians can say almost anything in a political speech without risking suppression or even arrest; in other democracies, calling out individual minority groups risks litigation or even jail.

Again, Americans are most deeply protected whenever they speak, privately or in public, but international companies like those that operate in America, Europe, and elsewhere must adjust the content of their speech based on local laws and regulations. In Europe, for example, hate speech is more condemned, and individuals have much higher rights of privacy, including the "right to be left alone" or the "right to be forgotten."[20]

The concept of free speech creates tension between speech and individual privacy rights. As noted by former journalist and now law professor Amy Gajda in her book *Seek and Hide: The Tangled History of the Right to Privacy*,[21] American courts are wrestling with that tension. In some cases, judges strike down unbridled speech. For example, the online website Gawker published private videos of a former pro wrestler showing sexually explicit scenes. The wrestler sued for breach of privacy, and despite First Amendment defenses, the wrestler prevailed. Gawker entered bankruptcy. These cases are rare but might become less so in the years ahead.

---

20  *Google Spain SL, Google Inc. v Agencia Española de Protección de Datos (AEPD), Mario Costeja González*, Case C-131/12 [2014], ECLI:EU:C:2014:317.

21  Amy Gajda, *Seek and Hide: The Tangled History of the Right to Privacy* (New York: Viking, 2022).

America continues to protect almost all versions of speech, whether uttered by individuals or on behalf of private companies. The Supreme Court has established that political campaign contributions constitute a form of speech. This principle[22] acknowledges that financial contributions in politics have expressive value. As a result, regulations on these contributions must carefully balance electoral integrity with the essence of free speech. The Court has held that while such contributions are vital for political expression, they remain subject to regulatory oversight to maintain democratic fairness.[23] Moreover, these determinations occur partly due to American public opinion that wishes free speech to be mostly protected. Time will tell, but we think this view won't change.

How can speech in America best be managed under an environment of vigilant enforcement? Before we answer, we remind readers that we are only paying attention to how governments can manage speech—if they can manage it at all. Private actors are always free (unless they otherwise commit themselves, such as via contract) to restrict or constrain speech. So, social media sites like Facebook and X (formerly Twitter) are free to restrict content and even block speakers if

---

22  See *Citizens United v. Federal Election Commission*, 558 US 310 (2010), and *Buckley v. Valeo*, 424 US 1 (1976).

23  Key cases illustrate this balance: In *Buckley v. Valeo* (1976), limits on personal and independent campaign spending were deemed unconstitutional, whereas direct contribution limits were upheld. *Citizens United* (2010) further extended political spending as speech, prohibiting government restrictions on independent expenditures by corporations and unions. And *McCutcheon v. Federal Election Commission*, 572 US 185 (2014), struck down overall contribution limits from individuals, highlighting the ongoing interplay between free expression, campaign finance, and regulatory boundaries in American democracy.

they choose. Private companies and individuals can prevent speech on their private properties unless they agree to offer it.

The government has limited power to legislate freedom of speech. We allow even hateful speech, often under the assumption that "bad" speech can be offset by "good" speech that more speech can usually limit the damage otherwise. Today, we face challenges of censorship, even in public spaces. This is especially true for university campus environments. Private universities, like private individuals, can offer or restrict speech in any fashion they choose. Public universities—those owned and operated by governments—must follow the government rules if they try to restrict or limit speech. Any limitations on speech must be content-neutral and narrowly tailored to address a core interest. For example, a public university might restrict speech to a certain time of the day and/or certain places based on content-neutral criteria, but it cannot and should not restrict speech absolutely.

Unfortunately, it seems that too many students and employees of universities condemn and try to exclude certain speakers. Today, this problem seems to mostly involve speech from those who appear more conservative than the average student on campus, but at times, this belief can exclude those on the left who are a bit more liberal than average.

We argue strenuously for a policy that encompasses this guideline: That more speech, not less speech, is the answer—especially on American high school and college campuses where minds are educated and opinions are shaped. This should be true in the public sphere but also in private realms. Although those in private realms are free to restrict speech as they choose, we hope that good practices will renew our faith in the power of speech—to support, defend, anger, inspire joy, and bring on tears—and find new ways to invigorate American life with different voices.

We continue to assume with optimism that our country will support an environment across America where the power of ideas wrestles and resolves, where those ideas can lead to better ideas and better outcomes for all. And we can now insert another notch in the belt that encompasses American optimism.

## FREEDOM OF THE PRESS

This freedom is conjoined with free speech under the First Amendment. There is very little daylight between these two freedoms. The Founders knew how vital a free press was to their emerging democracy. Madison described it as "one of the great bulwarks of liberty."[24] He and other Founders used the word "press" in the business sense, namely a publisher of information and thought.

The Founders, like Americans today, at times struggled with what a free press had to say. That included Jefferson, but in one of his most famous quotes (at least well-known in media circles), writing from Paris in a letter dated 1787, he noted:

> The people are the only censors of their governors; and even their errors will tend to keep these to the true principles of their institution. To punish these errors too severely would be to suppress the only safeguard of the public liberty. The way to prevent these irregular interpositions of the people is to give them full information of their affairs thro' the channel of the

---

24   James Madison, "Report on the Virginia Resolutions," *Writings*, ed. Jack N. Rakove (New York: Library of America, 1999), 608.

public papers, & to contrive that those papers should penetrate the whole mass of the people. The basis of our governments being the opinion of the people, the very first object should be to keep that right; and were it left to me to decide whether we should have a government without newspapers or newspapers without a government, I should not hesitate a moment to prefer the latter. But I should mean that every man should receive those papers & be capable of reading them.[25]

Like all politicians and public figures, Jefferson faced public criticism, especially from the press, yet like Madison's "bulwark," he believed a free press was core to American democracy. He also underscored his belief in literacy, that the people should be capable of reading and understanding what is written, able to discern critically.

It's curious why the Founders linked free speech and free press in the Bill of Rights. It's curious that they even separated them at all. The separation suggests different perspectives between the press and individual rights to speak and write. Justice Potter Stewart concurred with this view in the 1978 case of *Houchins v. KQED, Inc.*:

That the First Amendment speaks separately of freedom of speech and freedom of the press is no constitutional accident, but an acknowledgment of the critical role played by the press in American society. The Constitution requires sensitivity to that role,

---

25  Thomas Jefferson, "Letter to Edward Carrington," January 16, 1787, in *The Papers of Thomas Jefferson, Volume 11: 1 January to 6 August 1787*, ed. Julian P. Boyd (New Jersey: Princeton University Press, 1955), 48–49.

and to the special needs of the press in performing it effectively.[26]

Like free speech, the rights of a free press can be limited, but only in narrow, content-neutral ways. As noted by Justice Holmes in the 1919 case of *Schenk v. United States*:

> The most stringent protection of free speech would not protect a man in falsely shouting fire in a theater and causing panic.... The question in every case is whether the words used are used in such circumstances and are of such a nature as to create a clear and present danger that they will bring about the substantive evils that [a law passed by Congress] has a right to prevent. It is a question of proximity and degree. When a nation is at war many things that might be said in time of peace are such a hindrance to its effort that their utterance will not be endured so long as men fight and that no Court could regard them as protected by any constitutional right.[27]

At that point, early in the twentieth century, the Supreme Court set a framework for balancing the individual and corporate rights of free speech and free publication against the collective interests of society; in that case, it was about prosecuting the Great War (World War I). Later cases moved to the

---

26 *Houchins v. KQED, Inc.*, 438 US 1, 17 (1978) (Stewart, concurring). In this concurrence, Justice Stewart echoed Jefferson's sentiment on the importance of a free press, recognizing its critical role in a democratic society.

27 *Schenck v. United States*, 249 US 47 (1919). In this landmark decision, Justice Holmes articulated the "clear and present danger" test as a means to evaluate the limits of free speech, a principle that also applies to the freedom of the press under certain circumstances.

concept of "strict scrutiny" when government laws or regulations impacted speech content.

Even earlier, the country attempted to limit such freedoms. The most important moment for freedom of the press occurred shortly after the founding of America. Congress passed several laws, including the 1798 Sedition Act,[28] which made "seditious libel" a crime for criticizing government actions. Members of the press were arrested and convicted under those laws. The acts were not challenged directly in the Supreme Court, but numerous states lobbied to overturn them, arguing their violation of the First Amendment. Most of the acts ceased to be enforced or otherwise expired during President Jefferson's terms in office.

Even before our founding, American courts considered whether "truth" would be a defense to a claim of libel by the press. In 1735, John Peter Zenger (who printed a weekly newspaper) was arrested for libeling a government official. Hamilton defended Zenger, arguing truth as a defense.[29]

Under English law that prevailed at the time of the writing of the Constitution, defamatory statements were presumed false. The defendant carried the burden of establishing truth. There was no "good faith" belief in the truth as an accepted defense to a claim of libel or slander. But Zenger was acquitted, and American libel law moved away from its English precedents, allowing for a "good faith belief in the truth" defense.

Justice Hugo Black declared this separation from English law and precedents in the 1941 case of *Bridges v. California*.[30]

---

[28] *An Act in Addition to the Act, Entitled "An Act for the Punishment of Certain Crimes Against the United States,"* Chapter 74, 1 Stat. 596 (1798).

[29] *The Crown v. John Peter Zenger*, 1735.

[30] *Bridges v. California*, 314 US 252 (1941).

Justice Black had tussled with Justice Holmes over when the government could intervene to prevent or condemn disclosures, under the "clear and present danger" framework. He narrowed the "clear and present danger" standard in this case that presented the conflict between free speech/press and fair trials, described as two of civilization's "most cherished" policies. Justice Black, in response to reliance on various English precedents, noted:

> There are no contrary implications in any part of the history of this period in which the First Amendment was framed and adopted. No purpose in ratifying the Bill of Rights was clearer than that of securing for the people of the United States much greater freedom of religion, expression, assembly, and petition than the people of Great Britain had ever enjoyed.[31]

And from that statement and beyond, the separation from English doctrine moved American free speech and press freedom to a different plane of understanding. As Abrams noted in his book:

> English law was no longer the locale for American judges to visit to receive guidance as to how to apply the First Amendment. America was on its own, and First Amendment law grew ever more expansive and more distinct from that applied abroad.[32]

Later, the Supreme Court, in its decision in *New York Times Co. v. Sullivan*,[33] required for liability that the press engage in "actual malice" if the subject of a story was a public

---

31   *Bridges v. California*, 314 US 252 (1941): 264–265 (opinion of Black).
32   Abrams, 2017.
33   *New York Times Co. v. Sullivan*, 376 US 254 (1964).

person (such as a politician). That is, liability failed to attach unless the press knew a story or fact was false, or it "recklessly" disregarded whether a story or fact was true or not. And since the press (which in later years was deemed to include all forms of media including radio, television, cable, social media, and individual publications) generally receives facts and develops stories over time, the Supreme Court addressed whether society (for example, the government) could restrain the press in advance from running a story.

The Supreme Court concluded (generally) that society could not; that where information was received by the media, it was generally free to publish or otherwise report its story, even in cases of national security. Whether to publish a story or not, or whether to include specific facts or not in a story, is generally thought of as best left to the judgment of the press.

In America, individuals and other private entities are mainly free to speak or print or report on almost anything they deem fit. There are a few exceptions, and they are narrowly tailored ones. In some cases, while the press may be free to report on information they receive, they might be subject to challenges based on how that information arrived. For example, while a newspaper might receive certain information surreptitiously, the individual who gathered and disclosed such information might be subjected to criminal charges (for example, theft or trespass).

Members of the press can be charged for trespassing or theft under the right facts. But even in those cases, the speaker or the press is left to choose whether to disclose or not. There are many examples where individuals and companies choose not to disclose information for various reasons. In some cases, they might have had concerns about possible liability, such as defamation. In others, they might have paused to protect national security or other secrets. In others, they might have used good judgment not to share damaging information about another American.

In America, those choices are mostly left to the speakers, and we are better off because the government does not censor the flow of information to our eyes and ears. We need more information, more accurate information, better information to offset poor, bad, or wrong information. In America, we have those opportunities; citizens in other countries—even in some liberal democracies—do not. These freedoms are additional American democratic advantages.

## FREEDOM TO ASSEMBLE PEACEABLY AND FREEDOM TO PETITION THE GOVERNMENT FOR REDRESS

The rights to assemble and petition were known well by the American colonists. Petitioning for redress had existed for centuries under English law. But before the Revolution, at least one governor in Massachusetts restricted assembly and petitioning via proclamation. Adams observed:

> The most alarming Process that ever appeared in a British Government...declaring it Treason for the Inhabitants of that Province to assemble themselves to consider of their Grievances and form Associations for their common Conduct on the Occasion.[34]

---

34   *The Works of John Adams, Second President of the United States: With a Life of the Author, Notes and Illustrations* Volume 4, ed. Charles Francis Adams (Boston: Charles C. Little and James Brown, 1851), 195.

"Petitioning" describes legal means, especially non-violent means, to encourage certain actions by the government or to oppose actions. All actions taken to influence government—letter-writing, speeches, lobbying, peaceful protests, collecting signatures for initiatives—qualify as petitioning.

Like petitioning, peaceful assembly includes protesting and other activities to spur government decisions. It also includes the simple freedom to gather with friends, neighbors, and so on.[35] Like the rights of free speech and free press, petitioning and assembling can occur for intolerant or odious reasons, such as when promoting white nationalism and/or communist interests.

Under the rules of the King of England and his representatives in the colonies, notably the governors, the American colonists had few rights to protest. The Declaration specifically underscored that concern:

> In every stage of these Oppressions [what the signers of the Declaration called the abuses of the King] we have Petitioned for Redress in the most humble of Terms: Our repeated Petitions have been answered only by repeated Injury.

As the Founders pondered the Bill of Rights and key individual freedoms, the rights to assemble peacefully and petition to redress grievances took central roles. Before the Bill of Rights was drafted, almost every colony allowed such a rule under their founding constitutions or charters. For example, the Maryland Constitution of 1776 included this language: "That every man hath a right to petition the legislature for the

---

[35] Neil Gorsuch, *A Republic, If You Can Keep It* (New York: Forum Books, 2019), 135–138.

redress of grievances, in a peaceable and orderly manner."[36] New Hampshire's 1783 Constitution provided:

> The people have a right in an orderly and peaceable manner, to assemble and consult upon the common good, give instructions to their representatives; and to request of the legislative body, by way of petition or remonstrance, redress of wrongs done to them, and of the grievances they suffer.[37]

Madison's initial proposal, articulated in his June 1789 speech to the House of Representatives, included this language:

> The people shall not be restrained from peaceably assembling and consulting for their common good; nor from applying to the legislature by petitions, or remonstrances for redress of their grievances.[38]

During the debates in the House and Senate on this language, members raised concerns that these rights were embraced in the other freedoms. Thus, they construed this draft language as trivial and unnecessary. But prior actions by and concerns with actions by the King of England's representatives swayed the language towards that finalized in the First Amendment.

Later debates addressed members' concerns that both assembling and petitioning the legislature might require that the legislature accept the views of the people rather than use their independent determination. The Founders clearly

---

36  Maryland Constitution of 1776, Article 45, adopted November 11, 1776.
37  New Hampshire Constitution of 1783, Part I, Article 32, adopted June 2, 1784.
38  James Madison, "Speech to the House of Representatives," June 1789. This speech was part of his initial proposal for the Bill of Rights.

defined that America would be a "representative democracy," that the people could raise issues and concerns, but their representatives in the House and the Senate retained their independence to make decisions as they deemed right on behalf of the people, whose redress included continuing peaceful assembly, petitioning, and voting out those who failed to represent them properly.

Throughout the years following ratification of the Bill of Rights, the courts continued to recognize peaceful assembly, protest, and lobbying via petition as core rights of the American people.

# CHAPTER 7

# EQUAL PROTECTION OF THE LAWS: AMERICA'S "SECOND FOUNDING"

THE AMERICAN EXPERIMENT IN FREEDOM, liberty, democracy, and representation started from positions of contention and painful battles, especially over the status of slavery in parts of America. Ultimately, those battles and the journey itself continue to inspire us today, especially as we citizens keep moving toward (but never reaching) a "more perfect" union. The Declaration and Constitution addressed some of the most basic questions, including how a group of individuals could best manage a common society for the greater good. These documents speak to first principles that remain core to America and those worldwide who look to American liberty and freedom for inspiration.

The Constitution was based on the morality of the Declaration. The Declaration placed individuals at the center of the revolution, stating that "all men are created equal." Every individual has the right to dignity. Every individual has the right to be treated equally by the government. These principles created conditions to guide American progress for centuries and to continue to guide those elected representatives who must respect their oaths to the Constitution itself.

Slavery was debated but not resolved in the Constitution, and the Declaration was non-discriminatory. Based on the ideal that "all men are created equal," and that all people are deserving of dignity, the collective morality of our Founders made it inevitable that slavery could not survive. Discrimination against people based on race, gender, and sexual orientation could not be endured because all people deserve the same dignity.

Since our founding, we have made much progress on this democratic journey, a journey no other country has taken in this manner. From our founding, and at the core of American democracy, we have struggled to progress toward extending the founding ideals to every member of our society. On the eve of his assassination on April 4, 1968, Martin Luther King Jr. delivered his final speech, a sermon, where he noted that the Declaration of Independence dug a well of great intention to ensure all men were created equal.[1]

For too many decades, slavery left indelible marks on America. While some Founders wished to excise slavery at the beginning of the nation, others refused, and the Founders entered horrific compromises, including counting enslaved persons as three-fifths persons in the states where they resided and allowing under the Constitution a return to slavery for those who escaped to other states, using the Fugitive Slave Clause (we note again that while this is a shorthand name for this provision, neither the words "slave" or "slavery" are mentioned in the Declaration or the original Constitution).

---

[1] Martin Luther King Jr., "I've Been to the Mountaintop," Speech, Mason Temple, Memphis, TN, April 3, 1968.

Peace in America after the Revolutionary War didn't last. Southern states continued mining human misery, eventually leading to the Civil War outbreak. During that war, America was given new chances to center its freedoms for every Black man (but not yet many other minority groups or women) under the Thirteenth, Fourteenth, and Fifteenth Amendments.

The Framers intentionally created our Constitution to be difficult to amend. Amendments occurred twenty-seven times (including repeal of the Prohibition amendment, the Eighteenth Amendment). Amendments require approval by two-thirds of both House and Senate members, then ratification by three-fourths of the states. This framework differs from state constitutions, which are easier to amend and are often done by a majority vote of its citizens. But that difficulty couldn't sway Congress, and especially President Lincoln, from blotting the stain of slavery left inside the original Constitution.

Scholars rightfully describe the three Civil War and Reconstruction Amendments, the Thirteenth, Fourteenth, and Fifteenth, as the "second founding" of America.[2] The Thirteenth Amendment, ratified in 1865, provides in major part:

> Section 1. Neither slavery nor involuntary servitude, except as punishment for crime whereof the party shall have been duly convicted, shall exist within the United States, or any place subject to their jurisdiction.

---

[2] For a thorough and excellent discussion of these issues, see Eric Foner, *The Second Founding: How the Civil War and Reconstruction Remade the Constitution* (New York: W.W. Norton & Company, 2019).

The Fourteenth Amendment, ratified in 1868, provides in part:

Section 1. All persons born or naturalized in the United States and subject to the jurisdiction thereof, are citizens of the United States and of the State wherein they reside. No State shall make or enforce any law which shall abridge the privileges or immunities of citizens of the United States; nor shall any State deprive any person of life, liberty, or property, without due process of law; nor deny to any person within its jurisdiction the equal protection of the laws.

Section 2. Representatives shall be apportioned among the several States according to their respective numbers, counting the whole number of persons in each State, excluding Indians not taxed. But when the right to vote at any election…is denied to any male inhabitants of such State, being twenty-one years of age… the basis of representation therein shall be reduced in the proportion which the number of such male citizens shall bear to the whole number of such male citizens twenty-one years of age in such State.

Section 2 of the Fourteenth Amendment has never been used against any state despite continuing voting discrimination. That section precludes the counting of Native Americans, women, and individuals aged under twenty-one, conditions remedied via future amendments and legislation. But this section was specifically designed to, and did, overwrite the Three-fifths Clause in the Constitution. As that happened, gender ("male") was written for the first time into our Constitution.

While the Constitution remains difficult to amend, the efforts by prior leaders that led to passage of the Fourteenth Amendment need underscoring, for it is this amendment, more than almost any other than those found in the Bill of Rights, that assured American freedoms for all, and will continue to shine brighter lights.

One overlooked provision is that the Fourteenth Amendment established birthright citizenship. This constitutionalized the idea that virtually everyone born in America (or in American territories) immediately becomes an American citizen, regardless of race or ethnicity. The United States stands almost alone on this; almost all other countries, including almost all other liberal democracies, limit automatic citizenship.

America's birthright citizen provisions underscore America's founding philosophies, including why immigrants should aspire to become Americans, a powerful idea that aids in assimilating all groups in the vision of American democracy. And it remains a powerful repudiation that, in America, "whiteness" is not the source of citizenship. Some wish to ignore this aspect of the Fourteenth Amendment, but they will fail and they should fail. We should continue to celebrate this version of American uniqueness.

The Fifteenth Amendment, ratified in 1870, provides in major part:

> The right of citizens of the United States to vote shall not be denied or abridged by the United States or by any State on account of race, color, or previous condition of servitude.

Despite its seemingly clear language, the Supreme Court continued to narrow its interpretation in the latter nineteenth century. States remained free to determine who voted; thus, they remained free to continue vestiges of discrimination. And many states did just that, blocking equal rights for many decades. Remember, the Founders punted on the question of who the voting "People" would be under the Constitution, leaving the question of voting to individual states, an error that may still haunt us today. The Fifteenth Amendment did, however, ensure that all states expanded suffrage beyond white men.

Each of these three amendments attempted to refocus the powers of Congress. Recall that the First Amendment says, "Congress shall make no law...." These amendments attempted to inject power into the relationship between the federal government and the states. Each stated that "Congress shall have the power" to enforce the provisions of the amendments via "appropriate legislation."

These three amendments created a second founding moment (or decades) that could have ushered in a more perfect union. Our leaders during this period failed to do so. The US Supreme Court, in addition to continuing resistance from the secessionist southern states, bears the primary responsibility for failing this vision.

First, the scope of the Thirteenth Amendment narrowed when the Court addressed the *Civil Rights Cases* of 1883.[3] The Court noted that the amendment had the potential to eliminate all vestiges of slavery across America but chose instead to narrow its interpretation, determining that the vestiges of slav-

---

3    *Civil Rights Cases*, 109 US 3 (1883).

ery (such as equal accommodations and public transportation) did not end due to its passage. The Fourteenth Amendment, as enacted by various congressional laws and as interpreted by the Supreme Court, remained to sort out American discrimination. Justice John Harlan dissented and opined:

> If the constitutional amendments be enforced according to the intent with which, as I conceive, they were adopted, there cannot be in this Republic any class of human beings in practical subjection to another class with power in the latter to dole out to the former such privileges as they may choose to grant.[4]

Alas, the Supreme Court majority disagreed. It took until the World War II era and the rise of the civil rights movement in the twentieth century to reverse this error.

The Fourteenth Amendment was interpreted by Congress and the Supreme Court more broadly—but barely. And the Fifteenth was narrowed substantially.

For many today, the Supreme Court is the main protector of our individual freedoms. That was not true in the latter years of the nineteenth century. In many ways, the Court enabled daunting and continuing discrimination between white men and all other groups of Americans. That did not have to be the case.

---

4   Id. at 60 (Harlan, dissenting).

## THE CIVIL WAR AND LINCOLN'S GETTYSBURG ADDRESS

President Abraham Lincoln's Gettysburg Address is likely the most well-known presidential speech in history, and certainly among the shortest. The Battle of Gettysburg was fought in mid-1863. It was one of the bloodiest battles of the Civil War, with more than 50,000 casualties (dead and wounded). Delivered to dedicate the Gettysburg Civil War Cemetery, Lincoln ended this two-minute speech by saying:

> It is...for us to be here dedicated to the great task remaining before us—that from these honored dead we take increased devotion to that cause for which they here gave the last full measure of devotion—that we here highly resolve that these dead shall not have died in vain—this nation, under God, shall have a new birth of freedom—and that government of the people, by the people, for the people, shall not perish from the earth.[5]

This speech and related sentiments led the country to pass the Thirteenth Amendment and shortly thereafter follow with ratification of the Fourteenth and Fifteenth Amendments, as efforts to blot the stain on America caused by slavery and related racism.

Before the Civil War, abolitionist and former slave Frederick Douglass spoke at an Independence Day event in New York in 1852, noting:

---

[5] Abraham Lincoln, "Gettysburg Address," speech delivered on November 19, 1863, at the dedication of the Soldiers' National Cemetery in Gettysburg, Pennsylvania.

What, to the American slave, is your 4th of July? I answer, a day that reveals to him, more than all other days in the year, the gross injustice and cruelty to which he is the constant victim. To him, your celebration is a sham; your boasted liberty, an unholy license; your national greatness, swelling vanity; your sound of rejoicing are empty and heartless; your denunciation of tyrants brass fronted impudence; your shout of liberty and equality, hollow mockery; your prayers and hymns, your sermons and thanks-givings, with all your religious parade and solemnity, are to him, mere bombast, fraud, deception, impiety, and hypocrisy—a thin veil to cover up crimes which would disgrace a nation of savages.[6]

In 1857, seven out of nine justices on the Supreme Court ruled in *Dred Scott v. Sandford* that an enslaved person who resided in a free state was not thereby entitled to his freedom, and African Americans were not and could never be citizens of the United States.[7] The decision added fuel to the intersectional controversy and pushed the country closer to civil war. Among constitutional scholars, the *Dred Scott* decision is widely considered the worst decision ever rendered by the Supreme Court.

Lincoln and other Union leaders saw these ongoing failures and heard many cries and pleas. In 1863, Lincoln announced freeing enslaved persons in the Confederate states under the Emancipation Proclamation. Little changed then, but with the

---

[6] Frederick Douglass, "What to the Slave Is the Fourth of July?" speech delivered on July 5, 1852, at an event commemorating the signing of the Declaration of Independence, held at Corinthian Hall, Rochester, New York.
[7] *Dred Scott v. Sandford*, 60 US (19 How.) 393 (1857).

Union victory and end of legal slavery, and with the Second Founding Amendments in hand, many thought freedom and equality had finally been granted to Black Americans.

Alas, it was not to happen then, not truly for another century.

Post-emancipation, many of the southern state leaders continued their quests to define freedom for African Americans in narrow terms, especially related to voting rights. Several southern states passed "Black Codes" designed to preserve much of the plantation system and forced labor. The South's defense of slavery hinged on its perceived collective benefits, a common rationale in governments that infringe upon human rights under the guise of communal needs.

The Declaration of Independence, a testament to American moral values, posits individual rights above collective economic interests. Consequently, despite the South's economic arguments or even majority opinions, this fundamental American principle prioritized the rights of the oppressed individuals over the collective needs of the majority. Our Founders included this moral concept from the beginning; American brothers fought a terrible war to define it.

Despite the ratification of the Fifteenth Amendment, which was designed to enshrine voting rights irrespective of race, the practical realization of these rights for Black Americans has been persistently hampered, shaped in part by interpretations and rulings of the Supreme Court. The amendment, while groundbreaking, did not fully transcend the foundational principle that left the administration of voting mainly to individual states. This decentralization meant that the amendment's noble aspirations initially did little to alter the entrenched, racially discriminatory practices at the state level. It wasn't until the civil rights movement of the 1950s and 1960s and the subsequent passage of the Voting Rights Act of 1965 that a more effective legal framework was established to dismantle these barriers.

However, the saga of voting rights in America is marked by ongoing challenges. The Supreme Court's interpretations of the Fifteenth Amendment and subsequent voting rights legislation have often reflected a balance between federal oversight and state sovereignty. Relevant decisions[8] demonstrate the federal judicial deference to state authority in managing elections, even when such decisions arguably disadvantage minority voting rights.

These developments underscore the complex and evolving nature of voting rights in the United States. The Fifteenth Amendment, while a cornerstone in the quest for racial equality, did not safeguard against the suppression of Black voters. Instead, it represented a positive step in the ongoing struggle to fulfill the true spirit of American democracy—a struggle that continues to this day as the nation grapples with the balance between state autonomy and the protection of fundamental rights.

Many other legal and congressional actions were required to extend freedoms to oppressed groups beyond those discriminated against because of their skin color. It took passage and ratification of the Nineteenth Amendment early in the twentieth century to protect the right of women to vote; it took a federal law passed in 1924 to bring citizenship and voting rights to Native Americans; it took World War II and

---

[8] See *Shelby County v. Holder*, 570 US 529 (2013) and *Brnovich v. Democratic National Committee*, 594 US ___ (2021).

Japanese-American internment (in the name of national security) to ensure that such rights were available to all Americans regardless of race or national origin; it took ratification of the Twenty-Fourth Amendment in 1964 to eliminate poll and other taxes that stood in the way of minority Americans exercising their right to vote; and it took passage of the Twenty-Sixth Amendment, ratified in 1971, to bring the right to vote to adults in the eighteen to twenty age group.

Amending the Constitution remains difficult, but successful efforts were made to extend voting rights. Without a right to vote, no other freedom or right seemed secure. The power owned by white landowning men continued unabated for too many decades. Our country needed until the beginning of the modern Civil Rights era to create what has been called a "Second Reconstruction" to bring the vision of our Founders to many other Americans.

We wonder about the progress America would have realized sooner if only the Founders had tackled voting rights in 1775. And we wonder what other progress we could and should have made without celebrating the wonderment of a federal government intricately balanced with the so-called "fifty laboratories of democracy"—the states—where those smaller democracies resisted the America to come.

This is why we still journey toward the "more perfect Union."

Should we be depressed by the opportunities lost? No. We have progressed in the right direction to create a much better future for all citizens and immigrants who often choose perilous paths to become Americans. And our work, together, continues.

# CHAPTER 8

# CREATING OPPORTUNITIES FOR PROSPERITY

AMERICA HAS BEEN LUCKY—LUCKY THAT our Founders understood the underlying drivers that freedoms bring. They wrote founding documents to embed and communicate such freedoms. They understood that we would always strive to be more perfect in a republic (which America is). We are lucky that the American experiment of the eighteenth century, an experiment that benefited primarily white, landowning men, yet whose moral compass recognized that the Creator believed all humanity was born equal, evolved through growth, interpretation, and change to bring similar benefits to women and members of all races and religions.

There are several sources for the information provided in this chapter, including the work of author and geopolitical strategist Peter Zeihan, especially in his most recent book, *The End of the World Is Just the Beginning*.[1] Paul interviewed Zeihan on an *Optimistic American* podcast.[2] We also rely on

---

1  Peter Zeihan, *The End of the World Is Just the Beginning: Mapping the Collapse of Globalization* (New York: Harper Business, 2022).
2  Paul Johnson, "This Is an Extraordinary Time to Be an American: Discussing Geopolitics with Peter Zeihan," August 13, 2022, in *The Optimistic American*, podcast, 27:13, https://youtu.be/tRF4uccV6to.

Michael Beckley's work and his books *Unrivaled* and *Danger Zone: The Coming Conflict with China*.[3] Paul also interviewed Beckley on the *Optimistic American* podcast.[4]

But our focus in this book differs from theirs in that we focus primarily on what's *right* with America and why our optimism about the future reflects more than fortunate exogenous factors such as geography, waterways, and military might. What has made America the greatest superpower in the history of this planet has been founding our country around the rights of individuals and the protections provided through our Constitution and the rule of law.

## AMERICAN ORGANIZATIONAL STRENGTHS VIA THE CONSTITUTION

Americans are lucky our Founders did not stick with a confederacy but instead decided that the new country would require that the otherwise independent states cede some of their rights and responsibilities to unify collective action for the soon-to-be American people who, in many cases, were remarkably diverse. In Article 2 of *The Federalist Papers*, John Jay, Founder and first US Supreme Court chief justice, wrote about how a free people often ceded some natural rights to create a government to serve their overall interests. He commented on the many American advantages as the country declared its independence:

---

[3] Beckley, 2018; Hal Brands and Michael Beckley, *Danger Zone: The Coming Conflict with China* (New York: W.W. Norton & Company, 2022).

[4] Paul Johnson, "America's Strengths are Unrivaled: With Michael Beckley," May 21, 2022, in *The Optimistic American*, podcast, 1:06:35, https://optamerican.podbean.com/e/america-s-strengths-are-unrivaled-michael-beckley/.

It has often given me pleasure to observe, that independent America was not composed of detached and distant territories, but that one connected, fertile, widespreading country was the portion of our western sons of liberty. Providence has in a particular manner blessed it with a variety of soils and productions, and watered it with innumerable streams, for the delight and accommodation of its inhabitants. A succession of navigable waters forms a kind of chain round its borders, as if to bind it together; while the most noble rivers in the world, running at convenient distances, present them with highways for easy communication of friendly aids, and the mutual transportation and exchange of their various commodities.[5]

The strengths Americans (then and now) gained by the states uniting are incredible. Through this unity of different regions and people, America became the leading light of liberal democracy. A liberal democracy couples the rights, powers, and wishes of a majority of its citizens with individual rights deemed sacrosanct and untouchable by the majority's will. It was as close to the ideal of a social contract among its people as any philosophers might have imagined.

Today, we are both more diverse and more inclusive. Civil rights, equal rights, and human rights moved our country forward and these rights also created more producers, consumers, and higher productivity factors. As rights expand to others, property and ownership rights (for example, intellectual property rights) ensure that the people are incentivized to create, innovate, and build. Expanded education trains workforces

---

5   *The Federalist Papers*, Article 2.

and grants new opportunities outside anyone's "class" or "station in life." The rule of law ensures that all are treated fairly and that companies cannot create monopolies that block innovation and its byproducts: more creativity and wealth.

We underscore (again!) that the most incredible thing the Founders of America did was to empower individuals over collective interests and over the government itself. America's extension of individual rights and freedoms created our superpower status. But we were aided by some special factors. For example, the US is a net oil exporter thanks to shale and compressed natural gas. We are much better positioned to capture renewable energy (solar and wind) than most of the world.[6]

The US is the most stable and powerful industrial power in history. The global COVID-19 pandemic and industrial friction elsewhere have driven America toward re-industrialization at epic proportions. Many offshore factories and industries are now moving back home, a great benefit to present-day and future American workers.

Today, America's authoritarian opponents find they need to become either imperial or mercantilist economies.[7] They reached social agreements with their citizens to give up political and individual freedoms in exchange for growing econo-

---

[6] See David J.C. MacKay, *Sustainable Energy—Without the Hot Air* (England: UIT Cambridge, 2009); US Department of Energy, *Wind Vision: A New Era for Wind Power in the United States* (Washington, DC: US Department of Energy, 2015).

[7] Both mercantilist and imperialist economies involve the control and influence by powerful nations over weaker countries, although they have distinctly different underlying philosophies. For additional information about these economies, see Benjamin J. Cohen, *The Question of Imperialism: The Political Economy of Dominance and Dependence* (New York: Basic Books, 1973) and Eli F. Heckscher, *Mercantilism*, translated by Mendel Shapiro (London: Routledge, 1994).

mies that claim to improve their quality of life. But that agreement can't continue without force-feeding their products into other nations to maintain their growth, which is a disastrous path according to history. China and Russia's mostly extractive economies require access to consumers in other countries, often at the point of the spear (or missiles or drones). Thus, their governmental operating systems push other countries toward Western democracy for mutual benefit.

## GEOGRAPHIC STRENGTHS

Humbly, we agree that America is the world's greatest superpower, maybe of all time. Whether we are or are not, it's obvious that no other nation has ever had the geographic advantages of the United States. If we are, we surely are the only one in the Western hemisphere, with blue water oceans on our east and west and a land mass connected exceptionally well by rivers and ports. All other superpower candidates (China, Russia, and maybe the European Union) share borders with friendly countries but also potential enemies or rivals. None are protected like America is by its oceans.

America is the perfect country from a security position. There may be no more difficult nation to invade than the United States. Our northern neighbor, Canada, is more than an ally of the US; its people are almost in brotherhood with us. On the south border, Mexico is also friendly to the US, with a population significantly younger than America's.

Early settlers found many safe and deep-water harbors along those oceans. As they traveled toward the country's interior, they found many navigable rivers emptying into those oceans. As the settlers became farmers in the interior of North

America, they were able to move their crops and other goods toward urban regions and later trade with foreign countries.

Today, the US has over twenty ports connected to our shores, of which many are connected to rivers, allowing for cheap transport of goods throughout the country. These rivers stretch over 2,000 miles inside the United States territory. America's rivers offset the transportation costs of goods by many factors over what it costs to transport on land. America's rivers and ports give the US the ability to industrialize without being forced to sell products overseas; the US industrialized base simply can sell its products to itself.

That simple geographic dimension enriched generations of Americans. In addition, much of the American continent is arable. The US has more arable farmland than any other country in the world.[8] As one of the largest food exporters, Americans have few worries about feeding themselves in times of external turmoil. Our technologies allow for the growth of more food per acre than most of the world's.

However, we should only gauge a country's success and superpower status by comparing it to its rivals. While China is about the same geographic size as America, it has about one-third of the arable land.[9] China has a challenging topography, with many regions not being suitable for growing food. Its coasts have fewer deep-water ports and rivers, many of which are barely navigable and often face flooding or drought.

---

[8] David Brown, *America the Bountiful: A Focus on US Farmland and Food Security* (Washington, DC: US Department of Agriculture, Economic Research Service, 2020).

[9] See Dwight H. Perkins, *Agricultural Development in China, 1368–1968* (London: Aldine Publishing Company, 1969); Lester R. Brown, *Who Will Feed China? Wake-Up Call for a Small Planet* (New York: W.W. Norton & Company, 1995).

Other potential superpowers face rivals on their borders. Today, Russia is at war with Ukraine in part to protect its borders from perceived enemies. The NATO alliance's primary mission is managing Russian aggression and threats. China, too, is surrounded by potential enemies. While Russia and China are in alliance today, they haven't been in the recent past. China's rivals include Taiwan, South Korea, and Japan. Add India, Vietnam, and Australia to that list. China's abuse of much of its Muslim population causes friction with many border countries.

Notably, America's shale oil revolution has allowed it to be the world's leading oil and natural gas exporter. China has fewer land-based energy resources and relies on fuel imports. China is the leading importer of Russian oil and gas.

We agree with Zeihan, who, as noted in his book, *The End of the World Is Just the Beginning*, believes that while today's world benefits greatly from globalization, tomorrow's world will move to regionalize and de-globalize for many reasons. In this new world (that may seem like a return to yesteryear), America can feed itself, energize itself, and manufacture itself to continuing prosperity. The rest of the world cannot. Lucky indeed, we are. America is unrivaled![10]

## DEMOGRAPHIC STRENGTHS

American demography strengthens America's hand. In the earliest centuries, America was a destination for many people who sought greater freedom, and much of its early population growth was due to younger families (those long boat rides across the Atlantic were no picnic, especially for older folks!)

---

10  See citations at footnotes 1-4, supra.

who moved to America to succeed. They often grew large families because of their beliefs, family needs, and religions.

War rarely has been to our shores, and while the Revolutionary and Civil Wars cost millions of lives, they occurred many years apart, allowing the American population to continue upward. Even World War I and World War II had lesser impacts on American lives than what happened to the populations of countries in Europe and Asia. After World War II, as the war machine ended but the Cold War arose, America's industries drove substantial economic success, encouraging family formation and immigration. The baby boomers in America, the largest American generation ever, had children and gave rise to the millennial generation, leading to additional growth, something many developed and developing countries missed doing. America can grow quickly, continue to add population and jobs, and, as required or desired, open the spigots of legal immigration. For the foreseeable future, America will continue to attract people, and we have the space to house them all. Even today, we are one of the least populated nations on the planet.[11]

Zeihan and Beckley note the demographic challenges ahead for major countries, especially perceived superpowers. In addition, much of the world has been urbanizing for some time and moving toward smaller family sizes. America saw similar trends, evidenced by the creation of suburbs and residential outgrowths from urban centers. On average, suburban families incur lower costs to live than urban families.

As members of the baby boomer generation retire, millennials fill in with their large numbers. The demographic advan-

---

11   Ibid.

tage is bigger financial budgets, more workers, lower percentage deficits, and stronger markets and economies. China makes a great case study for its near- and far-term challenges. The pressures of urbanization, coupled with its one-child policy years ago, left it in a position of depopulating. Zeihan and Beckley believe China's population might fall by about half (more than six hundred million people) over the next thirty to fifty years.[12]

China now has the fastest-aging workforce in human history, and it will lose seventy million workers over the next several decades. In the past, China had ten workers for every retiree; that ratio will flip over the next forty to fifty years. China's demographic future is bleak, and the same is true of Russia.

America is different. Per Beckley, we are one of the only major countries whose workforce will continue to grow this century.[13] China again is in the worst position, possibly the worst in human history. Unlike China and Russia, America remains a country that attracts many immigrants; we will likely return to average growth through legal immigration. We both agree that our existing illegal immigration system needs repair. However, our legal immigration system can change to improve America's growth prospects dramatically. Focusing on recruiting the best minds in the world to move here is essential to ensure our technological edge. As more people retire over the upcoming decades, adding more people (including immigrants) who pay taxes is a solid way to lessen budget deficits.

---

12   Ibid. See also Jiayang Fan, "How Dissent Grows in China," *The New Yorker*, December 7, 2022, https://www.newyorker.com/news/daily-comment/how-dissent-grows-in-china.

13   Beckley, 2018, Chapter 2.

★ ★ ★

Demography and geography certainly will play significant roles in America's future success, but something else unique about America encourages growing families and additional people to come here. That something else is opportunity.

## RULES-BASED ORDER, NAVAL PROTECTIONS, AND THE WORLD AMERICA BUILT AFTER WWII

The horrors of World War I have been largely forgotten. Most people don't understand the causes of the war, and even fewer understand the years and challenges that followed. Over 16.5 million people died, a number only surpassed by World War II. The US and its allies won World War I, but our inability to win the peace led to World War II.

In the aftermath of World War II, the United States embarked on an ambitious, strategic, and ultimately transformative endeavor: to rebuild the devastated economies of Japan and Germany. These decisions, driven by strategic, political pragmatism, and humanitarian concerns, marked significant departures from the punitive approach adopted after World War I by the victors.

America's decision to rebuild the economies of Japan and Germany was a multifaceted strategy driven by lessons from the past,[14] a desire to counter the spread of communism,[15]

---

[14] William R. Keylor, *The Twentieth-Century World and Beyond: An International History since 1900* (England: Oxford University Press, 2011).

[15] Melvyn P. Leffler, *A Preponderance of Power: National Security, the Truman Administration, and the Cold War* (California: Stanford University Press, 1992).

a goal to establish a stable international order, self-interested economic benefits, and humanitarian concerns. Certainly, this approach stimulated American economic interests.[16] American leaders understood that this rebuilding not only facilitated the recovery of Japan and Germany but also laid the foundation for a new era of global cooperation and prosperity.[17]

After World War II, much of the developed world lay in ruins. America used the Marshall Plan to rebuild Europe and remained in Japan and Germany, insisting they install democratic systems. In both cases, we saw our former enemies regain incredible prosperity. The US continued to help other nations build prosperity, hoping such would bring peace and democratic reforms.

Today, Germany ranks third in nominal GDP, and Japan ranks fourth. Over and again, where liberal democratic values became the norm, their people prospered. This is most evident in North Korea versus South Korea. For centuries, Korea was a unified nation. For thirty-five years, it fell under the dominance of Imperial Japan. But at the end of World War II, it was divided into North and South Korea. These two Koreas highlight the benefit of democratic capitalism over authoritarian socialism. South Korea's liberal democratic country, which began as the more rural of the two regions, now has the twelfth largest economy; North Korea's authoritarian communist country is 107th, and its people continue

---

[16] Michael J. Hogan, *The Marshall Plan: America, Britain, and the Reconstruction of Western Europe, 1947–1952* (England: Cambridge University Press, 1987).

[17] See John Gimbel, *The Origins of the Marshall Plan* (California: Stanford University Press, 1976); John Dower, *Embracing Defeat: Japan in the Wake of World War II* (New York: W.W. Norton & Company, 1999).

to live in abject poverty.[18] Germany, South Korea, and Japan are three of America's strongest allies, with American bases in their countries that shore up our military strength in Europe and the Pacific regions.

But how did that all happen? Post-World War II, as America helped the world rebuild, we empowered other nations to democratize themselves. We helped them rebuild their economies based on free market principles. While this happened, another excellent power source began to imprison a part of the world behind an imperial "Iron Curtain," a phrase used by English Prime Minister Winston Churchill. Soviet Union General Secretary Joseph Stalin strengthened his grip over the communist Soviet Union, and the communists in China pushed Chinese democratic forces (allies of the United States during World War II) to the island of Taiwan. The USSR later developed its own nuclear weapons, and the Cold War commenced.

For anyone who visited those countries behind the Iron Curtain as we did, it can only be described as a war between light and darkness. East Berlin, Poland, and other Eastern European areas, which became satellites of the Soviet Union, fell into massive economic despair. Compared to nations that elected to follow the American world order, the differences were stark. Adopting liberal democratic values and free market principles dramatically improved the lives of the people living in those areas over the centralized control of communism. Where the rule of law existed, where the power of individualism took hold, economic conditions dramatically improved.

---

18    Central Intelligence Agency, "The World Factbook 2023," https://www.cia.gov/the-world factbook/ (accessed August 26, 2024).

The quid pro quo America required for its support resulted in a world today that, from a human standpoint, would have been unimaginable in 1945. In return for becoming or continuing as an American ally, America agreed to use its strengths, including its military might, to create a rules-based order to enable trade and protection worldwide. Many of today's larger economies accepted America's offer. Today, this order allows for international free trade, even by those who rejected American leadership. For example, without America's Navy continuing to protect the free and safe movement of goods across oceans, preventing nearby countries and privateers from attacking that kind of commerce, even our adversaries' economies would be negatively affected. Much of the Chinese oil supplies from the Middle East could not occur without America's worldwide protection nor its ability to ship its exports. Russia would not be able to have protection of its exported commodities. And during the 2023 Hamas/Israel war, the US again took the lead in protecting shipping routes.

This global exchange market was not by accident. The Bretton Woods agreement (signed in 1945)[19] created a global monetary system with stable yet adjustable currency exchange rates. The participants agreed to international rules regarding their currencies, agreeing to avoid deflating their economies and currencies to offset local economic challenges.

This had a consequential impact on the US dollar. US political and economic dominance and the destruction from World War II left no currency other than the dollar at the center of the system. The participants desired stability, with fixed

---

[19] See Richard N. Gardner, *Sterling-Dollar Diplomacy: The Origins and the Prospects of Our International Economic Order* (New York: McGraw-Hill, 1969), 14–17.

exchange rates considered essential for trade. The US dollar was deemed the world's reserve currency, and all other currencies were pegged to it. In addition, the Bretton Woods agreement created the World Bank and the International Monetary Fund to coordinate international financial cooperation.

America's power leadership after World War II created solid foundations for international cooperation and trade. The United States became the world's sole economic superpower. Even non-allies, including some ongoing enemies, were compelled to follow many of the rules made after the war to trade goods effectively across international borders.

Today, it seems globalization retreats. China's aggressive diplomacy and Russia's exploits have left the world in a position to take sides again. The loss of globalization will likely result in an increase in the costs of products and may slow human progress. Many countries may suffer as economic globalization recedes. However, the US is again in an extraordinary position. America can continue to feed itself, energize itself, and supply its citizens with the goods and services they expect by reaching out to import goods and services from elsewhere as is desired, although likely more regionally than in today's world. America has already begun a process of re-industrialization that will dramatically improve the industrial output of the US in the upcoming decade. The American dollar remains the primary driver of international currency strength; at the moment, no other currency is poised to replace it.

While some political movements in the US suggest a more isolationist perspective, we doubt this will happen because it is not in America's long-term interest. America will continue to play a role in reshaping the world. We will be the cornerstone in promoting Western liberal democratic values, resulting in greater prosperity and improving the human condition. We will do this, and America and those nations allied with us will benefit. America is one lucky country for sure.

## AMERICA'S MILITARY MIGHT

On January 17, 1991, hundreds of thousands of American troops lay off the southern border of Saudi Arabia's coast, along with tens of thousands of tanks, dozens of naval ships, fighter jets, and stealth bombers, all with Baghdad, Iraq, in their sights. The American military, which had not been in a major war since Vietnam, was about to show the world its overwhelming military strengths, including the strengths of American technology.

After Iraq's leader Saddam Hussein had invaded the nation of Kuwait, attempting to control and disrupt the supply of oil, and refused to leave, the world witnessed a "shock and awe" campaign never seen before. For those who doubted the US's strength, it was clear that our military might and technology set us dramatically ahead of other militaries. Moreover, the US organized a coalition of more than forty countries (with almost one million soldiers) to drive Iraq out of Kuwait successfully.

US General and Commander of Allied Forces Herbert Norman Schwarzkopf Jr., also called Stormin' Norman, later visited Phoenix City Hall to give Paul unexpected gratitude for his involvement with troops as they departed for Operation Desert Storm. Paul took the opportunity to download everything he could from the general. General Schwarzkopf described the astonishing American war machine in detail.

Early in January 1991, Task Force Normandy had nine AH-64 Apache helicopters from the US Army's 101st Airborne

Division and four Air Force Pave Low special operations helicopters. They flew a lightning-fast and low assault into Baghdad, wiping out Iraqi radar sites with Hellfire missiles and anti-aircraft guns with Hydra-70 rockets, creating a twenty-mile corridor without air defenses. America's military took advantage of this corridor to fly Strike Eagle fighters, Ravens, hundreds of US Air Force, Navy, Marine Corps, and coalition fixed-wing aircraft and cruise missiles, followed by massive B-52 strikes, pummeling Iraqi positions and supply lines.

What the world witnessed on television that early morning in January was like a video game with real-life consequences. The advancement in the speed of microchips gave our guidance missile systems accuracy that was not realized before in war. We asked General Schwarzkopf in 1991 if the US was at its peak strength. He told us that technology was changing combat in ways never imagined. He said what we saw in Baghdad during the early stages of the attacks was the tip of the iceberg for the advancements in American technological warfare. He said, "If you could see what I see, you would know you haven't seen anything yet."

By all indications, we now see exponential advancements in the capability of the US military. Thirty years after General Schwarzkopf's tip-of-the-iceberg comment, Beckley, a current expert on America's military might, made a similar point about America's military strength on the *Optimist American* podcast.[20] He explained why America's military might is unsurpassed and growing stronger. America continues to spend substantially more money than every other country to maintain the freedoms that our Constitution created (and

---

20   Beckley, *The Optimistic American*, 2022.

that our rules-based system exported worldwide), including the freedom of naval navigation, enabling the free flow of goods and services. Many countries like China import vast quantities of food and fuel and would starve or freeze without the benefits of the American order. Moreover, countries like China not only need to build more military might to catch up to the United States, but their continuing need to dedicate much of their current and future military investments toward maintaining peace at home and in nearby geographic regions hampers progress.

The world remains a dangerous place. Many of America's potential adversaries (China, Russia, North Korea, Iran) possess or will possess nuclear weapons. Maintaining world peace requires the United States and its allies to maintain advantages. China is growing its overall military might, including creating a bigger navy, using enhanced cybersecurity, and threats of space force weaponry (such as anti-satellite missiles). The latest American military, missile defense, and nuclear posture strategy (written in 2022)[21] opines that China is our main adversary. It is the only competitor of the United States and its allies with the intent to reshape the international order, and increasingly, it has the power to do so.

Moreover, much of the United States' defensive military assets are old. A recent (2022) report[22] by The Heritage Foundation describes the decline in our military hard power

---

21  See US Department of Defense, *2022 Nuclear Posture Review* (Washington, DC: US Department of Defense, 2022); US Department of Defense, *2022 Missile Defense Review* (Washington, DC: US Department of Defense, 2022).
22  The Heritage Foundation, *2023 Index of US Military Strength: Assessing America's Ability to Provide for the Common Defense* (Washington, DC: The Heritage Foundation, 2022).

and assigns low or marginal letter grades/ratings for preparedness to the US Army, the Navy, the Air Force, and the Space Force. Only the Marine Corps was well rated. While our nuclear arsenal is strong, it is aging.[23] The Heritage Foundation thinkers and other experts have called on America's leadership to continue to invest deeply in our military posture in the face of new and continuing threats from China, Russia, Iran, North Korea, and certain non-state (terrorist) actors.

This may beg the question: What type of optimism assumes we must always be ready for war? We doubt the world will ever be rid of the imperial tyrants who hope to expand their economic interests through geographic acquisitions. We doubt we will ever be completely free from the threat of terrorism. But we are optimistic that strength and deterrence can keep war, including nuclear exchanges, from happening in the first place. We are very optimistic that as long as we allow individuals to own what they create and promote the ideals of individuality, as long as we don't regulate many companies out of business, we will continue our advantages in technology. And as long as we have a technological advantage, we have the ideal deterrence.

The American focus on civil rights, equal rights, human rights, property rights, free markets, and free enterprise is vital to these advantages. But can we keep our freedoms without our technology and strong defenses? Post-World War II, America

---

23   Yet, the United States continues to spend more on nuclear weapons than any other nation, a lot more. According to a June 2024 report by the International Campaign to Abolish Nuclear Weapons (ICAN), in 2023 the nine nuclear-armed countries spent more than $90 billion on their nuclear weapons systems, with the US at $51.4 billion, more than the other nuclear countries combined, and with the biggest percentage increase at 18 percent. *Surge: 2023 Global Nuclear Weapons Spending (ICAN, 2024).*

established the "rules of the road" for trade and related freedoms. Enforcing those rules required strong allies—countries with mostly democratic governments committed to individual freedoms and peace, strong treaties and other alliances, and integrated military systems, including bases in worldwide locations to enforce the rules. Today, we remain optimistic that our leaders will continue providing these necessary resources to protect our country and enable us to trade worldwide. Even in an era of de-globalization, we can maintain a free, powerful, and everlasting America with rules that ensure peace and freedom. And we start, and possibly end, with the primary source of American strength: The Rule of Law.

## THE RULE OF LAW IN AMERICA

America is a land of hope and opportunity, inextricably linked to the rule of law. This nation's aspiration to be a place where everyone can excel to the best of their abilities hinges upon a rules-based order. Public education and the freedom to conduct business provide the essential pillars supporting hope and opportunity. Education acts as the great equalizer, granting citizens access to opportunities. The freedom to conduct business embodies the ownership of one's creations and minimizes corruption. Underlying all this success is the rule of law.

In America's business landscape, most benefits (including hard work, success, and income) are earned by and entrusted to the hands of workers, employees, and entrepreneurs. The rewards of free enterprise remain mostly untouched by the system itself. However, America's progressive tax system ensures that individuals with lower income levels pay a lower percentage of their incomes in taxes than those with higher incomes. Since it truly takes an American village for anyone to succeed here, sharing a portion of one's economic success compels such a system. Moreover, government support further alleviates some tax burdens on lower-income Americans.

America is a nation governed by laws. Federal, state, and local laws, and court interpretations of these laws, protect the rights and responsibilities that individuals need to succeed. In America, laws, not the whims of influential individuals, regulate behaviors. These laws are created and empowered by the collective will of the American majority. In America, everyone is subject to the same laws, as our Founders forbade "bills of attainder" that fail to apply universally. The Constitution's Tenth Amendment outlines the waterfall of rights within which the federal government operates, while individual states and, ultimately, the people retain sovereignty in other areas not assigned.

The Founders severed ties with their mother country, an English colony where the king and monarchy reigned supreme, even as they embarked on new lives in a distant land. The long-distance relationship with England proved untenable, prompting our early leaders to break free from oppression and tyranny, including unjust taxation.

Contemporary courts and scholars debate how much the constitutional language (and laws derived from it) can adapt as American society progresses. Most concur that the Constitution's interpretation should align with the eighteenth-century principles and the historical contexts of its amendments. The Supreme Court continues to deliberate and address these concerns, with the consensus that the Constitution remains relevant today, and most likely will tomorrow.

One of the numerous advantages of America's rule of law is that it provides clarity for anyone interacting with fellow Americans, delineating the rules to be followed. In cases of uncertainty, American courts offer guidance on interpreting these laws. The foundation of our legal system—the Constitution, federal, state, and local laws, and court or other dispute resolution mechanisms—played a pivotal role in propelling America to become the world's most robust economic system. While some countries resort to bribery to facilitate business transactions, America (although not completely immune to such issues) relies on an effective legal process to combat corruption. Most business transactions in America are executed expeditiously and fairly and, where needed, resolved through our nation's sophisticated dispute resolution system.

Our system of checks and balances is complicated. Our society is more complex than the agrarian system that primarily existed here in the eighteenth century. Yet our governing documents and the laws that were implemented consistent with them continue to support markets in as accessible a fashion as practicable. In America, any citizen is free to select a career path. Anyone can invent almost any business path. The ability to select one's own economic path is greater here than anywhere else.

Because of the freedoms democracy affords, America is a land of restarts. Not everyone succeeds with their first business plan or career. Sometimes, their choices can lead to ongoing economic challenges and risks. In America, however, clear paths exist to enable individuals to start over, begin again, experience resilience, and envision success anew. One of those paths includes the ability to declare bankruptcy. While some people see bankruptcy as a badge of shame, it is actually another opportunity to achieve the American dream. This is one of the fundamental freedoms the Founders placed in the Constitution (Article 1, Section 8).

America was not to be a place where debtors had no hope for the future. The American vision of success through hard work, good education, and business opportunities continues to be highly valued. We will have much more to say about America's justice systems and the rule of law in Chapter 12.

## MISCELLANEOUS THOUGHTS

We certainly see significant potential threats to our democracy. On foreign policy, a rising coalition among authoritarian governments creates a need to rethink our military-strategic interests and provide additional funding. Our nuclear arsenal needs updating to ensure the necessary deterrents. We hope there will be enhanced support from our current allies (and new ones) and a recognition that one significant military loss could undermine the American-led world order. We face alternative philosophies at home that threaten the individualism our country is based on and a partisan political system that enhances radical voices disproportionate to their numbers. Indeed, we see risks related to global warming, the need for reforms in our educational system, and the threats of immigration both from unregulated illegal immigration as well as the need to increase merit-based immigration. Most importantly, we see the danger to human progress if we abandon free market principles.

However, we don't believe in the worst possible outcomes on all these issues. We have faith in the outcomes based on the data. Based on the evidence, these issues are no more significant than the big challenges we faced in our past and yet somehow we found our way through the darkness.

We should never take the American system and history for granted. We could lose what has created the greatest prosperity in human history, designed around the rule of law, free elections, and people determining their destinies. If we don't convince the enemies of our resolve, we could find a new world order (with new economic rules and authoritarian controls) that displaces the values America's Founders and the citizens who benefited created. There would be a ripple effect across the world's democracies.

We remain optimistic that, in the future, our leaders will listen, talk softly but firmly, and stay firm in their resolve to protect world order based on the rule of law. Fortunately, the past seventy-five years of American history have given us that faith.

So, are we a democracy or a republic? America's current systems were built on majority votes coupled with the protection of minority rights. All public positions in America are elected via majority vote. Properly analyzed, America is a democratic republic.

We elect members of Congress (representatives and senators) by majority votes in individual districts and also by states. There is increasing criticism about our Electoral College system. Yet, the president and vice president are both elected by majority votes, namely votes by electors selected in individual states and citizen electors who cast ballots, where a majority of each set elects the president and vice president. Complex for sure, but the Founders were wise in how they created America's democracy.

Other democracies support different systems. One example is a parliamentary system where majorities vote for groups of individuals who then elect their top leaders (such as prime ministers). But look closely because those systems also have the hallmarks of democracy—namely, majority votes win!

We challenge anyone to argue successfully to the contrary. And we wonder why anyone would claim the American system is not based on democracy. You need only read our Constitution (and the constitutions for the various American states) to see how we elect political leaders and why our system is so fundamental to individual rights and freedom.

We do, however, recognize that democracy can be and is messy. While individual rights are often protected, large groups of individuals, or factions, as the Founders called them, may use their more limited power until they can align with others to capture a majority view. While the Founders were deeply concerned about political parties, they understood the benefit of factions and their power to organize, succeed in elections, and then be involved in the process of compromise through the legislative process. This wonderful system was designed to elicit compromise and allow sharing to reach common goals.[24]

Groups that criticize America sow discontent because a failed government is necessary before they can impose their radical, undemocratic ideas (at least as compared with the ideals of liberal democracies, including the protection of individual freedoms). Unfortunately, these groups control many of the power levers in today's American politics. Polling estimates that extreme factions on both the left and the right represent less than 10 percent of the public; however, they often

---

24  See Levin, 2024.

control majorities of the two major primary election systems, leading to more division.

Let us walk you through some math to illustrate how the extremes that represent 10 percent of America can control the two primary systems.[25] The US Census Bureau estimates that about 21 percent of eligible citizens are not registered to vote. According to Gallup, in 2023, about 43 percent of America's registered voters identified as independent, 27 percent as Republican, and 27 percent as Democrat. Individuals who turn out to vote in partisan primaries (Republican or Democratic) total about 30 percent. So now do the math: 79 percent of the eligible voters multiplied by the 27 percent in the Democratic or Republican Party equals about 21 percent. Of this 21 percent, approximately 30 percent will vote in the primary. This equals 6.4 percent of all eligible voters who will vote in a party primary, with a majority at 3.2 percent + 1.

Thus, less than 10 percent of the public can control both party primaries. There are an estimated 5,000 elected offices across America. Through "gerrymandering" (a process where the party in the majority aligns voting districts to benefit its members), only 30 percent of the candidates for those offices have real opposition in a general election. The remaining 70 percent cements partisan views and gives the more radical elements of our society the power to control the system at local, state, and federal government levels. These forces mean

---

25  See US Census Bureau, *Voting and Registration in the Election of November 2022*, Table 4b (*Reported Voting and Registration, by Sex, Race and Hispanic Origin, for States: November 2022*), https://www.census.gov/data/tables/time-series/demo/voting-and-registration/p20-585.html (accessed August 26, 2024); Gallup, "Independent Party ID Tied for High; Democratic ID at New Low," January 12, 2024, https://news.gallup.com/poll/548459/independent-party-tied-high-democratic-new-low.aspx.

less competition and fewer leadership choices for citizens and can result in elected representatives who don't represent all the people they are elected to serve.

So, while we strongly believe America is a democracy, we see appropriate changes ahead to the primary election system that exists today. Under the current system, the views of non-party affiliated or independent voters are left out. That must change.

★ ★ ★

We can't leave this chapter without saying something about immigration. Many other countries struggle with shrinking populations now and as projected over the next fifty years. This projection includes many European countries, Russia, and China. Those countries have fewer immigration options. Shrinking populations, with more people aging and fewer people working, sets a political and economic time bomb. America can always turn on its legal immigration spigot to bring in new workers and citizens, a benefit not always available to many other countries.

But we must be careful. Our current immigration policies are reactive and create instability that threatens political stability. We react where we should be intentional. Importantly, we must ensure that individuals coming to America support American values.

America is a land of many immigrants and children of immigrants. That was true during the founding years leading up to the Declaration and remains true today. Most immigrants eventually grasp the English language, if not in their generation, then in the following generations, and integrate as fully as native-born Americans.

We don't believe in open borders, and we know that our government has a role in protecting our borders. Yet, we think today that we're doing more to keep out the desirables than we are in keeping out the undesirables. We like the idea of a merit-based or market-based immigration system to bring the best into the US. Imagine if America had not allowed Albert Einstein to emigrate from Germany before World War II!

We should recruit the best from around the world, not try to keep them out. We should encourage all foreign student graduates of American universities to keep their talents and educational successes here. With a merit-based system, we can ensure America can lower its budget deficits by adding income earners to help pay the cost of our retirees. We can maintain US supremacy by maintaining our technological lead. But this will require Americans to understand the benefits of growing markets and abundance.

That so many individuals want to emigrate to America says that we still are one of the most desirable places on the planet to live, play, and thrive. The greatest indication of which nations are successful and which are failing is where the people and their money (capital) choose to go. Under those measures, there is no place like home—America!

# PART III

# AMERICAN GRIT: PROTECTING THE NATION

## CHAPTER 9

# ENTERING THE ERA OF INTERNATIONAL TENSION

WORLD WAR II DAMAGED EUROPE and Asia substantially. It changed America as well, but mostly positively. Looking back, it is difficult to recall the emotional climate of the Cold War that followed World War II, but the biggest fear was the possibility of global thermonuclear war. By the end of World War II in 1945, only America possessed nuclear bombs. At the end of the 1940s, the Soviet Union (USSR) developed atomic capabilities. This meant no country could win a "hot" Cold War. Few people know this story.[1]

★ ★ ★

Soviet Union Major General Dmitri Polyakov sat in a small fishing boat on the Yamuna River, which originated from the Yamunotri Glacier in the Lower Himalayas in Uttarakhand, at 14,800 feet. The water quality was good until it passed through New Delhi. Floating among the high reed plants known as bulrushes, Polyakov and his boat were out of sight and in an ideal fishing spot.

---

1   See Elaine Shannon, "Death of the Perfect Spy," *Time Magazine*, August 8, 1994, https://time.com/archive/6725778/death-of-the-perfect-spy/.

Polyakov ranked high as an officer in the Soviet Union's military intelligence agency, the GRU. He analyzed intelligence gathered by Soviet spies—information that included stolen or acquired data and technologies related to atomic secrets in the United States. Soviet spies who had defected and acted as double agents provided much of this information. Polyakov had access to that intelligence and much more. A former US Central Intelligence Agency (CIA) director described him as the jewel in the crown of intelligence spies.

As a flock of peacocks screeched in the background, Polyakov delivered a lecture while his fishing line danced under the water. The noisy birds drowned out his words, but a man sitting beside him in the boat heard and recorded his military briefings. Those recordings profoundly altered the Cold War. The man sitting next to Polyakov was a CIA officer.

This patriotic Russian, who despised the Soviet system, gave vital security information to the CIA official to ensure that America won the Cold War and that it did not turn "hot." Although Polyakov's motives for helping in the Cold War were puzzling, he rejected asylum offers, saying he loved Russia and never planned to leave. His payment mainly came in power tools, overalls, fishing gear, and shotguns, all valued at less than an estimated $3,000 yearly. He drank little and was faithful to his wife; he was not a man to sell out his country for cash. He'd fought in World War II but was greatly disillusioned by the Soviet government, which he believed was corrupt. He feared the USSR would become totalitarian without checks and balances or dissenting voices.

The infamous American double agents Robert Hanssen and Aldrich Ames betrayed Polyakov. Hanssen and Ames turned their loyalty against America for a simpler reason—

money. They earned millions of dollars for passing along information, including military and nuclear secrets and the identities of several double agents, including Polyakov.

Long after the Cold War, in 1998, the public learned that Polyakov was sentenced to death for treason and executed. But he was a hero, for he had provided the US with information that altered the potential course of nuclear destruction during the Cold War. There is an unmarked grave somewhere in Russia cradling this Soviet soldier who played a significant role in Western democracy—and maybe even the survival of the Earth's living populations.

By 1945, World War II had destroyed much of the world. The United States lost 420,000 enlisted men and women, while an estimated forty to fifty million people died elsewhere, and another twenty-five million were injured because of the war. This war destroyed roads, bridges, farms, livestock, and cities across Russia, China, India, Europe, Japan, and many other parts of the world. The US was mainly spared thanks to the big, vast, blue Pacific and Atlantic Oceans, which served as practical barriers against attacks by adversaries. American infrastructure—government, industry, agriculture, citizenry—remained unscathed compared to those systems in other countries.

Given World War II's destruction, a new world order was necessary. The US, with its unparalleled power and resources, was uniquely positioned to lead. Yet, America chose not to become the next global empire of the mid-twentieth century because empires and democracies are incompatible.

Instead of pursuing an empire, US government leaders allied with other nations. On behalf of Americans, they offered other world leaders a grand bargain: accept our financial capital and leadership through the Marshall Plan (and the reconstruction in Japan, led by US General Douglas MacArthur) to rebuild the world, and, in exchange, America would provide access to the world's biggest market (perhaps the only viably functioning market left at the time). In addition, the US Navy ensured that allies could safely trade among themselves without risking attacks from privateers, pirates, or hostile neighbors. The offer came with a catch: America would provide those benefits only to countries that supported American interests against the Soviet Union and its authoritarian government.

The world divided into two spheres. The American sphere promoted a global market, allowing for the free exchange of goods. American ports, as well as those of its allies, bustled with commerce and goods. Entrepreneurs innovated new products and developed systems to make products more efficient, resulting in a rise in the quality of life among all people in the free world and an overall improvement in the human condition.

In contrast, those living within the USSR's sphere witnessed ominous signs of a world of darkness. Those who opposed the Soviets' wishes were imprisoned behind what was called the Iron Curtain. The USSR presented a significant threat to democracy.

The extractive policies of the USSR were vastly different from the inclusive policies of the US and its allies. Property rights, patents, copyrights, and other intellectual property are essential in developing technology and progress in a free society. Inventors and creators have incentives to innovate, knowing they can commercialize their ideas. Competition and businesses develop because of it, creating a virtuous circle of innovation.

## CHINA AND RUSSIA AS ALLIES

China aligned with the USSR during most of the Cold War. In 1950, Chairman Mao Zedong of China and Stalin of the USSR entered an alliance known as the Treaty of Friendship. This treaty strengthened military and economic ties between those two nations and united them against a common enemy, the United States and its allies.

Through Polyakov, Americans discovered that Communist China and Communist Russia diverged in interests. As the US focused on exploiting weak points in the division, scenarios unfolded that ultimately led to the collapse of the Soviet Union. When Stalin died in 1953, his successors challenged his policies. In late February 1956, Nikita Khrushchev delivered a secret speech denouncing Stalinism, criticizing Stalin's purges that resulted in the deaths of hundreds of thousands of USSR citizens, including members of the Communist Party.

An Israeli intelligence agency uncovered and leaked Khrushchev's speech, causing turmoil and rioting among Soviet citizens, devastating the Communist Party in the US, and significantly damaging relationships with other Iron Curtain countries. As a result of the speech, Aleksandr Solzhenitsyn, a Soviet soldier (a captain in the Soviet Red Army who had been exiled for criticizing Stalin), was released and exonerated. Solzhenitsyn went on to write *The Gulag Archipelago*,[2] which portrayed the brutal nature of the Gulag prisons and Stalin's policies.

---

2  Aleksandr Solzhenitsyn, *The Gulag Archipelago 1918–1956: An Experiment in Literary Investigation*, trans. Thomas P. Whitney (New York: Harper & Row, 1974).

Khrushchev's speech also upset Mao, who had adopted policies similar to Stalin's. Mao based his Great Leap Forward on Stalin's purge policy, resulting in millions of Chinese deaths through persecution, starvation, incarceration, and execution. Mao believed Khrushchev had abandoned the principles of communism.

In early 1960, Mao pushed Khrushchev to be more militant with then-US President Dwight Eisenhower after the USSR shot down an American U-2 spy plane that had been photographing USSR military bases in Cuba. When Khrushchev failed to act aggressively, he lost face with Mao, the Chinese communists, and the People's Republic of China (PRC). In 1962, relations between the USSR and China broke down because Mao wanted the USSR to go to war with the US over the Cuban Missile Crisis. Khrushchev felt Mao was pushing the world toward nuclear war; Mao believed Khrushchev was weak.

Communist elites in the USSR finally deposed Khrushchev in October 1964. After his removal, Mao found no peace with the new leadership of the USSR. Leonid Ilyich Brezhnev implemented more oppressive policies against political dissidents and engaged in feuds with other communist countries. This resulted in the Sino-Soviet border conflict of October 1969 (in the area of the Ussuri River in Manchuria), which the USSR won when it assumed control over disputed territory. The win drove a wedge between the USSR and China. USSR's premier, Alexei Kosygin, met with China's premier, Zhou Enlai, to restore communication between the two powers—but the damage was done. By the early 1970s, Mao knew China could no longer rely on the USSR as an ally.

In 1971, President Richard Nixon's administration capitalized on the split, partially based on information Polyakov revealed on the Yamuna River riverbanks. Then-Secretary of State Henry Kissinger traveled to Beijing to arrange Nixon's visit to China, changing the bipolar geopolitics of the Cold War into a tripolar world—from the USSR and the US to China to US to USSR. This juxtaposition profoundly affected the Cold War.

Nixon's agreement with China offered similar terms to that provided to other allies in the Marshall Plan from 1945: naval protection for the transportation of products, access to capital markets, and the ability to sell into the US market. Many Americans believed that as China became a free market, it would become more democratic. This did not happen.

The American-led alliance sacrificed some American assets to create a world order that helped generate a détente with the USSR to end the Cold War. The agreement between the US and China had questionable direct benefits for individual American citizens. Overall, America benefited from China's efficiently and cheaply made goods and services in a much safer world, but the agreement arguably sacrificed American jobs.

Before the deal, China was barely a preindustrial power. Since then, China has grown substantially. Most informed observers believed that opening Western democracy markets to China significantly increased the growth of the Chinese economy over the following decades.

With clear-eyed hindsight, the case often is made that the alliance's tradeoffs greatly enhanced US growth. However, by the beginning of World War II, the US was hitting its stride. It escaped destruction throughout the war and, thanks to production during the war, became an industrial giant. The US had vast, undeveloped lands full of incredible resources. Americans were one of the world's largest food producers; we produced significant amounts of fuel, electric energy, and raw materials. The US was going to be a world power, regardless.

The positive results following World War II on America and its citizens were undeniable. The Bretton Woods agreement in 1944 created a new monetary system based on the American dollar. At the end of World War II, with a significant portion of the world destroyed for a second time, the United States provided allies with all the goods they needed, so long as they paid in gold. This led to massive gold reserves in the US. With the US controlling most of the world's gold, nations agreed to base their currency on the US dollar, which based its currency on gold.

It was a new world order, unprecedented in history. Combined with American naval security for the transportation of goods, efforts to rebuild war-torn nations, and opening US markets to allies, Americans built a period of unprecedented world growth. Later, China benefited greatly from that world order. When the USSR fell, US leaders offered Russia the ability to participate, and it accepted.

Today, however, China and Russia overlook those historic benefits and instead see the American-led order as an existential threat. For authoritarian governments, all that matters is staying in power, and democracy threatens that goal. Their leaders believe America's focus on individual freedoms makes us corrupt and weak. They believe collective interests should prevail over the individual.

In January 2022, in response to Russia's war against Ukraine, Russia and China declared a new era in the global order. They released a 5,000-page document that described their renewed friendship. While this "statement of friendship" does not fully endorse Russia's invasion of Ukraine, it captures much of the territorial ambitions of both Russia and China. It challenges the leadership of the North Atlantic Treaty Organization (NATO) and the United States, hardening attacks on liberal democracy. In 2023, Americans could interpret the latest statements of friendship and support by Chinese President Xi Jinping and Russian President Vladimir Putin as the opening salvo of a "new" Cold War. On the global stage, the world's two most powerful authoritarians, whose leadership has driven their nations into totalitarian states, announced a sweeping long-term agreement that challenges the international order.

Some American economists and industrialists romanticize China's rise. They see China and the US in relative terms and view the current state as one of international relativism—a world where no morality exists among nations, only different constructs. Justice, human rights, free elections, and the natural rights endowed on America by the Creator are America's truths. They are not necessarily universal truths, some say. The authoritarian view that supports a more collectivist state is equally valid under this view of international relativism.

In the relativist view, gravity pulls everyone and everything toward those with power. In simple terms, it's a new world order. It wants to replace the old order, led by America. Superpowers rise and fall, and new ones grow in their place; relativists opine that this is just the natural order of world leadership.

Geopolitical experts and economists believe Russia's and China's threats are not coming from nations determined to flex their muscles as inevitable superpowers. Instead, they are countries in decline, driven to act while they can. Significant data convinces many observers that Russia and China face challenges demographically, geographically, and economically.

## CHALLENGES OVER THE NEAR TERM

These vulnerabilities likely make the two countries more dangerous, especially over the next decade or two. Challenges from shrinking demographics, debt, reversals on free market trends, and extractive policies require them to become more ambitious to maintain export levels and extraction efforts that drive the growth in their economies. But the rest of the world, especially democratic countries, are responding. One result is China's encirclement by other nations that are unwilling to accept their dominance. Western and Eastern countries (such as Japan, South Korea, and the Philippines) understand the risks ahead and maneuver for advantage, again led by the US.

Authors who have been guests on *The Optimistic American* podcast, Peter Zeihan, in his book *The End of the World is Just the Beginning*,[3] and Michael Beckley, in his book, *Danger Zone: The Coming Conflict with China*,[4] argue that China suffers geographically and demographically, with limited information provided to its citizens from corrupt, isolated government practices that purged detractors. Demographically, they are facing a disaster; for example, China's Shanghai Academy of Social Sciences predicts China's population will decline to fewer than six hundred million, less than half of what it is today.[5]

---

3  Zeihan, 2022.
4  Brands and Beckley, 2022.
5  Ibid. See Stephen Chen, "China's Population Could Halve Within the Next 45 Years, New Study Warns," *South China Morning Post*, September 30, 2021.

While China has made significant progress in industrialization, its economy remains inefficient. Under a central planning model that continues to drive China, state-run investments rarely make an economy more efficient. Too often, companies favored by the PRC, not the marketplaces, continue to receive government investment. China took on extraordinary debt to centralize control, dramatically flooding its currency markets. They also loaned money to other nations and domestic companies; many loans will not be repaid.

China's agricultural system is inefficient. One out of three workers in China works in agriculture, while less than 1 percent of Americans work on farms. China remains the world's most extensive food importer, while the US is one of the largest exporters.

The United States entered this new Cold War as an unprecedented superpower. Geographically, demographically, militarily, and economically, the US is vastly superior to China and Russia combined. Our advantages are enormous, yet we still face significant risks. And if it is a war we are to meet, even a Cold War, American leadership continues to matter.

## NUCLEAR ARMAGEDDON (OR NOT)?

On August 6, 1945, much of Hiroshima, Japan, was destroyed by an atomic weapon dropped from a US military airplane. On August 9, 1945, a second atomic bomb was dropped on and destroyed much of Nagasaki. Shortly after that, the Pacific Theatre's portion of World War II ended. Japan formally surrendered to the United States on August 15, 1945.

Historians estimate there were 140,000 casualties in Hiroshima and 70,000 in Nagasaki by the end of 1945.

To date, only the United States has ever deployed a nuclear weapon in armed conflict, but this caused a worldwide proliferation of atomic armament arsenals. We are fortunate to still live on an Earth mostly unscathed by nuclear holocausts as had happened in Japan. Yet, in what may be a new Cold War, we may be closer today to a nuclear exchange than we were during the first Cold War. This is why we are choosing to study the lessons of the last Cold War now to avoid catastrophic consequences.

From 1945 until 1949, the United States was the only country in the world that owned the potential to use nuclear power as a tool of war. The USSR tested its nuclear bombs in 1949, followed by Great Britain in the 1950s (much of the work on the Manhattan Project included scientists and engineers from Great Britain). France and China developed their nuclear weapons in the 1960s. Today, the nuclear club includes India, Pakistan, North Korea, and (most likely, but not yet confirmed) Israel.

Following World War II and the destruction of much of Hiroshima and Nagasaki, President Harry Truman determined that the choice to use nuclear weapons or not must remain in civilian rather than military hands, primarily those of the president of the United States. Yet, Daniel Ellsberg, a former military planner turned anti-war activist, identified twenty-five times when American presidents threatened to use nuclear weapons in conflicts.[6]

The world remained (and likely remains) on the razor's edge of a nuclear Armageddon. While most of the world's cit-

---

6     Daniel Ellsberg, *The Doomsday Machine: Confessions of a Nuclear War Planner* (New York: Bloomberg Publishing, 2019).

izens believe that nuclear war is a last resort, in the decades following World War II (and especially after the USSR joined the nuclear club), the limited use of nuclear weapons was often considered a first option by American and Soviet military and civilian leaders.

The Korean War (1950 to 1953) was one of the first major conflicts of the Cold War. The US contemplated then using nuclear weapons to push back Chinese forces, with a recommendation by General MacArthur, commander of the US and United Nations (UN) forces, to do so. President Truman rejected his recommendation and later relieved MacArthur of command.

During the Suez Crisis in 1956, after Egypt nationalized the canal, America was drawn into the conflict that included Britain, France, and Israel. Our leaders, along with the Soviet Union, proposed a resolution to the United Nations, which Egypt rejected. War planners in the United States considered using nuclear weapons to force Egypt to comply. During the Vietnam War, two presidential administrations, Johnson and Nixon, contemplated a limited nuclear strike.

In the conflict with Ukraine, Putin overtly continues to threaten to use nuclear weapons. Many Americans must again face the eerie feeling of a world where nuclear war is possible. Will Putin use them? We don't know, but we should question the threat.

When threatened by a nuclear power, especially one that has as many nukes as China or Russia, when and where will America draw a line? Should we capitulate because Russia's and China's leaders are more committed to ending humanity than American leaders are? And, if we show them that the threat of using nuclear weapons is enough to make us back down, will it provide an incentive for them to threaten again to use them?

These threats matter. But if we back off because of the threat of nukes in Ukraine, why wouldn't Russia threaten again in Lithuania, Taiwan, or Poland? If Russia or China believe we are weak regarding this threat, where does it end?

During the Cold War, when America's leaders faced authoritarian threats, instead of firing off a few (or hundreds or thousands) of nuclear bombs, we answered through a strategy called containment. Containment was designed to block further geographic expansion of Soviet power, inducing a retreat from Soviet control and influence and fostering the seeds of destruction within the Soviet system. We knew their system was corrupt. The USSR outlawed free enterprise and, through corruption, murder, and restricting the human desire to create and innovate, we believed that if we contained them, they would eventually fall of their own accord.

Two American leaders during this period, John F. Kennedy and Ronald Reagan, understood the need to lead from a position of strength to make the authoritarians believe that their threat of nuclear weapons would not deter us. It was like a game of poker where the stakes were the survival of humanity. And in poker or negotiation, if your opponent knows you will fold your cards even when you have the winning hand, they will almost always go all in.

Many believe that the Cuban Missile Crisis in 1962 was perhaps the closest the US and the world came to nuclear annihilation. The USSR installed nuclear missiles in Cuba to prevent a US invasion of the island and to threaten the US mainland. President Kennedy rejected calls for a direct military strike and imposed a naval blockade. Backchannel diplomatic conversations led to the USSR's agreement to withdraw their missiles in return for the US agreeing never to invade Cuba and to remove nuclear missiles from Turkey (a fact long held secret). But the keys to success were Kennedy's strength and resolve while pursuing diplomacy.

It has been estimated the USSR's nuclear stockpile was about 40,000 warheads by 1986. The United States reached its peak stockpile in 1967, estimated at approximately 31,000. As of 2021, according to the Federation of American Scientists, those numbers stand at 6,257 for Russia and 5,500 for the US. Most of these weapons yield destructive power many times more than the bombs that detonated in Hiroshima and Nagasaki.[7]

The reduced number of weapons was purposeful. Growing and maintaining a nuclear arsenal is expensive. The USSR (now Russia) and the United States had economic interests in reducing those costs. Beyond economics, both countries understood that the end of the world might follow from one or the other making a tactical mistake by launching such weapons, whether directly at each other or indirectly in conflicts in other countries.

Under President Nixon, in 1969, détente became a core element of America's foreign policy. The Nixon administration promoted more productive dialogue with the Soviet government to facilitate negotiations over arms control and other bilateral agreements. Although Reagan ran on a platform to

---

[7] Robert S. Norris and Hans M. Kristensen, "Global Nuclear Weapons Inventories, 1945–2010," *Bulletin of the Atomic Scientists* 66, no. 4 (2010): 77–83, https://doi.org/10.2968/066004008; Hans M. Kristensen and Matt Korda, "Status of World Nuclear Forces," *Federation of American Scientists*, last modified 2021, https://fas.org/issues/nuclear-weapons/status-world-nuclear-forces/.

end détente, during the later years of his presidency, he saw an opening to negotiate additional nuclear weapons reductions with Soviet General Secretary Mikhail Gorbachev, outcomes that dramatically reduced nuclear weapons owned by both countries. Again, a policy based on both strength and diplomacy is what worked.

Following the collapse of the Soviet Union in 1991, the United States and the surviving leadership in Russia undertook significant measures that included various treaties toward disarmament and non-proliferation of nuclear weapons sent to other countries. Many non-nuclear powers pushed to reduce these risks when the Non-Aligned Movement (NAM) was created to moderate tensions between the major nuclear powers. NAM defined geographic regions (Latin America, the South Pacific, and parts of Asia) as Nuclear Weapon-Free Zones and, with the cooperation of the countries that held nuclear powers, created the Nuclear Non-Proliferation Treaty in 1968. The treaty recognized only the first five countries (US, USSR, UK, France, China) as nuclear states. Most countries worldwide are signatories to the treaty and, in return, receive help to develop the peaceful use of nuclear power.

From that point forward, the two major nuclear powers entered various treaties, especially after the fall of the Soviet Union, to reduce the number of nuclear weapons they actively managed. They also created other procedures to reduce the risks of a nuclear Armageddon. Before the collapse of the USSR, leaders from the United States, the Soviet Union, and the United Kingdom signed the Limited (or Partial) Test Ban treaty to ban nuclear weapons in the air, outer space, and underwater, effectively limiting testing to underground locations to reduce radioactive fallout from such testing and de-escalating the Cold War nuclear arms race.

In 1972, the Strategic Arms Limitation Talks (SALT) between President Nixon and Soviet General Secretary Brezhnev produced two agreements: one limiting the deployment of anti-ballistic missile (ABM) testing to defend against nuclear attacks but also compelling an enhanced nuclear arms race, and the other capping the number of ABM launchers.

After the Soviet Union collapsed in 1991, the United States and Russia signed treaties to reduce their nuclear arsenals. The first Strategic Arms Reduction Treaty (START) was signed in 1991, and the second, START II, was signed in 1993. However, Russia withdrew from START II in 2002 after the US. withdrew in late 2001 from the ABM Treaty. Still, efforts to reduce nuclear stockpiles continued.

In addition to direct negotiations, key leaders launched efforts to limit the risk of nuclear weapons falling into evil hands. For example, in 1991, two US senators, Sam Nunn of Georgia and Richard Lugar of Indiana, created the Nunn-Lugar Cooperative Threat Reduction (CTR) Program, an initiative aimed at securing and dismantling nuclear and other weapons of mass destruction and destroying associated infrastructure in former Soviet Union countries, including Belarus and Ukraine. This created a landmark program to reduce the risks of nuclear attacks. The CTR led to deactivating thousands of nuclear warheads, securing fissile materials, eliminating bomb delivery systems, and destroying chemical and biological weapons.

The US and Russia signed the Strategic Offensive Reductions Treaty (SORT) in 2002, replaced by another in 2010, the New START, which set lower limits on deployed warheads and launchers. That treaty also included updated verification measures. New START was renewed for five more years in 2021.

As President Barack Obama once said about managing the decision to use or not use nuclear weapons, "[l]et's stipulate that this all is insane."[8] From President Truman's time in office through the years of President Trump, and then with President Biden, many presidents faced the dilemma of nuclear weapons—deterring bad actors from getting their hands on nuclear weapons as a limited approach to solving existing challenges, while maintaining massive nuclear arsenals to deter other perceived threats.

Civilian leadership of this decision in America keeps those decisions balanced by the risks to the world after a nuclear Armageddon. In other nuclear-armed countries, we believe similar factors held and hold that deciding to use such enormous power might be the ultimate error.

During the four years of the Trump administration, nuclear Armageddon again seemed a possibility. Trump threatened to annihilate North Korea, possibly with nuclear weaponry, if that country continued to threaten America and the world. Fortunately, that did not happen either, as it had not occurred in more than seventy-five years since the end of World War II.

As noted in Fred Kaplan's excellent breath-stealing 2020 book, *The Bomb: Presidents, Generals, and the Secret History of Nuclear War*:

---

8   Jeffrey Goldberg, "The Obama Doctrine," *The Atlantic*, April 2016, https://www.theatlantic.com/magazine/archive/2016/04/the-obama-doctrine/471525/.

The [nuclear] bomb...has co-existed with humanity for three quarters of century with no catastrophes, as yet, since the two explosions, over that Hiroshima and Nagasaki, that set the nuclear age in motion.

...

[E]very president has decided that the risks are too enormous.... They decided that they would not push the button, unless it was absolutely, unavoidably necessary, if then.

...

At the dawn of the nuclear age, Harry Truman wrested control of the bomb away from the generals, entrusting it to the top civilian authority, because he understood that, as he put it, "this isn't a military weapon...." The story of the bomb ever since has been—and will continue to be—the story of presidents and generals grappling with [the fact that that the atomic bomb exists and the fact that it is the ultimate destructive power], figuring out the best way to maneuver around [these facts] or to reconcile them.[9]

While there have been setbacks and challenges in enforcing and continuing various treaties, their continued existence—and continuing ideas to create new treaties and understandings—demonstrates recognition by major nuclear powers of the importance of stability and the catastrophic consequences of uncontrolled atomic proliferation. There is hope for con-

---

9    Fred Kaplan, *The Bomb: Presidents, Generals, and the Secret History of Nuclear War* (New York: Simon & Schuster, 2020), 320–323.

tinuing wisdom and optimism that nuclear weapons will never again be used in anger.

\* \* \*

Our readers might find it difficult to assess where optimism lies in this challenging history since World War II. But for the authors, it lies in the simple fact that no leader, in America or elsewhere, has made what could be their final decision. The benefits of nuclear power, which is used positively to provide energy in the world, are clear. The risk of nuclear power being used for weaponry is that it could destroy all of us.

While we cannot ignore the risks, the best way to avoid catastrophe is to learn from the historical legacy of the Cold War. The diplomats, ambassadors, and political leaders must talk, but they must never let any of democracy's enemies doubt American resolve to protect the order it established. If the diplomats fail to convince America's enemies that we want peace, and if our nation, too, decides to go all-in to prevent them from bullying the world, the result will mean the end of the civilized world.

Protecting the world order necessitates a steadfast belief in the United States as a force for good. This conviction underpins the central purpose of this book. We must confront whether the core narrative that has united our nation since its inception still resonates. Do we remain a nation committed to universal truths and the principle that all people are created equal? Or do we succumb to the divisive ideologies of the alt-right and the woke left (discussed in the following chapter)? Will we forsake the ideal of equality for a belief that some people are more equal than others? Do we categorize individuals by their group affiliations, or do we uphold the principle of judging them by the content of their character? This book invites us to scrutinize and reaffirm our foundational narrative.

We need faith in who we are. There are inherent advantages to liberal democracy. We see the current authoritarians adopting the same flawed centralized systems that eventually destroyed other modern authoritarian governments. We believe and argue that oppression and extraction from individuals in time will always fail. So long as we don't end the world through the potential mistakes that can happen when two nuclear powers conflict, we hold the better cards.

America's focus on individuals created a force beyond the power of a normal government. Millions of people participate in innovation, creativity, discovery, and improving the human condition. Through these private sector means, we have created driverless cars, personalized medicine, reduced energy costs, grown more food, cured cancer, and extended human life span.

A new Cold War seems unavoidable, but to avoid catastrophe, we must try to avoid it or at least ensure it's not a "hot" war. If war arrives, we must win it as peacefully as possible, allowing democracy and free markets to continue.

How can we do this? First, we must recognize the threats and face them with strength. Strength is more than armament. Strength is a citizenry that still believes in the ideal that is America. It comes from understanding our faults while understanding how dramatically better we are than the alternative. We must know and understand the great promise we still have to offer humanity and future generations.

For democracy to survive, Americans (and its leaders, especially political leaders) must compromise. We will never agree on everything, but we must find common ground at home. Doing so allows us to agree on the principles of who we are and what we need—and leaves room for optimism. Compromise in politics is necessary to preserve for posterity the gifts of freedom and liberty we inherited.[10]

In short, we must get our act together here in America. With the international new Cold War, we face a new world. A different world alignment may arise from the global order of the last fifty years. But together, the world remains better served by an American-led order that maintains the individual liberties that undergird Western democracies.

---

10   See Levin, 2024.

## CHAPTER 10

# PROTECTING AMERICANS AT HOME, AS WE REDISCOVER OUR "BETTER ANGELS"

The evening air was heavy with the scent of kerosene as young men ignited their torches, their khakis and polo shirts stark against the forming militant ranks. As the flames flickered to life, they felt a historic turning point reminiscent of the Brownshirts' quest for power in Nazi Germany. But this was not 1930s Germany; this was Charlottesville, USA, on August 11, 2017. Their march began with chants of "Jews will not replace us,"[1] marking a bold statement from the self-proclaimed alt-right.

October 7, 2023, was a horrific day, a day where 1,400 Jews were brutally massacred in their homes in Israel. Soon after, a startling response emerged on US college campuses. On October 15, long before any military response from Israel, at a pro-Palestinian rally, young people began to coalesce, defending the perpetrators. Coinciding with the day, a Cornell professor expressed, "I was exhilarated." He added: "What

---

[1] Anti-Defamation League, "After Charlottesville," *YouTube*, August 9, 2018, https://youtu.be/EiAT2IEzJAc?si=5HnKWA24nlp_qsSC (accessed January 6, 2024).

has Hamas done? Hamas has shifted the balance of power. Hamas has punctured the illusion of invincibility."[2] It was a preemptive defense for the murderers, remarkably from individuals who would abhor the alt-right demonstrators mentioned earlier.

Both groups of youths seemed unaware of the profound influence ideological movements had on their perspectives. Ideologies are formidable, especially when they bifurcate society into oppressors and oppressed. Few in either group recognized their susceptibility to manipulation by those embodying the dark triad traits of psychopathy, narcissism, and Machiavellianism,[3] willing to sacrifice rationality and factual assessment for a power-centric ideological view.

The manipulators are those seeking to acquire or maintain power. Politicians, who should ideally uphold America's virtues by checking their party's extremes, often vanish into a metaphorical fog. They either defend these extremes or, through cognitive dissonance, abandon moral principles to maintain group status.

To combat these potent forces, one must grasp both the philosophical foundations and the contemporary interpretations, along with understanding the dark triad personalities promoting them. Countering this domestic threat requires a deeper understanding of their motivations than they them-

---

[2] Sofia Rubinson, "Cornell Professor 'Exhilarated' by Hamas's Attack Defends Remark," *The Cornell Daily Sun*, October 16, 2023, https://cornellsun.com/2023/10/16/cornell-professor-exhilarated-by-hamass-attack-defends-remark/.

[3] Delroy L. Paulhus and Kevin M. Williams, "The Dark Triad of Personality: Narcissism, Machiavellianism, and Psychopathy," *Journal of Research in Personality* 36, no. 6 (2002): 556–563.

selves possess, encompassing not just the politicians but also the ideologues shaping them.

★ ★ ★

America's framework is one of federalism. "The People" begin with all the power; they cede some of it to state governments for certain rules enforcement—generally the day-to-day aspects of safety and intersections with others. The Founders set up the federal government as a limited government, with its powers delineated in the Constitution itself. And to underscore those limits, the states adopted the Bill of Rights, including:

- Ninth Amendment: "The enumeration in the Constitution of certain rights shall not be construed to deny or disparage others retained by the people."
- Tenth Amendment: "The powers not delegated to the United States by the Constitution, nor prohibited by it to the States, are reserved to the States respectively, or to the people."

It is clear and simple language.

Neither the Declaration nor the Constitution mentions "politics," "politicians," or "political parties." The Constitution established procedures for the election of leaders, the people's representatives. It provided for the election by the people of electors who would vote (subject to the initial determination of a majority of the people in each state) for the president and the vice president.

*The Federalist Papers*, written mainly by Hamilton and Madison, expressed concerns about the political parties and related systems, but parties did not come into much power at the beginning of the American system of government. That changed during Washington's presidency, and he expressed some concern about the party system in his farewell address:

> However [political parties] may now and then answer popular ends, they are likely in the course of time and things, to become potent engines, by which cunning, ambitious, and unprincipled men will be enabled to subvert the power of the people and to usurp for themselves the reins of government, destroying afterwards the very engines which have lifted them to unjust dominion.[4]

Washington highlighted his concerns about parties based on regional differences rather than political philosophy, but his concerns share common bonds with those of today's political parties. Ultimately, he wanted an America that worked and endured: a "national Union" where the people resist "every attempt to alienate any portion of our country from the rest...."[5]

★ ★ ★

The political group concepts of the alt-right, the radical left, and other extreme groups within them make up a very small portion of Americans. Groups like the white nationalists, identity politicians, and politically correct authoritarians want to reform liberal capitalism or Western liberal democracy values.

---

[4] George Washington, "Farewell Address," September 19, 1796, in *The Papers of George Washington*, ed. Dorothy Twohig, vol. 41, 269-270 (Charlottesville: University Press of Virginia, 1996), 269-270.

[5] Washington, 1939.

They represent small portions of Americans, but with today's social media platforms, they have very large megaphones.

In recent times, it seems that Americans stand at the bottom of two giant tectonic plates that are slowly moving toward one another. We appear to be on a collision course, a catastrophe that may crush the incredible society that has been built between them. At the tops of those plates are two factions that, given the choice, would destroy America as we know it. They are angry, yelling, and unwilling to listen to one another or even to reason, while most of us simply want them to stop the anger and rage.

We refer to these camps as the "alternatives." Found within both liberal and conservative ideologies, these camps share many similarities. They prioritize collective interests over individual ones. They harbor bigotry toward groups they perceive as having harmed them. They oppose the free speech rights of those with differing views. Despite representing only small minorities in America, they receive disproportionate attention in the media. Moreover, they are willing to harm others through violence or reputation destruction to achieve their goals.

These alternative groups exploit the primary election system of the country's two major political parties by taking advantage of the fact that only a small number of citizens vote in those elections, which allows them to have a voice that outweighs their numbers.[6] Both alt factions intentionally seek to undermine liberal democracy because they can't sell their views to the majority of Americans.

---

[6] For a discussion of the "math" surrounding this concept, see the discussion on page 194, supra.

For a long time in America, politics resembled a team sport. You could belong to the red team or the blue team, yet after any competition, you could be coworkers, share meals, marry one another, and even enjoy a cold brew together. Most Americans share a deep sense of pride in our American identity. They aspire to make progress and provide equal opportunities for everyone. They express gratitude for the countless blessings our country bestows upon them, and although they recognize the challenges that lie ahead, they believe they are part of a greater purpose.

Our citizens need a unifying narrative. America has long been known as a cause for good. Without unifying truths and ideals, citizens falter and ultimately fail to reach consensus on difficult issues such as immigration, taxes, and social programs. The alternatives reject absolute truths and any form of unifying cause. For the nation to remain united, we must answer the questions: Who are we? What do we believe in? What do we stand for?

Part of the answer reflects the abundance created by a society that prioritizes the individual. While this aligns with the traditional right and left views within liberal democracies, the alternatives' rants often drive the exact opposite message.

★ ★ ★

The threat to individualism arises from two ideologies that position themselves on opposite ends of the political spectrum. On one side, there is the self-identified alt-right. On the other side, there is an unidentified extreme left, referred to as the alt-left.

The traditional right and left have long embraced the concepts that democracy, individual rights, free markets, and self-governance are gifts to humankind. The alternatives oppose them. The traditional left and right prioritize the individual. The alt-left and the alt-right place greater value on the collective interests based on their respective groups. Consequently, both reach the conclusion that the ends justify the means. Indiscriminately, they harm others.

But we can't succeed at changing the narrative unless we better understand what these alternative voices oppose—namely, rationalism, equality of opportunity, and optimism. We can't understand the pressures we face without understanding them.

## THE ALT-RIGHT

The alt-right, as they self-identify, has witnessed a surge in popularity since the Great Recession of 2008. The alt-right encompasses various organizations that espouse anti-democratic doctrines, including several violent groups such as the Proud Boys, Oath Keepers, Aryan Nation, and the American Nazi Party.

Incidents involving far-right extremist groups have experienced a significant increase. According to the Anti-Defamation League's Center on Extremism, 71 percent of the 387 "extremist-related fatalities in the United States" from 2008 to 2017 were perpetrated by members of far-right and white supremacist groups.[7] In 2023, right-wing extremists committed all such murders.[8] The Biden administration

---

[7] Anti-Defamation League's Center on Extremism, "Murder and Extremism in the United States in 2017," *Anti-Defamation League*, January 12, 2018, https://www.adl.org/resources/report/murder-and-extremism-united-states-2017 (accessed December 3, 2024).

[8] Anti-Defamation League, "Murder and Extremism in the United States in 2023," *Anti-Defamation League*, February 20, 2024, https://www.adl.org/resources/report/murder-and-extremism-united-states-2023 (accessed December 3, 2024).

designated these groups, advocating for white supremacist ideology and anti-government militia ideology, as America's primary domestic terrorist threat.[9]

While violent left-wing groups and individuals also pose threats, far-right networks appear to be better armed, larger in size, and more prone to violence. These criminals target religious figures and institutions, primarily focusing on Muslim or Jewish individuals and US or foreign government entities within the United States. Their motivations stem from opposition and immigration policies to conspiracy theories such as "white genocide" and "replacement theory." The propagation of the Big Lie, which refers to debunked theories about the fraudulent nature of the 2020 presidential election, is integral to the arguments of these right-wing and far-right factions.

The alt-right and other associated organizations are at a philosophical war with the concepts of the Enlightenment, including science, rationality, free markets, and free elections. The theories behind these beliefs are expressed in the "Dark Enlightenment." The Dark Enlightenment, conceived by software engineer Curtis Yarvin in 2008 and expanded upon by philosopher Nick Land, espouses racism and the rejection of democracy.[10] The Dark Enlightenment is dedicated, along with other extremist views, to dismantling democracy.

---

9    US Department of Justice, "National Strategy for Countering Domestic Terrorism," released on June 15, 2021.

10   Curtis Yarvin, "The Path to (Dark) Enlightenment," *Unqualified Reservations* (blog), March 29, 2013, https://www.unqualified-reservations.org/2013/03/the-path-to-dark-enlightenment/ (accessed December 3, 2024); Nick Land, "The Dark Enlightenment, Parts 1–4," *The Dark Enlightenment* (blog), 2013, https://www.thedarkenlightenment.com/the-dark-enlightenment-by-nick-land/ (accessed December 3, 2024).

Land argued against the foundations of Western liberal democracy to discredit the rational basis of American democracy. He contended that American ideas of individualism are merely an offshoot of religious beliefs. Specifically, he dismissed the Jeffersonian statement, "We hold these truths to be self-evident, that all men are created equal," because he considered it an orthodoxy tied to religious values.[11] Proponents of the Dark Enlightenment hope to legitimize unequal treatment of people based on race, gender, or group, and aim to replace democracy itself with a business-led type of government. Under this version of the alt-right, women are relegated back to traditional gender roles. Ultimately, while Dark Enlightenment advocates may draw inspiration from certain libertarian ideas, they miss the core principles of libertarianism.

The modern fascism movement can be traced back to the 1880s, during the *fin de siècle* (the end of the century). This period marked a revolt against materialism, rationalism, positivism, and liberal democracy. The generation of the fin de siècle[12] embraced emotionalism, irrationalism, subjectivism, and vitalism. Intellectuals and philosophers of this era criticized urban society, condemned rationalistic individualism, and viewed modern society as unstable and corrupt. They regarded individuals merely as part of a larger collective.[13]

---

[11] Yarvin, 2013; Land, 2013; see Jamelle Bouie, "The Enlightenments Dark Side," *Slate*, June 5, 2018, https://slate.com/news-and-politics/2018/06/taking-the-enlightenment-seriously-requires-talking-about-race.html (accessed December 3, 2024).

[12] Robert Wohl, *The Generation of 1914* (Massachusetts: Harvard University Press, 1979), 18–20.

[13] Carl E. Schorske, *Fin-de-Siècle Vienna: Politics and Culture* (New York: Random House Inc., 1981), 4–6.

Social Darwinism became a cornerstone of significant intellectual influence during this period. Survival of the fittest became a fundamental principle in the intellectual mindset of the fin de siècle. They challenged the idea that human nature was governed by rational choice, instead arguing that it was determined by heredity, race, and environment. Joseph Arthur de Gobineau developed the theory of the Aryan master race and scientific racist theory. And Friedrich Nietzsche's theory of Übermensch (superhuman) and the "Will to Power"[14] also influenced it.

Similar to today's alternatives in both liberal and conservative parties, fascists and Marxists may have despised each other, but linking the two ideas politically strengthened them. Both factions disdained rationalism, enlightenment, modernism, and liberal democracy. Georges Sorel, a French intellectual, not only advocated violence in his book *Reflections on Violence* (1908),[15] but attempted to bridge the two factions. Initially a member of the radical left, Sorel greatly influenced fascism and eventually shifted to the radical right to merge the two ideologies. Sorelianism was considered the forerunner of fascism.

The fascist coalition in Italy merged nationalism and socialism with Sorelianism. By 1912, supporters of the Italian Revolution began advocating for a "New Man" and a "New State." The country was gripped by fascism and Benito Mussolini following the onset of World War I and the subsequent destruction of the Italian economy. In nearby Germany,

---

[14] Michael Biddiss, *Father of Racist Ideology: The Social and Political Thought of Count Gobineau* (New York: Weybright and Talley, 1970), 35–39.

[15] Rüdiger Safranski, *Nietzsche: A Philosophical Biography* (New York: W. W. Norton & Company, 2003), 182–187.

led by Adolf Hitler, the Nazi Party (which stood for National Socialist Party) was modeled after Mussolini's fascist model, following a Sorelian model.

World War II devastated the philosophy of fascism, but it didn't extinguish the ideals. The alt-right today argues that they are engaged in a life-and-death struggle against Marxism. This serves as a dog whistle to both economic conservatives and religious conservatives. However, at the core of the alt-right and fascism lies racial and class exclusion. Both movements can adopt socialist theory when it suits their interests. Yet, the true objective of both fascists and the alt-right is to dismantle rationalism, individualism, and the liberal democracies founded upon those principles.

Today, the new philosophy of the right is forming through groups like the Heritage Foundation with Project 2025 and right-wing academicians. Harvard Law Professor Adrian Vermeule argues that the Constitution aimed to promote the rule of law rather than protect individual rights. His theory, common good constitutionalism,[16] has gained significant traction among intellectuals within the traditional Republican party, attempting to inject into interpretations of the Constitution a sense of religion-based morality.

Originalism is a concept in current Supreme Court interpretations of the Constitution that the meaning of a constitutional provision should be determined based on how the citizens at the time of the Constitution's ratification (or amendment) would have understood it to mean. Supreme Court Justice Antonin Scalia's advocacy of originalism became

---

[16] Adrian Vermeule, *Common Good Constitutionalism* (Massachusetts: Polity Press, 2022), 12–15.

the backbone of the conservative legal theory. Common good constitutionalism, the new conservative theory, is more the antithesis of originalism than is the "living constitutionalism" form of interpretation historically used by progressives appointed to the Supreme Court by Democratic presidents. Living constitutionalism posits that the Constitution has a dynamic meaning and that its interpretation can adapt to contemporary circumstances and societal changes. Both originalism and living constitutionalism advance individuals' maximum liberty and freedoms to differing degrees.

The advocates of common good constitutionalism don't bother with what the Founders intended. They believe the liberal order that maximizes free elections and personal liberties hinders their view of a better government, a government based on religious morality. This doctrine advocates expanding governmental powers and argues that authoritarians are not necessarily detrimental to a free society. Vermeule presents the theory of "subsidiarity," wherein powerful federal authorities possess the right and duty to intervene when less influential political authorities fail to safeguard the common good, even if it requires overriding the views of State or local jurisdictions.

## THE ALT-LEFT

The alt-left and the alt-right share several areas of philosophical agreement. Both reject the rationality of the Enlightenment years and base their beliefs on groups and the power of the collective, rather than the fundamental power of the individual.

The alt-left encompasses various radical theories and ideas, including postmodernism, post-structuralism, wokeism, and critical race theory. Anarchists are also considered part of the radical left. They often oppose globalism, capitalism, profit-driven organizations, and even representative democracy, instead of supporting direct democracy.

Postmodernism, the foundation of alt-left ideology, posits that there is no universal rationality or objective truth. It is associated with relativism, viewing reality as a subjective construct. Postmodernism challenges modernism, rationality, morality, human nature, and universal truths, emphasizing multiple cultural identities. In the 1950s and 1960s, postmodernism emerged as a competing ideology against modernism and the prevailing Enlightenment views.

Postmodernist and post-structuralist philosophers, such as Jacques Derrida, Michel Foucault, and Jean Baudrillard, rejected all the principles of modern philosophy that focused on the individual. They rejected overarching stories and ideologies that claim to explain large swaths of human history and experience.[17]

The postmodernists disliked metanarratives and dismissed universal truths. They saw these narratives as simply a way to control the oppressed. They also rejected the Enlightenment as a metanarrative and considered Western liberal democracy's claims of incredible growth, reduction of poverty, illiteracy, and child mortality as dogma. According to Foucault, any benefits that existed primarily favored oppressors, dismissing the Enlightenment's impact on reason and human rights as

---

[17] Jean-François Lyotard, *The Postmodern Condition: A Report on Knowledge* (Minneapolis: University of Minnesota Press, 1984), xxiii–xxv; Jacques Derrida, *Of Grammatology* (Baltimore: Johns Hopkins University Press, 1976); Michel Foucault, *The Archaeology of Knowledge* (New York: Pantheon Books, 1972); Jean Baudrillard, *Simulacra and Simulation* (Ann Arbor: University of Michigan Press, 1994).

a tool for white men to dominate others. Like Marxism, this philosophy centered on the oppressed and the oppressor.

Post-structuralists, like postmodernists, approach philosophy from a group mindset. Economic status, racial identity, and values determine an individual's identity, rather than each person being seen as unique and deserving of equal treatment by society. This explains why the alt-left embraces politically correct authoritarians who employ words like bigotry, racism, misogyny, or white privilege to destroy reputations.

In this view, it is not individuals that matter but instead power. Intent has no purpose.[18] According to this view, people should not be judged by their good intentions or charitable actions but solely by the group to which they belong. The listener gets to interpret what is offensive and the authority on what is said.

This radical left is a departure from traditional liberalism. Liberalism believes that through civil rights, equal rights, and human rights, we can promote the equal opportunity of all individuals. Unlike the fascist alt-right, which desires to restore power to the white race, postmodernists aim to transfer power to the oppressed. Like the alt-right, they are identitarians who classify individuals based on the groups to which they belong.

Postmodernism extended into various academic disciplines, shaping a range of theoretical frameworks. One such theoretical framework was post-colonialism. A significant figure in this intellectual shift was Edward Said, whose book *Orientalism*[19] used postmodernist concepts to critique

---

18   Michel Foucault, *The History of Sexuality, Volume 1: An Introduction* (New York: Vintage Books, 1990), 92–95.
19   Edward W. Said, *Orientalism* (New York: Pantheon Books, 1978).

Western perceptions of Eastern societies. Said argued that Western society had abused Eastern societies and justified this by creating a dichotomy between the "enlightened West" and the "backward East."[20] Said's work designed a defense of radical Islamic culture in the West Bank and Gaza. It ignores the radical practices of the Revolutionary Islamic groups that practice honor killings, the persecution of those who identify themselves as LGBTQ+ individuals, the suppression of women, and the glorification of martyrdom. We disagree vehemently and believe that acknowledging these differences is crucial, as some values—like equality and human rights—are inherently superior and universally applicable.[21]

In a postmodern, postcolonialism, post-structuralist world, you will hear language that equates reason with violence and coercion and portrays liberal democracy as oppressive. Critical race theory and intersectionality (which we won't define here) are offshoots of postmodern thinking, asserting that all institutions created by the Constitution, including capitalism, are racist and serve the interests of only one group.

Postmodernists, post-structuralists, and colonialists have one big thing in common with the alt-right; they argue for a world not based on universal values, rationalism, science, and a society based on the individual. They disregard evidence that democracy and the free-market system have successfully lifted more people out of poverty, reduced illiteracy, and decreased child mortality than any other system in history.

---

20   Said, 1978, at 1-28. Said critiques how Western scholarship and culture constructed a dichotomy between the "enlightened" West and the "backward" East to justify domination and exploitation.
21   Said, 1978.

★ ★ ★

Martin Luther King Jr. dreamed that individuals should be judged based on their character rather than the color of their skin.[22] His dream has become an enduring belief of both the mainstream of the right and left. However, this concept of valuing individuals is anathema to the proponents of the alt-left, who believe people should be judged solely based on the group to which they belong, specifically based on the color of their skin.

King's concept that we can cure racism and inequality only with love, not hate, eludes the politically correct authoritarians. The alt-right focuses on violence, while the alt-left focuses on destroying reputations.

Among Western liberal democracies, free speech is how we organize ourselves. We create a free marketplace of ideas where ideas compete with each other, enabling us to discover the truth. This reflects more than just an idea of individual rights; it is practical. But the postmodern left and collectivist groups reject free speech.

Polling data[23] presents an interesting truth: Americans are not as divided as it seems on the significant issues that truly matter. The right and left of America, although they struggle to recognize it, agree on the fundamental issues of individuality. They both, to varying degrees, support the ideals of the Constitution, which include free speech, property rights, free markets, equal rights for all regardless of gender, race, and sexuality, and the belief that every individual deserves dignity.

---

22   King, "I Have a Dream."
23   Ezra Klein, *Why We're Polarized* (Maryland: Avid Reader Press, 2020), 150–153.

It is a common and relatively effortless task to pinpoint the flaws in others. However, recognizing one's shortcomings requires a robust character and a profound sense of personal agency. This challenge becomes even more arduous when the subject of scrutiny is one's own "tribe" or political party. See if you can point out the excesses of the political party with which you are affiliated. Can you objectively assess its shortcomings and excesses without succumbing to the temptation of deflecting criticism by pointing out the failings of its opposition? Can you hold your party accountable for its extremes while avoiding the pitfall of justifying these excesses by comparing them to the other party's perceived greater wrongs?

Now, see if you can push this self-examination further. Ponder the wisdom of the Founding Fathers, valuing individualism through ensuring free elections, free enterprise, freedoms of speech, assembly, gun ownership, property rights, and upholding civil and human rights. Can you see how all these were simply reflections on the importance of the individual? Evaluate how the extremes within your political party might be contravening these principles.

Research underscores the immense power of self-agency,[24] showing that it can improve psychological well-being, financial stability, and interpersonal relationships. Self-agency is not merely a personal attribute; it is the most effective means to address societal divisions and counteract destructive hierarchical alternatives that threaten cherished values. By continuously exercising self-discipline in holding both oneself and one's political affiliations accountable, an individual can make a meaningful difference.

---

24   See Chapter 11.

When we participate in a political party or other groups, we risk abandoning personal values for the sake of tribal loyalty, which leads to a collective bubble. Stepping away from such extreme tribalism requires holding firm to moral authority and humility, which can steer American democracy toward a healthier, more inclusive state.

A simple yet profound rule for nurturing patriotism is to stop insulting other Americans if you want to be patriotic. True patriotism fosters respect and understanding among the populace, transcending partisan divides and personal biases.

Our journey through history is illuminated by the contributions of leaders like George Washington, Thomas Jefferson, Alexander Hamilton, Harriet Tubman, Frederick Douglass, Abraham Lincoln, Susan B. Anthony, Harvey Milk, and Martin Luther King Jr. Each, with their own set of imperfections, shared a unifying belief in the equality of all people. This belief has been a guiding light in our collective American story, helping to transform a flawed union into one ever striving for perfection. Through their and many other combined legacies, we recognize the awesome nature of what, together, we have built American success and world leadership.

We must continue to learn from our historical blunders, ensuring they serve as lessons rather than shadows that darken our collective spirit. This requires balanced perspectives that understand and acknowledge past wrongs while never losing sight of the noble ideals and sense of individualism that form our foundation. In reflecting on our history, we should remember that our mistakes, while significant, do not eclipse the greater good and the progress we have achieved.

As we move ever forward, we should recognize that the story of our country is not just about the "me" but profoundly about the "we." Our American narrative is one of collective effort, yet through individual contributions and purpose, however imperfect, we converge to create something truly magnificent and more robust. This realization serves as a powerful reminder that we are part of something much larger than ourselves, a dynamic and evolving journey toward a more perfect union. By embracing this collective identity, we can continue building, learning, and growing together, aspiring to the ideals that unite us in our shared humanity.

All the data we have researched says that focusing on the individual first is the most powerful way we move human progress forward. "We" believe that everyone matters. Every human being is worthy of dignity, freedom, and the right to make decisions. Watch for the warning signs at each end of the political spectrum. These alternatives on the far left and far right are not simply an extension of these ideals. They are the end of the road we know as civilization.

# CHAPTER 11

# HONORING OUR INDIVIDUALISM

WHILE GOOD LEADERSHIP MATTERS IN Western liberal democracies, a society's ultimate success or failure is determined by its citizens' performance and how they manage their individual self-agency. Ideology—and its effects on mass consciousness—poses the greatest threat to American society and progress. Conversely, there is nothing greater that you can do for your life than to find self-agency. We address how in this chapter.

This book supports and was inspired by The Optimistic American. On this regular podcast, led by Paul, various newsmakers and experts are interviewed, many of whom discuss the impact of these ideologies and the importance of self-agency. In addition, Paul co-authored (with Emily Bashah, Psy.D.) a book, Addictive Ideologies,[1] that analyzes how most ideologies strip individuals of their sense of agency (or personal responsibility and accountability).

The manipulators of addictive ideologies exploit various theories based on prejudice to amass power through their followers. They identify victims of the existing status quo and

---

1   Dr. Emily Bashah and Paul Johnson, *Addictive Ideologies: Finding Meaning and Agency When Politics Fail You* (California: Legacy Launch Pad Publishing, 2022).

exploit their vulnerabilities, usually around race, class, or gender. They convince those supposedly harmed by the status quo that they are victims, persuade them that they are being persecuted, and by objectifying the "out" group, they allow them to objectify the "oppressors."

Someone addicted to such ideologies (and we do use the word "addicted" intentionally) feels they have permission to retaliate under the promise of relief or even prosperity and a better life. They don't realize that the price for this is that they surrender their individual agency and their opportunities to reach different conclusions.

★ ★ ★

In a society centered around the individual, agency is of paramount importance. What is agency? It is a belief in one's ability to take actions that shape their destiny. It is an exercise of free will. In a world that upholds rationality, making decisions based on reason and a sense of personal responsibility provides a reliable chance for an optimistic future.

Fascism, socialism, communism, authoritarianism, totalitarianism, postmodernism, post-structuralism, and other alt-right and alt-left ideologies all prioritize the benefits of the collective over those of the individual. They consolidate power within the group. In his book, The Gulag Archipelago,[2] Solzhenitsyn recounted the horrifying impact of ideologies that led to unfathomable atrocities. As a member of the Communist Party of the Soviet Union, Solzhenitsyn served on the frontlines of war, surrendered to the Germans, and was

---

[2] Solzhenitsyn, 1974.

subsequently imprisoned by them. Upon his release, Stalin sent him, along with millions of other Russians, to the Gulag.

Solzhenitsyn dutifully served the Communist Party. Nevertheless, the government sentenced him to endure separation from his family, sub-zero temperatures, surpassing the brink of starvation, imprisonment, and performing hard labor by the very party he had faithfully served.

Instead of playing the victim, Solzhenitsyn took account of his responsibility. He examined his actions and questioned his accountability. He accepted that he unquestionably and loyally played his role as a soldier for the Communist Party. Solzhenitsyn helped relocate 10,000 families—almost 60,000 people—to Siberia. Most of them perished due to harsh conditions. By Solzhenitsyn's count, these atrocities led to the deaths of over sixty million people. And then, when he returned from the German front, he too was imprisoned there!

Solzhenitsyn chose to understand himself. He questioned why he'd participated in such injustices. He liked to say he became a free man even before he left the Gulag.

You own the capacities of both good and evil. Ideology allows people to abandon personal accountability and view others as evil or as external forces to defeat. It separates everyone into groups, labeling one's group as good and another as evil.

According to communist ideology, the poor Russians who had their properties stolen by the government were not seen as individuals but rather as part of an evil group. Property owners, along with other business leaders, were labeled as evil oppressors over the oppressed. Their intentions, hard work, youth, or innocence did not matter. Ideology promotes a duality—seeing good and evil as external forces. God and the Devil are considered equal forces, each attempting to attract people to their side. In the West, however, this perspective has been largely rejected by Christian-Judeo values, which emphasize that each person is given free will by God and can choose to do good or evil.

Immanuel Kant offered one of the first secular theories of evil in his book, Religion Within the Boundary of Pure Reason.[3] Kant saw evil as stemming from human will that was not entirely good. He tried to reconcile humanity's free will with its inclinations to do both good and evil.

In an individualistic society, members are accountable for their actions. Western liberal democracies create societies that grant individuals the freedom to choose what they say, whom they associate with, how they exchange value for goods or services, and what beliefs they hold. They ensure the freedom to work and to own what they create, empowering individuals to discover, innovate, and advance human progress.

## FREEDOM AND EQUALITY

Freedom is expandable when we give everyone an equal opportunity to succeed. But to guarantee everyone equal outcomes, we have to limit freedom. In his seminal work, The True Believer,[4] Eric Hoffer delves into the heart of revolutionary movements, positing that they invariably are driven by the pursuit of either freedom or equality of outcomes. Hoffer presents these two ideals as residing on opposite ends of the political spectrum. He articulates that your freedom

---

[3] Immanuel Kant, *Religion Within the Boundary of Pure Reason*, trans. J.W. Semple (Edinburgh: Thomas Clark, 1838).

[4] Eric Hoffer, *The True Believer: Thoughts on the Nature of Mass Movements* (New York: Harper & Row, 1951).

to shape your life according to your choices and efforts also requires you to acknowledge that this freedom inevitably leads to varied economic outcomes. Conversely, the quest for true equality in outcomes or status often demands relinquishing freedom, typically ceding it to collective authority to manage.

Freedom is more fragile than equality. Individuals who perceive their lives as irrelevant or futile may gravitate away from freedom and toward equality of outcomes. Freedom becomes a means to an end—establishing equal outcomes and uniformity. The peril of this approach is that once freedom is relinquished (for example, based on a return promise of equity), those in power are seldom inclined to return the freedoms forfeited.

Equity, defined as assuring equal outcomes, stands in the way of agency. Equity requires the individual to depend on the collective. Societies will not remain free for long unless their people believe they have the power to determine their destiny. And that only happens with understanding self-agency, their right to choose. Freedom, free will, and agency are interconnected.

## FINDING/REDISCOVERING PERSONAL AGENCY

At our core, we believe in the power of agency and individual responsibility—a cornerstone for the thriving of any society. This narrative extends beyond the political sphere, as explored in Addictive Ideologies, advocating for personal empowerment in the face of political disillusionment.

We call on each reader to cultivate these attributes within themselves and foster and respect them in others as the only real means of preserving the freedom that we have cherished for so long. The following are the key factors that will help everyone find their personal agency.[5] For a more detailed explanation, please refer to Addictive Ideologies.

## Know the Truth

"Know the truth" posits that the foundational step toward self-agency is the pursuit of truth. This is difficult with the deluge of negative information that bombards us daily. Political entities, news outlets, and social media platforms—all driven by economic motivation—perpetuate narratives of despair to maintain audience engagement and, thus, advertising revenues that support their businesses.

These organizations intentionally try to terrify you, leveraging humans' biological predisposition in the face of perceived threats and related fears. This primal response, known as the "amygdala hijack," disrupts our capacity for rational and creative thinking. Moreover, these addictive ideologies intentionally skew facts to create a disproportionate sense of fear or despair. "Know the truth" encourages you to challenge the sometimes-prevailing narrative of American decline, questioning the pervasive opinions that future generations will be worse off. When you know the truth, you can uncover how key individuals in politics and the media strategically use fear to engender tribalism, turning individuals into loyal followers of specific economic or political agendas, often through exaggeration or outright deceit.

To prosper in an individualistic society, you must know the truth and gain perspective. While threats certainly exist, you must dig deeper and question assumptions. To achieve

---

5    For more information, please see https://optamerican.com/agency-hierarchy/.

this, you must diminish the darkness and actively seek the light, optimism.

## Be Accountable to Yourself

Accountability to oneself begins with recognizing that each person is not just a member of a collective but a unique entity with intrinsic value and rights. This requires acknowledging and embracing the dual aspects of one's nature—the capacity for both good and evil.

Self-accountability demands that we recognize the dignity and rights of others. Seeing others as equals with the same rights and responsibilities requires an active effort to rise above our fears and prejudices. Our actions have a rippling effect, influencing not just our own lives but also those around us. By holding ourselves accountable to the potential good and evil inside each of us, we contribute to our potential and that of others around us.

## Find Meaning

If you believe that happiness is the destination of your life, you may find it elusive. We suggest that a more enduring and profound pursuit is the search for meaning and purpose. Meaning is a constant, a beacon that can guide you across life's tumultuous seas. It emerges from your choices in four fundamental areas: what you create, who or what you love, the service you provide for the betterment of others, and the struggles you face. We choose what we create, who or what we love, and the service we provide. While struggle chooses us, we choose how we interpret it.

Meaning is intrinsically tied to the exercise of free will—the profound ability to choose your life's path. In every moment, with every decision, you sculpt the narrative of your existence. Each aspect is a brushstroke in the masterpiece of your life, and this journey nurtures your well-being. Self-care is not an act of selfishness but the foundation upon which the capacity to contribute meaningfully to others is built.

The American struggle today is less about economics than it is about relevancy. We don't want to dismiss the very real financial struggle that many Americans face but, quite simply, the lives of most Americans, compared to individuals in most other countries and compared to any other time in history, are amazing. Yet most of us struggle with relevance, which can create pain. One key to dealing with this potentially chronic pain is by finding purpose and meaning.

## Empower Yourself: Embrace Strength Over Caution

Purpose gives you relevance, friction gives you resilience, and power is born of strength. Strength only happens by confronting the friction of life's challenges. By engaging with and listening to those with whom we disagree, we cultivate true power. This journey toward self-empowerment is seldom found by remaining isolated and seemingly safe.

While it is the duty of parents to protect their children, there is a growing consensus that contemporary society often errs on the side of over-protection. As we increasingly prioritize safety, our children lose the ability to work through the challenges they face in life. More challenging, this is creating a risk in our schools and even in our universities, where other fundamental values such as free speech, fairness, due process, critical thinking, and justice are given less emphasis. That is a mistake.

It is precisely through engagement with diverse ideas, challenges, and people that one's potential for success is maximized. Exposure to various viewpoints and experiences builds a robust foundation for understanding and navigating our world's complexities.

## Find Power in Love and Connection

Love, in its myriad manifestations, holds a transformative power. It has the capacity to break barriers, heal wounds, and bridge divides. The journey of life is, in many ways, a journey of learning to love more deeply, more inclusively. This quest is not just about the affection shared between individuals but extends to a broader, more encompassing love—a love that reaches beyond personal boundaries and embraces the larger human family. It is a love that recognizes the inherent worth and dignity of every individual and, in doing so, uplifts and unites.

We find this love in tolerance for people with different opinions. We find it in civil rights, human rights, and equal rights. We find it in free markets where people can own what they create, even if they have more material goods than we do. And we find it by recognizing that none of us got here alone. We stand on the shoulders of those who came before us. Love is a force that does not seek defense or justification; its truth is self-evident in the harmony it fosters. Love, in its purest form, is an enduring source of power—a power that enlightens, ennobles, and transforms. Through love, we not only discover our deepest strengths and connections but also realize shared humanity and the boundless potential that lies within this realization.

## You Are Part of Something Awesome

As Americans, we are part of an extraordinary fabric of freedom, woven through time by the collective endeavors of flawed and formidable figures. Our country's history is marked by grave errors, of which slavery is a particularly egregious example. Yet, our moral compass is calibrated by acknowledging such mistakes and the recognition of the inherent dignity of every individual.

## CHAPTER 12

# DEFENDING DEMOCRACY AND THE RULE OF LAW

It was an exciting day. After years of hard work, they saved the money to buy a new home. Yet it was overwhelming—contracts, title policies, warranties, loan agreements, and deposits to various utilities. Homebuilders, realtors, contractors, and title companies all over the country follow a similar process, one designed by the rule of law.

Before the homeowners arrived, engineers designed the property's lot, surveys were completed to ensure correct property boundaries, and soils were engineered to ensure compaction and stability. Various studies assured no environmental contamination; title policies ensured the homeowners were transferred property without liens or easements not disclosed to them. Construction standards engineered the home to withstand wind, earthquakes, and other defects. All this and more developed through the legal system over many years to ensure developers and lenders—not the ultimate homeowners—were held liable when a house sank, construction defects developed, environmental problems occurred, bad actors sold the same property twice, or boundaries were wrong.

The benefits of the American rule of law are even greater. Eliminating potential defects and ensuring that lenders are repaid properly result in lower interest rates. These routine activities create markets for developers to finance an inventory of homes at profitable levels. The homeowners, unknowingly and without any need to know, gain better pricing, better interest rates, and higher value than they otherwise might if no rule of law existed.

These property-related rules of law allow transactions to be completed at a speed unprecedented in history. These protections, built into over 200 years of legal precedent, allow homeowners to buy a home often without meeting any of the people involved behind the scenes. While the homeowners need these actors to fulfill their obligations, few recognize their importance to the result: purchasing a good home at a fair price, all assured by the rule of law.

An economy is really nothing more than the sum of the transactions that take place within it. Each of us conducts many transactions a day. The total number of transactions in an area creates a market. And the combinations of all the markets create an economy. The speed with which those transactions can take place significantly impacts the size of a market and, thus, the size of the economy. The judicial system's role in increasing assurances between parties increases the speed of completed transactions.

Anyone doing business today in China knows that Chinese businesses emphasize relationships more than businesses do in the US. One might cite various cultural reasons as a central concept of relationships at the heart of business dealings in China. This includes complex values of hierarchy, mutual benefit, "face," and respect. But the economic reason for focusing on relationships is that Chinese businesses cannot count on the rule of law to protect them. Hierarchy and Communist party concerns matter more than the law does.

American businesses and investors that have invested trillions of dollars in China are just starting to understand this as China confiscates data, documents, staff, and property. For the first time in 2023, more money is leaving China than going in.[1]

Regarding homeownership in China, a residential owner may have the right to use residential housing land, but the land is collectively owned. In China, there are no official procedures for registering land use rights, and thus, you may find different interests that register the same land. And while ownership rights of Chinese property may be protected, those rights must comply with "laws and social morality."[2] The real guarantor of one's property rights isn't a constitution, a court, or the law, but the Chinese Community Party.

In the US, our judicial system, property rights, patent rights, and the rule of law quicken business transactions. We can rely on the law even if we never meet our partners, vendors, or sellers. The effects of this are profound, from faster transactions to smaller businesses' ability to succeed. It assures that those who invent and create will be rewarded.

This discussion reflects merely one important example of the guarantees we have as Americans. The rule of law provides the context for everyday life in America, and such guarantees are not assured in many other countries.

★ ★ ★

It is easy to overlook how valuable America's judicial system is to our society. We intuitively know its value but rarely need to

---

[1] Annabelle Laing, BBC, "Why Businesses Are Pulling Billions in Profits from China," November 13, 2023.
[2] Peter Ho, *Unmaking China's Development: The Function and Credibility of Institutions* (England: Cambridge University Press, 2017), 118–120.

think about it. But the system's role goes way beyond simple examples of its effectiveness across the country. It enforces the rule of law, essential for a democracy to survive. The judicial system plays a key role in interpreting what the Constitution and related federal, state, and local laws mean for Americans.

Our Constitution is an outline of how our government is organized and how it protects individuals' rights. It establishes limitations for each of the three branches of government and serves as a check and balance against improper powers exercised by a legislature or chief executive. Without a judicial system to referee disputes, the Constitution would be hollow. Moreover, the judiciary ensures that the power of the majority, through its elected officials, cannot become tyrannical toward the minority.

This begs the question: Should a majority be able to take rights from the minority? If the majority disagrees with what you want to say, or with your religious practices, or your domain over certain property the majority wants but doesn't want to pay for, should a majority have the right to trample your interests?

In the US, these questions sound rhetorical because minority rights and freedoms are protected, but in most of the world, throughout history, they could not be assumed. Over and again, in world history, speech was oppressed, judges and the rule of law had no power, and morality and humanity failed. This included Russia's Gulag, a Cambodian society that resulted in almost two million murdered citizens (nearly a quarter of the population), and China's Great Leap Forward, which murdered millions of innocent people. This reflects collectivist agendas, not determined by a constitution and the rule of law but by one party and by one man. This kind of horrific history occurs rarely in Western democracies.

America's judicial system frequently saved us from authoritarian rule. At times, leaders themselves stress the legal system itself, but the independence endowed upon our judiciary allows it to challenge and correct bad behavior. Based on the evidence we have seen, we believe that it will continue to play its role in protecting the Constitution, regardless of threats that may come from the political branches and other actors who wish the independent judicial system only supported their views.

## LAWYERS IN A DEMOCRACY

America could and would not be the greatest country in the world today without the Founders' expectations and outlines of the American judicial system and its independence from the legislative and executive branches under the Constitution. It was fundamental to establishing a grand vision for this country's future.

The principal job of independent courts and judges is to protect the rights of those in the minority—including ethnic minorities, property owners, owners of ideas and patents, and even individuals charged by the government with a crime. Practicing lawyers play critical roles in American society. They help to enforce laws.

Without a robust system of justice—judges, courts, rules of evidence, and rights of appeal using objective, reasoned evaluation methods—there would be few successful ways to uphold the rights of fair dealings between and among individuals. The American sources of law (the Constitution, state constitutions, and laws passed in Congress and by state legislatures, as interpreted by the judicial system, case law, administrative rulings, and mediations/arbitrations) create the necessary foundation for enforcing rights that protect all Americans.

While it is true that certain laws ensure safety for American citizens (for example, standards set by the Food and Drug Administration), what really keeps us safe are the overall enforcement mechanisms of our judicial system. Lawyers are the people who are tasked with ensuring safe, fair, and equitable treatments. That's an important reason why America has, on a per-person basis, more lawyers than any other country. Of course, Larry, a lawyer, feels that having more lawyers would be a very good thing for America. And Paul, a business guy, tends to disagree.

## THE ROLE OF JURISPRUDENCE IN CHECKS AND BALANCES

Recall the structure of the Constitution as it created our federal government's tripartite system of branches: Legislative (Article 1) to debate and pass laws, Executive (Article 2) to enforce laws, and Judiciary (Article 3) to interpret laws. Per Montesquieu and other philosophers relied on by the Founders, the powers of federal governance needed to be separated. The Constitution specifically established only the Supreme Court; it then authorized Congress to set up additional courts, which it did under the Judiciary Act of 1789 during the first session of Congress.[3] Each state established its courts under its own constitution and related laws.

---

3    Judiciary Act of 1789, Chapter 20, 1 Stat. 73.

The Constitution also established that federal judges were to be appointed for life by the president and confirmed by the United States Senate. Hamilton, in Article 78 of *The Federalist Papers*, noted the critical requirement of life tenure for federal judges:

> If, then, the courts of justice are to be considered as bulwarks of a limited Constitution against legislative encroachments, this consideration will afford a strong argument for the permanent tenure of judicial offices, since nothing will contribute so much as this to that independent spirit in the judges which must be essential to the faithful performance of so arduous a duty.[4]

But Hamilton also viewed the judicial branch under the Constitution as the "weakest of the three [branches of government]," citing Montesquieu (from his book *The Spirit of the Laws*). He wrote, "the judiciary is next to nothing," but opined on the important role the judicial branch must play to determine that "whenever a particular statute contravenes the Constitution, it will be the duty of the judicial tribunals to adhere to the [Constitution] and disregard the [particular statute]."[5]

The creation of a strong judicial system as part of the separation of powers under the Constitution was controversial. Some of the debates concerned how judges with lifetime appointments might support a system of national tyranny. Concerns were such that half of the Bill of Rights (the first ten amendments to the Constitution) dealt primarily with judicial matters. Despite these and other concerns, Congress agreed to establish a robust, independent judiciary.

---

4  *The Federalist Papers*, Article 78.
5  Ibid.

The Judiciary Act of 1789 also established the original rule for six justices to sit on the Supreme Court, including a chief justice; it also created lower courts and the various ways those courts had jurisdiction over certain disputes (so as not to conflict with the powers of state and local courts). Later laws passed by Congress set the number of Supreme Court justices at nine, which is where this Court's membership remains as of today. As America's population grew, later laws increased the number of federal judges and courts.

Although the federal courts historically have not gotten as much attention from the public as the other two branches of the federal government, decisions by the federal courts, especially the Supreme Court, profoundly affected Americans' lives. The Supreme Court is the highest court in our federal system and the final word in analyzing the impacts of the Constitution as the "supreme Law of the Land,"[6] including over cases that begin in state court systems but that affect federal issues, under the Constitution's Supremacy Clause.[7] Since federal judges are appointed to serve for life, unless they retire or resign, the only legal check on them is through the power of impeachment under the Constitution.[8]

During the early years of our country, it was unclear whether the judiciary had the power to declare federal laws unconstitutional. The Supreme Court seized that power early in the nineteenth century,[9] and ever since then, federal courts have reviewed various laws and even struck some out

---

6 *Marbury v. Madison.* 5 US (1 Cranch) 137, 177 (1803).
7 US Constitution, Article 4, Clause 2.
8 As of 2024, fifteen federal judges have been impeached with eight convicted and removed from office. See Federal Judicial Center (www.fjc.gov), *Impeachments of Federal Judges* (accessed August 13, 2024).
9 See *Marbury v. Madison,* 5 US (1 Cranch) 137 (1803).

of the books. Congress also has the power to pass new laws to overturn decisions by the federal courts—unless their further action is later deemed unconstitutional.

Before the American Revolutionary War, judicial systems were emerging in many countries. However, in America, the judicial system's powers reached a zenith that continues to provide another advantage for the United States. The rule of law in America may be the most important reason financial capital flows into the US.

The role of our judiciary system and the undergirding provided to our society by the rule of law are great examples of why the winner of any new Cold War matters to humanity over the long term. But the speed and safety of transactions, as mentioned in the story of housing, are why the judiciary matters directly to you, almost daily.

The American judicial system, including rights enumerated in the Bill of Rights, focuses on protecting the freedoms of Americans. It is not unusual in our history that the judiciary had to protect those rights from attack by a majority of Congress members, as well as enforcement by the president and their executive team. In 2020, the judiciary had to preserve our right to free and fair elections. The overall protection of freedoms, including the freedom to work as one deems best, is based on the intersection of many parts of our founding vision, including the broad vision captured in the Declaration, the structure created under the Constitution, in all states under their constitutions, by laws of Congress, and the courts themselves. We Americans are the beneficiaries, a decisive reason why there is nowhere else in the world where it is better to live, work, and succeed than America.

We understand that to many, there seems to be a crisis today, that our election system, the rule of law, and the balance of power might be in question because of the next election. We trust the institutions, the history, and the ability of key stakeholders to supersede the forces of evil, the abuses of power, and bad decisions made by elected officials. But the foundation of America is based on the rights of individuals, including civil rights, equal rights, property rights, free markets, and free elections. We see nothing that leads us to believe these values are at risk.

**JUSTICE BENDS TOWARD FREEDOM**

In November of 2003, at the twentieth anniversary of the National Endowment for Democracy 2003, President George W. Bush spoke about the founding ideals of America and about how we emerged from the Cold War in the 1980s with the failure of tyranny and especially communism, noting that humans always bend toward freedom. Bush confirmed his views and those of political observers that the past generations saw the greatest advancement of freedom in the 250-year story of American democracy. In his view, "[l]iberty is both the plan of Heaven for humanity, and the best hope for progress here on Earth."[10]

---

10   George W. Bush, "President Bush Discusses Freedom in Iraq and Middle East," speech delivered at the twentieth anniversary of the National Endowment for Democracy, US Chamber of Commerce, Washington, DC, November 6, 2003, available at *The American Presidency Project*, https://www.presidency.ucsb.edu/remarks-the-20th-anniversary-the-national-endowment-for-democracy.

During his speech to business leaders, Bush opined on the democratic movements in the Middle East. He noted that modern democracies may or may not look like Western democracies, that "[d]emocratic nations may be constitutional democracies, federal republics, or parliamentary systems. And working democracies always need time to develop...." He noted that successful democratic societies protect key freedoms, implement the impartial rule of law, often privatize their economies, and secure private property rights.

Bush suggested that the countries of Iraq and Afghanistan (which America's military invaded after the September 11, 2001, attack on the World Trade Center in New York) were well on their paths toward democracy, that America would help them "secure democracy."[11] But we now know, from the benefit of hindsight, that these values Bush spoke of failed in both Iraq and Afghanistan to varying degrees, despite our commitment of trillions of dollars and thousands of military lives during the twenty-year period of war. Yet, we ask, why did freedom fail in these places? You might answer this question yourself.

In our view, freedom can't succeed in the long term if free people do not value it enough to protect it with their lives. The work of democracy is hard and must continually be defended against challenges from within and without. Alas, it cannot be imposed from the outside. The sacrifice must come directly from the beneficiaries. If you are an American, you are a great beneficiary of young men and women from one end of this country to the other who gave their lives so you could enjoy the benefits.

---

11   Ibid.

As Americans, we believe that freedom is a universal value. Because we worship at the altar of freedom, we struggle to believe that liberty isn't a human instinct. Yet, in other times and in other situations, there seem to be interests that other societies value more than freedom. Often people surrender freedom for the feeling of security. Historically, power has been more a universal value than freedom. And while we value freedom of religion, most Americans don't value religion over freedom. They are tied together. This is simply not true in most places in the Middle East.

The commitment to liberty must be long-term. The prosperity that comes from liberty and the focus on the individual takes decades, maybe even centuries, to mature. But prosperity cannot be secure without the rule of law that protects the rights of individuals over the powers representing the majority. This is no small accomplishment, and we have had to defend it repeatedly.

So, we can learn some lessons from these two countries where democracy mostly failed. Bush certainly was not suggesting that helping Iraq and Afghanistan build democracies was simple or straightforward. But many at that time thought it would be easier than it has been. "Never easy" is probably the best lesson we can learn, leaving us with deeper admiration for the vision and work of the Founders and the subsequent work of future generations. Our freedoms and democracy are always subject to attack from within the US and from outside. In the future, America's democracy will most likely require protection by the individuals who receive the benefits—all Americans.

## SIGNIFICANT AMERICAN JUDICIAL HISTORY

We believe that the contents of this chapter, including a difficult discussion of why a judicial system is important across all sectors of society, sets an optimistic view of how an independent judicial system drives stronger democracies. Every American should understand that the right and power to determine which laws are constitutional and which are not and what freedoms to protect comes with deep concerns. While the courts act as backstops to keep majority rule from trampling minority rights and freedoms, they also can damage or destroy a society's progress and protection. During many decades throughout our history, the judicial system has constrained progress. This was especially true following the Civil War, as the country attempted to extract itself from the horror of slavery.

Following the Civil War, Congress passed, and the states ratified (even states that attempted to secede from America) the Thirteenth, Fourteenth, and Fifteenth Amendments to end slavery's stain. However, later interpretations of those amendments failed to embrace the broad vision for change. The Southern states that attempted to secede from the Union passed laws that restricted the rights, freedoms, and liberties of formerly enslaved people.

Imagine what this country could have become if what happened after the Civil War negated the historic decisions of our Founders and changed America's direction permanently. The Supreme Court, in the decades following the Civil War, narrowed interpretations of the language of those Second Founding amendments (Thirteenth, Fourteenth, and Fifteenth), enabling discrimination and racism to continue, underlining not only the initial legal concepts of slavery but the continuing failure to interpret the founding freedoms of America broadly.

Do you wonder, as we did, why that was the case? As Hamilton in *The Federalist Papers* (Article 78) noted, the federal court system was established with lifetime tenure for its judges to remove the pressures that otherwise existed to block challenges to laws passed by Congress and signed by the president. The salaries of such judges (and justices on the Supreme Court) could not be reduced during their years of service, again removing the pressures possibly felt that would prevent more objective reviews of various provisions of the Constitution, laws passed under its authority, and state laws that implicated federal issues. While Hamilton perceived the judicial branch to be the weakest of the three, its independence and determination to review laws and ensure Constitutional compliance remained fundamental to preserving the founding conditions of America.

By the framework established by the Founders, judges and justices are appointed by the president and are affirmed by US senators. By nature, that process is a political one. But after their appointments, the judges and justices' lifetime tenure and continuing salaries are meant to ensure necessary independence. And mostly those two factors do that job, even in times when hindsight showed a failure to help America progress. But can you also see the hesitation in moving the country quickly in new directions? Majority rule might try to drive the country to move more quickly at times, but the judiciary ensures that such movement complies with the limited powers of the federal government under the Constitution.

While court decisions from the decades of the latter nineteenth century seemed to challenge individual freedoms under the Constitution, as amended, the twentieth century led to many decisions that did protect our rights and freedoms. You can judge the beneficial speed (and even the failure of the speed), but overall, the judicial arc in America has bent toward justice. There is further to go, for sure, but only in America (and possibly in a few other democratic countries) can the people proceed with confidence that actions inconsistent with the Founders' vision will not damage America's freedoms.

One of the quirks of America's founding was that the Bill of Rights applied to the federal government only ("Congress shall make no law..."). The first ten amendments were designed to check the power of the federal government vis-à-vis the power of the people and the power of state governments. Madison believed these rights should extend to state power, but at our founding, most states included such rights in their constitutions to be interpreted by state courts.[12] The horrors of slavery and continuing discrimination against racial groups (especially in Southern states) led to changes in state constitutions and laws to preclude equality. While the Constitution is difficult to amend, most state constitutions are not. Many of them were amended to preserve the power of white men after the Civil War and Reconstruction.

It took many years after passage of the Fourteenth Amendment for the courts, especially the Supreme Court, to catch up to the need for societal change. The Supreme Court

---

[12] James Madison, "Speech Proposing Amendments to the Constitution," *Congressional Register*, June 8, 1789, in *The Founders' Constitution* Volume 5, eds. Philip B. Kurland and Ralph Lerner (Chicago: University of Chicago Press, 1987), 14–17.

narrowed its interpretation of that amendment in many ways. In part, the Fourteenth Amendment provides that, "No State shall make or enforce any law which shall abridge the privileges or immunities of citizens of the United States...." This tracks the language of Article 4, Section 2 of the Constitution: "The Citizens of each State shall be entitled to all Privileges and Immunities of Citizens in the Several States." During the latter eighteenth century, this was limited by the Supreme Court to underlying federal rights only (although some historians suggest that that change from "and" to "or" was merely grammatical).

There was a general sense by the drafters of this language that equality across the states would be realized, but those hopes diminished with the Supreme Court's decision in the *Slaughterhouse Cases*[13] late in the nineteenth century. Justice Samuel Miller, appointed by President Lincoln, issued a decision that affirmed the police powers of the States, narrowing the intended meaning of the Privileges or Immunities Clause in the Constitution. And while most members of Congress who passed the Fourteenth Amendment assumed the language provided broad federal oversight over the actions in the states, Justice Miller (in a close decision, 5–4) narrowed the interpretation substantially. The four dissenting justices responded in brutal fashion, but this Privileges or Immunities Clause remains mostly unused today.

In the twentieth century, the Court breathed larger lives into the Fourteenth Amendment, finding that the Amendment applied individual freedom protections, including those in the Bill of Rights, to the states. Later, courts interpreted the word

---

13  *The Slaughter-House Cases*, 83 US (16 Wall.) 36 (1873).

"liberty" in the Amendment to allow "incorporation" of those rights to state matters, beginning in 1925, with the freedom of speech and freedom of the press rights, with further incorporation of other rights following. In particular, the Court found substantive due process rights under the Fourteenth Amendment that enabled privacy rights, including abortion, gay marriage, and other rights that were not recognized at our country's founding.

Yet, the question of state rights and state action under the yet-to-be-reversed *Slaughterhouse* cases raises concerns for future interpretations of our freedoms. For example, Chief Justice William Rehnquist's decision in 2000 in *United States v. Morrison*, which struck a remedy of the federal Violence Against Women Act, ruled that Congress did not have the power to pass this law under the commerce clause of the Constitution or the Fourteenth Amendment. The Rehnquist decision noted:

> [T]he language and purpose of the Fourteenth Amendment place certain limitations on the manner in which Congress may attack discriminatory conduct. These limitations are necessary to prevent the Fourteenth Amendment from obliterating the Framers' carefully crafted balance of power between the States and the National Government.[14]

So there remains work to do—judicially and individually—to ensure that the freedoms Americans enjoy are fully extended to all. We do and you should remain fully optimistic that this successful journey will continue. For example, consider the right to privacy, a right not specified in the

---

14   *United States v. Morrison*, 529 US 598, 619 (2000).

Constitution, as amended. We believe that protecting such an important right is key to the future of freedom in America.

## THE LEGAL RIGHT TO PRIVACY

What are the Constitutional implications of individual privacy? How might they affect our freedoms in the future?

In June of 2022, the Supreme Court overruled *Roe v. Wade*[15] with the *Dobbs v. Jackson Women's Health Organization* decision.[16] A liberal-leaning court's decision in *Roe v. Wade* allowed and protected a federal right to abortion (in the first trimester of pregnancy, or for the health of the mother and child) for fifty years. The Court majority (5–4) ruled in *Dobbs* that while the Constitution protected the freedoms and liberty of Americans, it did not establish a federal right to privacy and that state laws could restrict abortion access.

For some, this is a disastrous ruling. For others, even people who support abortion choice, the turn to state lawmakers for legal permission seems a better outcome because they see it as a better way to support American democracy. Still, the American system is a liberal democracy, where individual rights and freedoms are first principles, followed by collective rights under majority rule. Certain freedoms, such as rights afforded by the First Amendment, can never be overtaken.

So, what does this mean about the right of privacy with respect to the private choice involved with abortion? As the Court journeyed throughout the mid-twentieth century, especially during the civil rights era, it found federal protections by breathing a substantive right into the due process clause

---

15   *Roe v. Wade*, 410 US 113 (1973).
16   *Dobbs v. Jackson Women's Health Organization*, 597 US ___ (2002).

found in the Fourteenth Amendment: "...nor shall any State deprive any person of life, liberty, or property, without due process of law."[17] Even to those who seek aggressive protection of individual freedoms, the notion that "process" includes "substance" seems oxymoronic. For many years, even commentators who supported the Court's decision in *Roe v. Wade* concluded its logic was flawed. The current Court majority agreed and overruled *Roe*.

There are many cases where the Court upheld personal privacy matters under similar substantive due process analyses: gay marriage, consensual sex, contraception, and interracial marriage. Yet many observers worry that the Court will continue to remove these other protections that have been in place for decades. It would be tragic if that turns out to be the case, but need it be? You have the right to freedom of speech. It can be used to prevent and correct. For America and its moral arc to move toward justice, ever forward, we, the people, can and will—collectively and individually—continue to move toward equal opportunity and justice for all. We believe that the Supreme Court and, as needed, federal and state lawmakers, will continue to protect personal rights on private matters. We have work to do because we see a small glimmer of hope that arises from the *Dobbs* case.

Justice Clarence Thomas is currently one of the most conservative members of the Court. For many years, he railed against what he perceived as an activist majority that used substantive due process as a weapon of judicial intrusion.

It's true that he suggests that, now that *Roe* has been overturned, the Court should take another look at cases where

---

17   US Constitution, Fourteenth Amendment.

certain rights were preserved by substantive due rights protections. He notes, in a concurring opinion:

> The Court well explains why, under our substantive due process precedents, the purported right to abortion is not a form of "liberty" protected by the Due Process Clause. Such a right is neither "deeply rooted in this Nation's history and tradition" nor "implicit in the concept of ordered liberty."[18]

He argues that due process merely means "process" and can be nothing substantive, calling it an oxymoron. He then notes that in future cases, the Court should reconsider all cases where it upheld rights based on a flawed substantive due process analysis.

Those comments raise great concerns across America, that additional individual freedoms are now at risk. We agree. However, *the courts do not create freedoms*. Most of the freedoms are based on the "natural rights of man" and are protected by the Constitution and legitimate federal and state laws. If the federal government doesn't protect such rights, the courts can deem any such laws unconstitutional. The states can choose to act or not, consistent with the wishes of most resident citizens, to be checked by overall constitutional concerns.

Many people, including you, might overlook what Justice Thomas noted. While he believes there are no substantive due process rights protected under the Fourteenth Amendment, it's not obvious—at least to us—that he thinks there are no bases for federal protections. Justice Thomas went on to write:

---

18   *Dobbs v. Jackson Women's Health Organization*, 597 US \_\_\_, \_\_\_ (2022) (Thomas, concurring).

After overruling these demonstrably erroneous decisions, the question would remain whether other constitutional provisions guarantee the myriad rights that our substantive due process cases have generated. For example, we could consider whether any of the rights announced in this Court's substantive due process cases are "privileges or immunities of citizens of the United States" protected by the Fourteenth Amendment.... To answer that question, we would need to decide important antecedent questions, including whether the Privileges or Immunities Clause protects any rights that are not enumerated in the Constitution and, if so, how to identify those rights.[19]

In many of his written opinions (including dissents), Justice Thomas has signaled that the Privileges or Immunities Clause may have been wrongly decided in the *Slaughterhouse* cases. This could be a feint to reject all such federal rights, but we doubt it. Can the Court breathe new life into that clause, continuing to protect many individual rights Americans have come to expect and rely on? It can and often has done so as it expanded protections for all Americans under the Fourteenth Amendment.

We remain confident and optimistic that the Court will move in this direction. The country, as, at times, checked by the judicial branch, always has. The path is never straight and sometimes reverses on itself; however, it does always bend, over time, toward even greater justice. That underscores what America has been all about since its founding almost 250 years ago.

---

19   *Dobbs v. Jackson Women's Health Organization*, 597 US ___, ___ (2022) (Thomas, concurring).

# PART IV

# AMERICAN GENEROSITY AND FORESIGHT: THE HORN OF PLENTY

## CHAPTER 13

# ENSURING THE PROSPERITY OF AMERICA

HAVING BEEN ELECTED PHOENIX'S MAYOR in the early 1990s, Paul was sent to Poland by the US Department of State to help restore democracy after the Iron Curtain came down. His actual job was to teach the city of Warsaw's leaders what he knew about governing a city in a democratic system.

When he walked through the old town of Warsaw, Paul saw beautiful five- and six-storied buildings lining the streets and squares. Originally constructed in the fourteenth and fifteenth centuries, they had been meticulously rebuilt after brutal bombings during World War II. Yet in 1992, they were falling apart from lack of attention and maintenance. Nearby trees looked like the skeletal remains of a nuclear holocaust. So much smoke rose from the tops of industrial factory stacks that the sky could barely be seen. When it rained, acidic soot fell on the once healthy, leafy trees, perpetuating their misery.

Farther north of the city, Paul saw a river that had turned brown with sewage. As the filth flowed into the Baltic Sea, the only form of a water treatment plant was a man with a pitchfork who was trying to pull out some of the sludge. His effort did little to improve the condition of the shores of Poland. The water was so polluted that swimming, fishing, and living near it were much too dangerous. On the streets, Paul noticed that cargo was still being transported by carts and horses. People were heating their homes with wood stripped from the forest. It was like visiting Poland during the Dark Ages in history.

After communism left Poland, it was up to local leaders to create governments that would shift from figuring out where to put a barbershop or a gas station to learning how to attract investment. The Soviet Union's puppet government ruled Poland after World War II. It implemented practices based on the theory of dialectic materialism, which removed property and business ownership, with the state controlling all means of production.

Where people and capital want to go determines the successes (or failures) of nations. Countries where people want to escape, and capital is insecure, fail. In Poland, investment was not secure, and people wanted out. But many clung to hope as freedom from rule by the Soviet Union was realized. Poland's example of movement from communism to democracy supports the reason capitalism has worked as a foundation for America's model of democracy.

The Second Law of Thermodynamics (systems go from order to chaos over time) also applies to social order and economics. In the long run, nothing escapes the process of entropy. Everything decays. Without attention to detail, disorder always increases. Weeds overtake cities. Buildings crumble. Military equipment rusts. People age. With enough time, societies fall. The inevitable trend is that things become less organized.

The solution to this entropy is to expend energy to create stability and maintain structure. Energy requires investment, and investment requires return. This fights back the tide of entropy and creates a beneficial order.

When the Soviet Union took away from people what they owned and ruled the means of production, the impact and results of their actions were not immediate. Even though property owners and businesses expressed rage, they were in the minority—creators and property owners are always in the minority. Over time, investment declines due to a lack of personal ownership. Those systems destroyed the energy that stops entropy, destroying society and cities and leaving them subject to atrophy and apathy.

Paul found in Warsaw that there was no incentive to invest in buildings, energy, or businesses. This situation created a dearth of tax income for the government, so no money was available to build water treatment plants or install scrubbers on the smokestacks. Capitalism may not be perfect, but it is not the enemy of the environment; it can be its savior. When capitalism is absent, people will strip the environment, harming even further the interest to invest.

What eventually brought down the Iron Curtain in places like Poland? It was the very people whom communism and Karl Marx said they were there to save. The people were fed up with working conditions, no promise to do better, and the inability to determine their destiny. Laborers stood on the docks and said, "No more!" The destruction of potential for progress and investment eventually led to a suppression of labor. Inevitably, labor revolts against the form of government that labeled them as the oppressed, while labeling freedom and capitalism as the oppressors.

Over human history there have been many systems of governance invented and implemented. It is clear that the systems we have in the United States, under the mantle of democracy, are unusual. What is the norm? It is chaos, conflict, disputes over resources, entropy—and often revolt. Only through an orderly society, which recognition of the rule of law and that every man and woman wants to own what they create and to use that power to advantage mankind, has humanity been able to prosper. We then find abundance. In our research, we were unable to find examples of where or when socialism or communism, over time, resulted in anything but brutal treatment of its citizens, damage to its environment, and a failed economy. The jury remains out on China, but we have little doubt the general rule will apply.

America's democratic system offers many individual freedoms: speech, religious expression, responsible gun ownership, freedom to lobby elected leaders, freedom to gather peaceably and, most important for this chapter, freedom to engage in the work of your choice. A society based on individual freedoms is oriented toward free markets and the freedom to choose various economic paths to support entrepreneurship and create jobs that support individuals and families.

The Declaration asserts that governments are designed to secure these rights, including "Life, Liberty and the Pursuit of Happiness," but only with the consent of the people they govern. Locke's view of the natural rights of individuals was to preserve their life, liberty, health, and goods.[1] The Framers were concerned enough about this issue to require under the Fifth Amendment: "No person shall be...deprived of life, liberty, or property, without due process of law; nor shall private property be taken for public use without just compensation."[2] This protection was later extended to cover the

---

[1] John Locke, *Second Treatise of Government* (1689), ed. C.B. Macpherson (Indianapolis: Hackett Publishing Company, 1980), Chapter II, Section 6.
[2] US Constitution, Fifth Amendment.

activities of the states by the Fourteenth Amendment. For example, the concept of eminent domain requires paying fair value for private land or property taken for the public good.[3] At the time of America's founding, private rights of trespass didn't exist in most states. Years later, the concept of individual possession was backed by legal protections such as laws against trespassing.

Locke singularly influenced the Founders' thinking and how they crafted the infrastructure that became America after the American Revolution. His influence on overall political philosophy was and is profound in many ways. He deeply influenced modern liberalism—a free society, mostly ruled by a majority of its citizens but also one that protects individual rights and freedoms. He wrote about freedoms, arguing that government needed to be separate from any religion, such as the government-tied Anglican Church in England.

Like Hobbes before him, Locke believed that human nature must include both reason and tolerance, that human beings will inherently act in selfish/self-interested ways (what he called the social contract), that humans are simultaneously equal and independent, and that they have the right to their life, health, liberty, or goods/possessions.[4] He also supported the introduction of currency/money to allow for the free exchange of possessions, making unlimited property accumulation possible.

---

[3] *United States v. Miller*, 317 US 469 (1943). See *Kelo v. City of New London*, 545 US 469 (2005).

[4] "The reason why men enter into society is the preservation of their property...the people, who have a right to resume their original liberty, and by the establishment of a new legislative (such as they shall think fit) provide for their own safety and security, which is the end for which they are in society." Locke, 1980, Chapter 7, Section 87.

In so doing, Locke sketched the American free enterprise system, and he seemed to suggest that it is a governmental role to balance individual wealth accumulation with society's desire for equal opportunity. John Rawls picked up on this concept in his book, *A Theory of Justice*,[5] where he discusses how a just society might structure taxation to maintain fairness and support the overall institutions, an argument that some suggest defends the concept of America's progressive tax system.

History suggests that economic freedoms and rights were embedded in America and its institutions even before the Revolutionary War and the establishment of American independence. From the writings of Locke, from the founding rights of companies under various charters issued by the King of England, from other philosophies that go back to the start of Western philosophy under Socrates, Aristotle, and Plato, American individual freedoms became sacrosanct. They included both the right to decide what job to hold and the freedom of the overall economic markets, protected as a valid exercise of the powers of the government.

## ADAM SMITH

Adam Smith was a Scottish economist and philosopher, a contemporary of some of the other philosophers who influenced the Founders, and someone who lived shortly after Locke. He is widely regarded as one of the most influential economists and thinkers, often called the Father of Capitalism and the Father of Economics.

---

5   John Rawls, *A Theory of Justice* (Massachusetts: Harvard University Press, 1971), 245–251.

On March 9, 1776, Smith published *An Inquiry into the Nature and Causes of the Wealth of Nations*,[6] a seminal work formulated over seventeen years of meticulous observation and a decade of writing. This two-volume masterpiece laid the foundations of modern economic understanding, exploring the burgeoning industrialized capitalist system that was reshaping the global order and challenging the prevailing mercantilist system. Smith's insights profoundly influenced everything from the establishment of the United States to the development of communism in the early twentieth century.[7]

Mercantilism, which dominated global economics for three centuries from the 1500s, operated on the principle that national wealth was amassed through limited imports and increased exports, adhering to a notion of scarcity. Wealth was measured in gold and silver, finite resources that nations accumulated often at others' expense through new discoveries and favorable trade balances. Military might and colonization were key to this economic strategy, with colonies playing a vital role in wealth accumulation by the colonial powers.

In this context, the relationship between governments and large business entities became synergistic yet insular. Major businesses, aligned with the state's interests, augmented their

---

6    Adam Smith, *An Inquiry into the Nature and Causes of the Wealth of Nations*, ed. Edwin Cannan (Chicago: University of Chicago Press, 1976).

7    Smith's theories shaped the early United States and influenced the emergence of communism and socialism. Marx's *Communist Manifesto*, published on February 28, 1848, sought to address perceived capitalist exploitation and income disparity. Socialism and communism, while often used interchangeably, differ in their approaches to property ownership and government control. Communism advocates for the abolition of private property, while socialism allows it but promotes communal ownership of production. Both systems arose in response to the perceived failings of capitalism.

international market presence through exports while lobbying for policies that stifled import competition, including through imposition of taxes/tariffs on imported goods. This protectionist stance was seen as essential for maintaining a favorable balance of trade, ostensibly ensuring economic prosperity and national security.

This mercantilist approach had tangible, though paradoxical, effects on the populace. On one hand, it fostered employment opportunities, as robust export activities necessitated a steady workforce. However, the flip side of this coin was less favorable. The deliberate restriction of imports led to inflated prices for foreign goods, making them less accessible to the average citizen. As a result, while employment stabilized, the cost of living escalated, rendering a decent standard of living unattainable for many. Workers found themselves in a conundrum: employed and earning, yet priced out of the very economy they were helping to sustain.

Smith challenged the mercantilist orthodoxy, advocating for the principles of free trade and market liberalization. He posited that when producers—vendors or merchants—remain free to operate without onerous governmental constraints, not only does it lead to lower prices for consumers, but also fosters an environment where economic prosperity is not fixed. Instead, Smith argued, an unimpeded market could expand the benefits, creating wealth and opportunities that transcended mercantilist thinking.

Smith argued that economic growth and improvement in living standards could be achieved not through protectionism and hoarding but through the dynamism of a free market, where competition and innovation would lead to greater efficiency, lower prices, and an overall increase in wealth. This marked a pivotal shift from the zero-sum game of mercantilism to a more expansive view of economic potential, laying the groundwork for modern economic theory and practice.

The mercantilist world required that colonies buy the exports from the colonial power, and provide the raw materials needed. The debate over colonization, often mired in emotional narratives of victimization versus oppression, overshadows its historical significance as a central component of mercantilist strategy. The European colonization of the Americas, for instance, was not just about dominance over indigenous populations but also about control over how settlers could purchase from other countries.

In this context, England's trade policies with its colonies augmented its wealth, often at the expense of the colonies' economic health. Restrictive acts favored English trade and limited available products in the colonies, driving up costs. The insistence on gold and silver payments and heavy taxation to fund wars led the colonies to shift the economic paradigm away from mercantilism, ultimately in the United States leading to the Declaration of Independence and the Revolutionary War.

Smith's advocacy for achieving social outcomes through the efforts of individuals within a market, a concept reflected in the founding principles of the United States, was a key part of his economic theory. He argued that market prices, shaped by unbiased individual decisions, were more effective regulators of the economy than government intervention.

The US operates under a mixed economy, balancing private enterprise with government regulation and social programs like Medicare and Social Security, which serve as safety nets rather than comprehensive solutions. Government interventions in the economy, including environmental protection and workplace safety regulations, aim to balance social welfare with economic growth.

The mixed economy model, embracing private sector dynamism and government intervention for social welfare, has demonstrated its efficacy. While debates on the extent of regulation and taxation continue, the underlying belief by most American leaders in a private sector-led economy, moderated by government regulation and taxation to support societal benefits, remains central. This system, underpinned by investments in infrastructure and education, not only fosters immediate economic growth but also secures long-term global leadership, demonstrating to many the enduring power of a balanced economic approach.

The principles espoused by Smith in *The Wealth of Nations* helped create our modern economics of business. He argued that rational self-interest, with unrestrained destructive competition checked, leads to overall prosperity. He was a free trade enthusiast and a proponent of *laissez-faire* economics (a policy or attitude of letting things take their own course without interference) to establish a liberal economic model that could drive a country's wealth and prosperity.

The Founders were influenced by Smith's views of free markets and self-interest as the best tools to create overall wealth. However, as written, the Constitution did not provide the specifics for such a structure in America. In fact, the Constitution instilled a less-than-free market approach in some areas, such as support for patents and trademark protections. Yet, the Constitution did insist on free competition across America and individual states. Later, legislation and judicial interpretations expanded such free market interests.

## ANTITRUST LAWS, THE MAGNA CARTA FOR THE AMERICAN ECONOMY

Smith's concern that unfettered competition leads to destructive competition, unfair agreements, and monopolies was well-framed. America faced such challenges, especially later in the nineteenth century when various Americans used their powers to monopolize industries like steel, railroads, and oil products. During the latter nineteenth and early twentieth centuries, various members of the US Congress and some presidents passed laws to restrict such behaviors. These are known as the American antitrust laws.

In 1972, Supreme Court Justice Thurgood Marshall poignantly described, in a majority US Supreme Court opinion, federal antitrust laws in general and the Sherman Antitrust Act (which proscribed agreements between competitors to raise prices and certain monopolies) in particular, as:

> [T]he Magna Carta of free enterprise. They are as important to the preservation of economic freedom and our free-enterprise system as the Bill of Rights is to the protection of our fundamental personal freedoms. And the freedom guaranteed each and every business, no matter how small, is the freedom to compete—unfettered by the artificial restraints imposed by combinations of their competitors.[8]

American antitrust laws were enacted to protect the marketplace from actors whose self-interest damaged the markets overall. Another key principle of these antitrust laws is that they protect competitive markets rather than individual

---

8   *United States v. Topco Associates, Inc.*, 405 US 596, 610 (1972).

competitors. The application of these laws shows how governments can appropriately protect the freedoms of their citizens, including economic freedoms, without stifling innovation.

## MILTON FRIEDMAN AND THE CHICAGO SCHOOL OF ECONOMICS

Author Milton Friedman, in his book *Free to Choose: A Personal Statement*, which he co-wrote with Rose Friedman, said, "The story of the United States is a story of an economic miracle and a political miracle that was made possible by the translation into practice of two sets of ideas—both, by a curious coincidence, formulated in documents published in the same year, 1776."[9] He was citing the Declaration (mostly authored by Jefferson) and Smith's *The Wealth of Nations*. To Jefferson and Smith, the government's most important roles were to create laws to support the collective interests of its citizens and to serve as an umpire—to resolve disputes among individuals based on rules that they and others in their society agreed upon—and not as a direct participant in the market economy.

The Great Depression of the late 1920s and 1930s challenged and replaced that view of government as an umpire with that view that government should, as Friedman condemns, "serve as a parent charged with the duty of directing some to aid others."[10]

Both Jefferson and Smith believed that the growth of government at some point in history could destroy the prosperity

---

9 Milton Friedman and Rose Friedman, *Free to Choose: A Personal Statement* (New York: Harcourt Brace Jovanovich, 1980), 2.
10 Ibid., 136.

we often take for granted, including the other freedoms articulated in the Declaration and Constitution, especially the Bill of Rights. The challenge of our time and beyond is to imagine and re-imagine the right role for America's governmental system with respect to the economy.

James Robinson, a guest on *The Optimistic American* podcast,[11] co-authored a book with Daron Acemoglu titled, *Why Nations Fail: The Origins of Power, Prosperity, and Poverty*.[12] They argued (and we agree) that governments that allow or promote extractive policies harm growth. As an example, they noted that two of the world's richest men, Bill Gates and Carlos Slim, had very different effects on their local economies because of how their governments dealt with extractive policies. Gates's inventions, which faced significant competition, added several percentage points to the American GDP. Conversely, Slim, who had monopolies on cell phones in Mexico, actually reduced output. A successful society fully incentivizes creativity where neither the government nor monopolies extract from other entrepreneurs their ability to compete.

Over the past decades, we Americans have chosen a more restrained path of business that restricts unlimited competition but rewards individual initiative in ways that support a healthier economy and better fairness for all. Some observers (you can include us) have concluded that America ratcheted a bit too hard to protect against potential economic hardship caused by powerful individuals and businesses.

---

[11]  See https:// www.youtube.com/watch?v=yWEAebhkN-Y.
[12]  Daron Acemoglu and James A. Robinson, *Why Nations Fail: The Origins of Power, Prosperity, and Poverty* (New York: Crown Publishers, 2012).

The pinnacle of such restraints occurred following the Great Depression, mainly in the 1930s. President Franklin Delano Roosevelt and his economic team invented and launched many governmental agencies to check unrestrained business behaviors, implemented initiatives to move through the Great Depression, and imposed additional limits on overall freedoms. The 1930s certainly challenged the future of the American economy. Many people who suffered also believed our economic system had failed them; contemporaneously, fascism and socialism rose across Europe and Asia, eventually culminating in World War II.

Some suggest that Roosevelt's policies saved the economy at that time; others have suggested that World War II pulled us out of the tailspin and led to a flourishing economy post-war. Following that war, others, especially economists who worked at the University of Chicago, argued that some American freedoms, especially economic freedoms, had diminished.

Friedman was one of those economists. In 1962, he published a short book titled *Capitalism and Freedom*.[13] He followed it with another book (and TV series) called *Free to Choose*.[14] *Capitalism and Freedom* was based on his lectures in the 1950s that shaped his later views and writings. At that time, the role of government in America and across the world had exploded, in part due to the social welfare state that emerged from the Great Depression and views espoused by economists who believed (and whose views were implemented in many Western democracies) that business cycles and related

---

[13] Milton Friedman, *Capitalism and Freedom* (Chicago: University of Chicago Press, 1962).
[14] Friedman and Friedman, 1980.

challenges like unemployment could be managed by increased government spending.

Friedman and his colleagues disagreed. They argued that the key to a growing economy (and thus lower unemployment) was to return to a more privatized economic system, where the role of government was limited to serving as an umpire to resolve disputes. The post-war explosion in government, however, led to massive increases in government spending, which Friedman and others observed could destroy Western economies that were based on individual initiative.

Those Chicago School of economics arguments paved the way for the election of Margaret Thatcher in Great Britain and Ronald Reagan in the United States. While both of those leaders curbed the growth of the government, they could not reduce its overall size. Each took steps to reduce governmental power vis-à-vis business, and those years led to the fall of the Berlin Wall and the Soviet Union, arguably proving that the Western democratic economic systems (such as bottoms-up/initiative capitalism) beat a central planning system (such as top-down, communism, socialism). While many other countries faced similar explosions in the size of government, the pressures were on to give markets and the private sector more say in a country's economy.

Friedman believed that the government, limited in and checked by its design, should stay in the background. In addition to its limited role, he believed in the Founders' vision that the power of governments must be dispersed, ideally toward local government followed by state government, followed last (and limited) by the federal government.

Friedman and his colleagues argued for many changes in how a democracy manages itself. They argued that monetary policy is wrong-headed, especially as managed by America's Federal Reserve. He believed that the simplest explanation for inflationary pressures was too much liquidity—too much floating money—across the economy. He was absolutely a free trader; that is, he believed in the right of businesses to trade their goods and services across international boundaries freely.

Like Smith, Friedman believed the best way to coordinate the economic activities of millions was through a private system where cooperation rested on self-interest, where voluntary cooperation between and among individuals rested on the proposition that all parties benefit from it, provided the transactions were truly voluntary and informed. Much of what he and his colleagues argued for led to profound changes in America's direction, but some of his ideas remain worth pondering in the future.

## CAPITALISM AND PRODUCTIVITY

America's economic system is a capitalistic system based on private ownership of economic entities where the means of production are operated for individual profit. Capitalistic systems allow private capital accumulation, protect competitive markets, establish private property rights, and enable individuals to use their labor in the ways they choose, at the wages they choose to receive for such work. Prices and the availability of certain goods and services are determined mainly by private markets.

Capitalism developed in the mid-seventeenth century, just in time for an American injection through the Declaration and Constitution and various laws enabled by them. The American system is not 100 percent laissez-faire or free market capitalism; certain behaviors are checked by antitrust laws to prevent destructive competition that might generate individual wealth but at a too high societal cost.

We believe individual workers and the selfish interest of business owners must guide the best way to allocate goods and services. It is a moral system; it is the only system where the "invisible hand" can do its magic, identifying areas of shortages and excesses so that individuals can immediately decide what additional goods and services should be developed and others should not. As a default, we believe that truly free markets enable the best division of labor of individuals, meaning individuals are incentivized to work at skills that are best for them as they choose how to spend their time. Free markets allow a freer flow of individual work choices, including the careers they choose to match their skills and learning best, to serve their families better, and to create wealth. Moreover, free markets best set prices for goods and services based on production costs and customer demand.

We believe that government—which needs to be limited under the American framework—should resist placing its large regulatory finger on the pricing scale. The markets themselves and the companies and individuals who work in those markets are closer to the choices that should be made regarding pricing, including whether to reject certain products where the pricing is too high. When prices go up, producers increase production. When prices fall, production reduces. Government officials don't have the appropriate signals to react properly for the good of the overall economy.

We expect some to disagree with our views, but that is the beauty of living in America. Disagreement leads us to options to consider and, ultimately, to collective agreement by a majority on issues of importance. If you believe the government is better positioned to manage issues like the pricing of goods and services, you should demonstrate to yourself why that system will better serve the desires of the people.

It is in everyday business decisions that naturally adjust excesses and shortages when similar government-driven decisions or edicts often fail. Such edicts rarely increase supply and reduce costs; in general, they do the opposite. When more key items or services are needed, most prefer enabling individuals to move quickly and deliver them at prices they set, fully disclosed to their customers. If prices are too high, based on the required availability of goods, customers won't buy, and prices will fall. If prices are too low, demand will increase and prices will then rise, eventually reducing demand.

These everyday market forces flourish under the American system, and too often we overlook the powers that the system gives.

Under all economic systems, wealth is created over time as overall economic productivity increases. Productivity measures the efficiency of the production of goods and services. It is measured as the ratio of output over key inputs in a production or service process. One common example is the productivity of labor, generally measured by a country's GDP per the number of workers in that system.

Productivity is the factor that creates overall wealth for countries. Increasing productivity means that labor can be tasked more efficiently. Increased productivity raises a country's standard of living because it enables people to purchase goods and services, increases leisure time, and provides for better investments in societal programs. Efficient productivity increases a business's profitability.

On the measures of GDP by country, America is the leader by far, followed by China. However, when GDP is adjusted based on factors such as the cost of living in each country, China is number one globally, followed by the United States. All other countries fall well behind China and America.[15]

In other developments, America is advancing technology at an amazing rate today. We are shocked almost monthly by advances in artificial intelligence (AI) technology. Businesses are focusing on how to get more and more efficiency out of their existing workforces. As efficiencies increase, prices fall. That frees money to focus on other products, creating new economic and job opportunities. Moreover, sometimes the efficiencies are so great that the cost of the product becomes as close to free as possible. There are many examples of goods and services that used to be very expensive (think camcorders and cameras) that are now free as part of your cell phone.

Rawls addressed some economic fundamentals in *A Theory of Justice*.[16] He created a thought experiment to ask what system individuals would choose to operate society from an "original position," where no one knew the individual advantages or disadvantages they had, such as family wealth, existing education, higher intellect, and strong communities. He opined that such individuals would select an overall system that might look unfair at the individual level, providing

---

[15] "World Economic Outlook Database: GDP Based on PPP, Share of World Total," *International Monetary Fund*, April 2023, https://www.imf.org/en/Publications/WEO/weo-database/2023/April (accessed August 26, 2024).

[16] Rawls, 1971.

a stronger society and economic system that would benefit all despite individual unfairness, provided that equally situated individuals could seek and receive opportunities (such as jobs) that led to individual personal gain.

Rawls's ideas provide solid justifications for America's progressive tax system and social safety net system, which includes welfare payments for the poor, especially families who can access health care under Medicaid, and financial support for seniors through Social Security and Medicare.

Strong communities support members in need, inspire hope, and create opportunities to bootstrap success, even when success means the ability to pay for basic living expenses and have a bit of money left over for leisure. The creation of strong communities in America, based on a strong economy, supports the founding vision of America—equal opportunity for all men and women.

★ ★ ★

All this will mean an abundance of jobs and wealth creation in America. In 2022, more than ten million jobs across the United States were unfilled. Ongoing housing shortages continue to drive demand for workers skilled in the building trades. Manufacturing is returning to America. For all the fear of workers being replaced by robotics or technology, almost every indicator says there will continue to be shortages of workers in the US. Workers will see even better job opportunities, and employers will see pressures for wages to rise.

But as workers move up these ladders of opportunity, they will need ongoing education to acquire new skills. Jobs are plentiful today for those with the skills to engage them. They will remain plentiful as more baby boomers retire (on average, there are 10,000 new retirees every day). The future will be won by workers who have aspired to more complex jobs that require new skills and worker knowledge.

*We believe that our children's and grandchildren's opportunities will exceed the ones we were granted.*

## CHAPTER 14

# ENCOURAGING ENTREPRENEURIAL OPPORTUNITIES

IN 2022, OVER 5.1 MILLION Americans became new business entrepreneurs. Half of those business owners were minority enterprises. Over 16 percent of Americans own their own business. In the World Bank's "Ease of Doing Business Index," America ranks in the top ten.[1] While we would like to see us be number one, for as large and diverse a nation as we are, there quite simply is no better place to be an entrepreneur.

America, more than almost any other place in the world, enables anyone, regardless of sex or gender, race, ethnic background, socioeconomic status, education level, religion, physical ability, and/or age, to start a business and succeed or fail. The personal agency to dream up a business and take action to create it is available to all Americans. However, some of the work businesses do must be regulated to protect employee and customer safety.

That was not the case in America before the Revolution. Under the monarchy of England, permission was needed to start a business, and permission was granted based on family status, education, or religion. For two examples, the

---

1     See https://www.oberlo.com/blog/entrepreneur-statistics.

Massachusetts Bay Colony and the Virginia Company received royal charters from the King of England that controlled business in their colonies.[2] Despite that structure, America's Framers removed the need for such grants and charters. As the country expanded, the new government granted, on an equal basis, land not owned by the government to individuals for agricultural purposes.

It is never good to take things for granted—especially the opportunities America offers entrepreneurs. And it is a grave mistake to believe you could have done what you accomplished in America anywhere. Imagine for a moment the life of a Kulak, a Russian farmer who had the misfortune of operating a productive farm under Stalin's rule. Or imagine owning a business in China today under Xi or Russia with Putin. The value of operating under the US government only matters when you compare it to something else.

When the revolution started in Stalin's Russia, the capitalist system was blamed as the oppressor. The party represented the oppressed—the workers, the peasants, and the poor. The solution to ensure equality of outcomes was to replace the capitalist system with government and take control of the means of production.

Unfortunately, without the individual incentive to produce (and to keep what you earn), production declined. The government confiscated goods and crops, harming the producers and worsening the people's situation. They experimented

---

[2] See "Charter of the Massachusetts Bay Colony, 1629, Issued by King Charles I of England," in *The Federal and State Constitutions, Colonial Charters and Other Organic Laws of the United States Volume 3, 1846–1854*, compiled by Francis Newton Thorpe (Washington, DC: Government Printing Office, 1909); Ibid., "Charter of the Virginia Company of London, 1606."

with increasing profit incentives, which led to increased production but also diminished the state's power. By the time Stalin ascended to power, he had no intention of compromising further.

Communism was based on Marx's theories, which were designed for industrialized states. However, the Soviet Union lacked significant industry. Stalin's Five-Year Plan involved financing industrialization by extracting resources from agriculture.

Stalin's plan shifted the blame of prior failures to wealthy peasants. He targeted a group called Kulaks, defined as wealthy peasants. They were vilified as enemies of the people, their farms seized, and those lucky enough were sent to the Gulag. The unlucky ones, millions of defenseless families, were sent to Siberia without shelter, where they faced horrific deaths from the cold and harsh conditions. The remaining farmers were forced to work on state-run farms as part of this extraction process.

From an agricultural perspective, this worsened the problem, leading to decreased productivity and food shortages that caused mass starvation across the Soviet Union. Adding insult to injury, Stalin sold grain to other countries to generate revenue for industrialization, even when Russians lacked access to food.

The construction of industry infrastructure, including road building, relied heavily on massive amounts of slave labor from prisoners in the Gulag. Tens of millions of people died, either from being forced to live in the Gulag or from starvation caused by collectivization.

Within the Soviet Union, the failures of collectivization were not overlooked. As the state-controlled plan faltered, criticisms within the Communist Party grew. Stalin had already killed tens of millions of people. He had no problem eliminating another million party members who had become the critics. He mercilessly executed from 700,000 to 1.2 million individuals who had devoted their lives to the Communist Party.

Mao duplicated the process in China. The Long March, the Cultural Revolution, and the Great Leap Forward resulted in the deaths of possibly sixty million people. Anyone who spoke up against the failed policies was purged.

## CHINA'S OPPORTUNITY

In 1972, President Nixon removed China from America's strategy of containment. Americans allowed China to be a part of the world order, to ship products with the protection of the American Navy, participate in the Western democracies' financial systems, and sell goods to Americans (at a considerable cost of lost American jobs). This change in American attitudes provided China with an economic bonanza.

It was an amazing release of the human spirit when Americans welcomed China into the free trade market in 1976. After Chairman Mao's death, Deng Xiaoping realized the benefits of opening markets and participating in the American-led world order. Under Mao, from 1950 to 1973, China's GDP grew at an annual rate of 2.9 percent. Deng's economic reforms led to unprecedented growth from 1978 until 2013, with the economy growing by 9.5 percent yearly. The period of expansion created by the de-collectivization of agriculture, opening to foreign investment, privatization, contracting out state-owned industries, lifting price controls and protectionist policies, and operating under the rule of law, including joining the World Trade Organization (WTO), was unprecedented not only in China but possibly in world history.

Americans believed that as China's markets became freer, their society would follow suit. We believed that free markets would eventually lead to democratic reforms. We believed that as China saw the benefits of the rule of law promoting human progress, it would naturally extend free markets and liberal democracy.

How wrong we were.

As China's economic power grew, so did the psychopathy that naturally comes with autocracy. By the time Xi Jinping came to power, it was clear that Chinese leaders were more paranoid and intimidated by the power of the private sector. They turned to mercantilism or imperialism to make up for the extractive policies they imposed on their people. Xi made it clear that he wanted to overthrow the American-led world order. While the American order greatly benefited China, all authoritarians are the same—they crave control.

The shift we are watching in China now is dramatic. Critique of the government has led to the silencing or imprisonment of Chinese company founders. China depends on exports, yet under Xi, it is combative with the people it needs to sell to. He turns his back on the entrepreneurs who led to China's great expansion.

## THE VALUE OF ENTREPRENEURSHIP

Entrepreneurs are America's (and the world's) problem solvers. Companies founded by entrepreneurs seek to effectively solve unsolved problems that matter to other people, potential customers, for the startup's goods or services. When a startup is successful, the management team reaps financial rewards; when unsuccessful, the company fails, and its employees seek other jobs and often go on to tackle other important, unsolved problems. As venture capitalist Marc Andreessen noted, "Every day, the next new thing walks through our door."[3]

Startups differ from government activity, where successes rarely lead to individual financial gain and failures rarely lead to job losses. Governments must work to resolve big issues—things like immigration, trade between nations, and military protection—but the entrepreneurs of America find the best ways to solve other problems. America has a history of successful startups, some of which became large companies. Democracy supports entrepreneurs who are motivated to solve such problems for personal economic gain. This is a vivid example of Smith's invisible hand, hard at work.

## A SHORT HISTORY OF MONEY—AMERICAN FINANCE, BANKING, AND VENTURE CAPITAL

The invention of money began in early human history, even before written history began. Many things were traded in ancient markets as bartering or exchanging one thing of value for another. Over the centuries, barter management progressed by creating intermediate stores of value to better exchange goods that were unalike. Various metals provided accepted values, which allowed them to be traded for other objects.

Gold and silver have been the most common forms of money throughout history. Gold coins began to be minted in

---

[3] Sam Harris, "Debating the Future of AI: A Conversation with Marc Andreessen," June 28, 2023, in *Making Sense*, podcast, 54:17, https://www.youtube.com/watch?v=QMnH6KYNuWg.

Europe in the thirteenth century. During the fourteenth century, Europe changed from silver in currency to minting gold. Metal-based coins had the advantage of carrying the value within the coins themselves. The exchange rates between the metals varied with supply and demand. Value could be damaged or destroyed by some currency manipulation, but financial stability generally rose as countries standardized the currencies.

The origin of finance can be traced to the start of civilization, dating as early as 3000 BC, as financially fortunate or savvy individuals and families provided the ability for early businesses to start and thrive. One of the early Greek pre-Socratic philosophers named Thales recognized (according to legend, recounted by Aristotle) that correct predictions about future events could drive value and personal wealth. He studied weather patterns and accurately predicted when a glut of olives would occur so that he could rent olive presses at low prices in off-seasons, then turn around and rent the presses at premium prices, thus establishing value through the management of assets he didn't own.

Banking originated in the Babylonian empire, where temples and palaces were used as safe places to store valuables. Initially, grain was the only valuable that could be deposited, but cattle and precious materials were eventually included. During the same period, other merchants supported trade by lending money with interest. These early banks provided loans backed by a farmer's grain harvest and lent to farmers and other traders bringing harvests to other regions.

Our modern banking system can be traced to Italy (during the Renaissance in the fourteenth century) and the wealthy families in Venice, Florence, and Genoa. The Medici

Bank was established in 1397. Banking spread from northern Italy to other regions in the Roman Empire and to Northern Europe in the fifteenth century.

In the seventeenth century, as governments began managing currency directly to support their economies, they created centralized banking systems. The first central bank began in Sweden in 1668. The Bank of England, the world's oldest, continually-operated central bank, opened in 1694, followed by central banks in Spain and France.

★ ★ ★

Following the Revolutionary War, America was bankrupt. It owed millions of dollars to private investors and foreign governments. By 1780, the American economy and government were in deep financial trouble. Before the Constitution was ratified in 1787, Congress created a federally chartered Bank of North America under the Articles of Confederation in 1782. That bank helped finance the war effort but had too few powers to succeed.

Hamilton recognized that the federal Articles of Confederation failed to support a viable economy. In 1787, he wrote to ask for a new government for the United States that supported its economy and paid off war debts. Those letters, and those from other leaders, led to the Constitutional Convention and its passage of the Constitution.

Hamilton also called on the new federal government to create centralized power in a president and key departments, including a "treasury" department. He lobbied for a central bank, a "National Bank," of the United States. After the Revolutionary War, the country elected its first president,

George Washington, and Hamilton was appointed the country's first treasury secretary. He was thirty-two. Hamilton embarked on strategies to refinance the war debt to raise revenues for the country, which came from tariffs on imported goods. It was a financing plan that continued until the passage of the Sixteenth Amendment in 1913, and the country's first federal income tax was imposed.

The Continental Congress authorized the issuance of the US dollar in 1786 and required it as the currency across the country under the Coinage Act of 1792.[4] Hamilton also established a central bank in 1791, the First Bank of the United States. The Second Bank of the United States was chartered in 1816, but it took until 1914 before Congress approved and set up the Federal Reserve to manage America's economy.

Americans today owe debts of gratitude to Hamilton, the first treasury secretary. Hamilton led the country out of the financial wilderness during his five-and-a-half years as treasury secretary.

★ ★ ★

Government financing and private financing existed side by side for many years, with private money leading the way. Private investing led to the concept of venture capital, which can be considered an American invention. Ancestors of venture capitalists include wealthy families who invested in various business enterprises, including whaling expeditions.

Whaling agents served as intermediaries between wealthy individuals and ship captains and their crews by setting up ownership shares in numerous expeditions to increase the

---

4    Coinage Act of 1792, Chapter 16, 1 Stat. 246 (1792).

chances of success. From these early investments in expeditions emerged investments in other business activities, such as agriculture, especially cotton and textile manufacturing. In America, both of those investment vehicles were centered geographically in New England but drifted to other cities such as Pittsburgh and Cleveland as the invention and use of electricity enabled new technologies, such as steel manufacturing.

Early investments in hard technologies evolved to investments (often via public capital markets through the sale of company stock) in other technologies such as those used by Eastman Kodak and Ford Motor Company and various telephone companies. As the recipients of funds changed and evolved, so did the various agents that connected wealth to business.

Historians credit the founding of the American Research and Development Corporation (ARD) in Boston in 1946 as the start of modern venture capital investing. The company invested funds in technology and other businesses, which were its portfolio companies. Investors provided direct funds to support ARD's work, and then the investors became partners with ARD.

Today, most investors in venture capital firms are limited partners, those who provide funds in return for expected future capital returns but cannot manage the affairs of portfolio companies owned in part by those firms. As venture capital evolved from the 1950s onward, investing moved west, primarily into Silicon Valley in Northern California, as venture investing remained robust throughout the Boston and greater New England regions.

Venture capital investing today captures much of the lore of American startups, often with a delusional belief in the success of such financial mechanisms. But there is much truth to this heroic perspective, and we honor those who have risked billions of investor dollars to solve society's problems.

Silicon Valley is considered the world's leader in business startups through venture capital. Venture capital investing was almost exclusively an American idea until the mid-1990s.

According to the Center on Entrepreneurial Innovation,[5] there are six "superstar" startup hubs in the world: Silicon Valley/San Francisco, New York, Boston, London, Beijing, and Los Angeles. Companies based in the United States receive about half of those investments, continuing to drive more and more new company formations in America.

Today, nine of the top ten companies are American, ranked by their overall capitalization. Apple, Microsoft, and Nvidia lead this list. America has twenty of the top twenty-five companies and thirty-five of the top fifty; many started as high-tech enterprises. Only Saudi Arabia's partially owned oil company is in the top ten. These major companies continue to spin off profits and ideas, often creating new start-up businesses.[6]

The government's role in creating the world's greatest entrepreneur expansion in history was prioritizing the individual. Certainly, this played out in the preservations of rights, but it also came over the course of America's building universities, community colleges, vocational schools, and charter schools. In our financial systems, we created vehicles for

---

5   Richard Florida and Ian Hathaway, *Rise of the Global Startup City: The New Map of Entrepreneurship and Venture Capital*, Center for American Entrepreneurship, September 2018, https://startupusa.org/global-startup-cities/.

6   MSCI, *Global Market Capitalization Rankings 2023*, https://www.msci.com/market-capitalization.

research and development funding. Our government offered tax advantages. We had entrepreneurs who often showed a heroic approach to business planning, including formal presentations to organize longer-range thinking, our technology transfer capabilities from our enormous college and university system, and the presumption that research grants should enable the transfer of new ideas to improve the human condition.

Today, too many people in both political parties miss the power of (mostly) unconstrained private business. The most underappreciated market force is the power of market signaling. By raising prices in the face of higher demand or lowering them to stimulate demand, the markets adjust to balance supply and demand and minimize shortages.

Government price controls never work and almost always produce supply/demand imbalances and shortages. Governments can and should default to creating better conditions for the private sector to solve problems and tax gains to produce agreed-upon revenues.

In the 1970s, America's economy stagnated while Europe's governments consolidated power by owning many sectors of commerce (such as telephone companies, airlines, and power generation). It took President Reagan and British Prime Minister Margaret Thatcher to blow up those systems and re-energize businesses, economies, and even countries. Doing so led to massive growth and wealth creation.

We remain enthusiastic about the legions of American entrepreneurs, the companies they have started and will start, the problems they solve, and the overall successful companies they build. We worry about regulatory capture, where regulators are "captured" by larger companies and strangle startups by creating rules and enforcement that benefit incumbent businesses.

We believe politicians on both the right and the left who demonize business are missing a real opportunity. America does not want more government. Overall, a country benefits from its new business creation by using a light regulatory touch, limiting its regulation to protect the personal safety of affected customers and employees as much as possible. While we are concerned about new trajectories toward over-regulation, America still appears poised to create the world's greatest entrepreneurs over the remainder of the century.

## CHAPTER 15

# ENSURING AN ABUNDANT FUTURE

OUR GREATEST HOPE IN THIS book is to illuminate that Americans should have an abundance mindset. We see continual and existential competition for resources in the face of a scarcity mindset. Yet, the data is clear: In the history of mankind, no nation has done more than America to advance freedoms and the prosperity of its people and others worldwide. So, how do we maintain this abundance for the next generation of Americans?

We have prospered and created more wealth than any nation in history because we empowered the individual over the collective. This empowered unbelievable innovation and discovery and moved the human condition forward more than ever. But it was the focus on the individual that released this human spirit.

We empowered the individual in the Declaration of Independence with, "We hold these truths to be self-evident, that all men are created equal, and they are endowed upon by their Creator with certain unalienable rights...." We empowered the individual in our Constitution with the Bill of Rights, which protected, among other freedoms, the right to speech, peaceable assembly, the free exercise of religion, and property ownership. We empowered the individual with human rights, equal rights, and civil rights and, in the process, created more buyers and more sellers. We placed those rights above the rights of the government. We prospered because our courts limited government power, forcing them to observe those rights.

Around the world, we empowered other individuals by creating an American-led world order based on the rule of law. In the process of opening these rights to others around the world, we opened markets, increasing not only the prosperity of the world but also the prosperity of the United States. It increased our access to raw materials, reduced wars between nations, held nuclear war at bay, and increased the security of ourselves and others. Abandoning that world order would be harmful not only to progress but to the prosperity and security of the United States.

By holding the genius of the individuals above all else, we enriched the collective. We witnessed stark evidence of atrocities from those nations who put the collective first, and we played a pivotal role in throttling back those powers in our conflicts with communism and fascism. Almost as though in paradox, we watched the sacrifice of many individuals who put the collective over their own interests. These are the people we consider heroes.

As we close out this book, we wish we could have spent more time on two issues, ones that deserve more space than we can afford. The first is the importance of education and the second is the importance of bridging the divides that exist between us. We believe these two issues are tied together and deserve discussion in a few paragraphs here.

## EDUCATIONAL FOCUS AND ATTAINMENT WITHIN THE UNITED STATES

Many of the Founders believed in the importance of education for the long-term success of America. Some, especially Jefferson and Adams, wanted a federally organized education system. They believed the success of America would be based in part on the knowledge and competence of its citizens. A common education system would equalize opportunities and create more productive citizens, which would become a leading edge for the future of America. To preserve and grow our republican democracy—a democracy centered on the informed consent of the governed—the population must organize its civic life by delivering better information about key issues of the times to citizens who can reason and understand. Moreover, citizens need a well-rounded educational experience to vote thoughtfully and wisely and resist the allure of demagogues with tyrannical views. Here's a great reminder: The Founders also believed in all Americans' high character and high virtue.

In the United States, almost nothing determines an individual's quality of life more than their level of education.[1] Even lifespans differ greatly between those who complete college education and those who never attend.[2]

---

1    See, for example, Bill Hathaway, "Want to Live Longer? Stay in School, Study Suggests," *YaleNews*, February 20, 2020, https://news.yale.edu/2020/02/20/want-live-longer-stay-school-study-suggests.

2    Jenesse Miller, "Life Expectancy Declines for Americans without a Four-Year College Degree," *USC Leonard D. Schaeffer Center for Health Policy & Economics*, March 9, 2021, https://healthpolicy.usc.edu/article/life-expectancy-declines-for-americans-without-a-four-year-college-degree/.

Education is essential to creating more productive citizens and giving the US an edge in international competition. To preserve and grow our democratic republic—a democracy centered on the informed consent of the governed—citizens need a well-rounded educational experience to vote thoughtfully and wisely and resist the allure of tyrannical views. America's education system is where youth learn that all people are created equal and that our system supports such ideals.

Many great things happen in America's public schools, giving children advantages. Today, the American system of public education supports nearly 14,000 school districts and almost 100,000 public schools and enrolls about 90 percent of America's children.[3] All public schools are supported by taxation by state and local governments; to a small degree, they are supported with federal funding.

America has trained teachers, who are free to work almost anywhere in the nation. They do an admirable job in teaching most subjects, and we see significant improvement in areas of concern.

In the early 2000s, one criticism of the American educational system was related to teaching science, technology, engineering, and math, now well-known by the acronym STEM. At that time, the United States had no schools that ranked among the top schools in the world. China was winning the STEM race for educating talented students. America paid attention and created magnet schools and charter schools to concentrate on teaching the STEM curriculum. Educators

---

[3] "Digest of Education Statistics: 2021," *National Center for Education Statistics*, https://nces.ed.gov/programs/digest/d21/.

everywhere raised their standards, and some American schools rose in the rankings to join the other best schools in the world.

BASIS, a charter school founded in Tucson, Arizona, had four of the top ten high schools in the 2024 national STEM rankings and six of the top twenty-five STEM schools in the US, according to a US News and World Report study.[4]

This clearly was a result of charter school legislation in Arizona. These results help show that when goals are set, the American system (including public, public charter, and private schools) can meet and exceed expectations and history. Even though American students still lag behind those in other nations in math, these results provide evidence that additional progress will result in the years ahead.

Educational funding that "follows" an individual student—whether they choose public or charter school education—is a reasonable public policy. We believe competition creates success. More importantly, parents yearn for options to the standard public education environment, and many today choose (where it's enabled) options other than public education. We delight in seeing parents select the right options for their children, whether those options are public education, charter schools, or other education driven by religious schools. Education funding should begin to follow the individual student as those options flourish.

The educational system needs constant improvement to be successful in a competitive world. Beyond STEM, we must focus on the basics, such as language and reading. Recent research draws straight lines between the number of words a

---

[4] "Best STEM Schools—Top Science, Technology, Engineering, and Math Programs 2024," *US News & World Report*, https://www.usnews.com/education/best-high-schools/national-rankings/stem.

child knows upon entering kindergarten and long-term educational success, and between reading by the third grade at third-grade levels and later successes in school and life.[5]

We worry that the version of civics we learned years ago has radically changed in America, and it is drastically less flattering to who we are as Americans. According to a recent poll, [6] 48 percent of Americans between the ages of eighteen and thirty-four would leave the US if it were invaded by another country, similar to what Russia has done in the Ukraine. The poll also indicated that 57 percent of Americans aged thirty-five to forty-nine would stay and fight, as would 66 percent of those from fifty to sixty-four. Why have younger Americans remained uneducated about why our liberty and freedoms are worth defending?

It appears to be true that we have recently allowed criticisms of the American order and founding conditions to dominate discussions regarding the value of teaching civics. This situation puts Western liberal democracy and its oldest, strongest constitutional democracy under threat. There is hope, however. The National Endowment for Humanities and the US Department of Education have granted iCivics and its

---

5   Anne Fernald, Virginia A. Marchman, and Adriana Weisleder, "SES Differences in Language Processing Skill and Vocabulary Are Evident at 18 Months," *Developmental Science* 16, no. 2 (2013); 234–248, https://doi.org/10.1111/desc.12019; Annie E. Casey Foundation, *Early Warning! Why Reading by the End of the Third Grade Matters* (Maryland: Annie E. Casey Foundation, 2010), https://www.aecf.org/resources/early-warning-why-reading-by-the-end-of-third-grade-matters/.

6   Maggie Kelly, "Nearly Half of Young Americans Would Flee if Russia Invaded, University Poll Finds," *The College Fix*, April 5, 2022, https://www.thecollegefix.com/nearly-half-of-young-americans-would-flee-if-russia-invaded-university-poll-finds.

academic partners funds to form a roadmap for education and promotions in American values.[7]

There are more than 7,000 degree-awarding colleges and universities in the United States. Our country has the highest number of students enrolled in post-secondary education, the highest number of students who have graduated from college, and the highest number of international students. More than four million Americans graduate from college yearly, a number far larger than any other country. About 40 percent of America's population (one hundred thirty million) have college degrees.[8]

As for citizens who have earned advanced degrees, America continues its lead. More medical, legal, and MBA degrees are awarded to Americans yearly than anywhere else worldwide. According to US News and World Report in its best global universities rankings, Western universities capture all top ten spots (seven in the US), twenty-three of the top twenty-five (with one in China and one in Singapore), and forty-four of the top fifty.[9] There are various world university rankings, and one can quibble with this list, but no one truly can dispute the massive educational lead that America and other Western democracies have and continue to have.[10]

---

7   "About Us," *Educating for American Democracy*, https://www.educatingforamericandemocracy.org/about-us/who-we-are/ (accessed August 2, 2024).
8   "Educational Attainment in the United States: 2022," Table 1, *United States Census Bureau*, February 16, 2023, https://www.census.gov/data/tables/2022/demo/educational-attainment/cps-detailed-tables.html.
9   "Best Global Universities Rankings 2024–2025," *US News & World Report*, https://www.usnews.com/education/best-global-universities/rankings.
10  "The World Comes to Us for Higher Education," comment by Peter Herford, in *The Optimistic American* podcast, https://youtu.be/watch?v=M61q1PTpATA, August 9, 2024.

We believe that the American post-secondary educational environment is not in decline. However, the costs of this education are becoming increasingly an issue, especially for lower- and middle-class citizens. In the world we see coming, the most important answer to America's divisions starts with an educated population. However, our greatest worry is bridging the divides in America.

## BRIDGING THE DIVIDES

How we communicate with one another matters. Here is the bad news: In a democracy that values free speech, it will get messy. We only have two pieces of advice: Be open to listening to others you disagree with and try being nice.

Every government system, including authoritarianism and democracy, requires a means to communicate its authority. However, our democratic republic system that prioritizes the individual requires the ability to disagree with that authority. Despite its challenges, media free from governmental control and/or oversight remains our primary defense against potential governmental abuses, serving as a vital check on power essential for preserving democracy. The government holds significant and centralized powers capable of enacting policies and decisions that can deeply impact the lives of its citizens. A free press operates as a decentralized watchdog. It ensures transparency and accountability by investigating and exposing corruption, human rights abuses, and other forms of governmental misconduct.

While we both see the significant challenges in social media, we also see the benefits of a more democratic and free press. In democracies, social media enhances the media's ability to protect the public from government abuses by facilitating rapid information dissemination and enabling citizen journalism.

Nothing in humanity's history is as important as the ability to communicate. Scholars estimate that humans started speaking 100,000 years ago. Oral communication likely started with storytelling because it captures history and aspirations to be passed among families, tribes, and generations. Then came symbols—in the form of pictures such as cave paintings and petroglyphs—invented around 30,000 years ago.

Most likely, writing didn't begin until the Bronze Age, possibly a bit earlier than 3000 BC. The first alphabet began in Egypt around 2000 BC and was followed by the Greek alphabet. Initial writings were often on stone and copper. Paper was invented during the Han dynasty in China, in the first hundred years AD. Later centuries put quills and ink at the disposal of human hands. Many of the earliest writings were done by members of various religious groups who had the time to distill verbal stories into written language.

In 1450, Johannes Gutenberg invented a printing press in Germany with metal moveable type. Early news (reported as facts, not just opinions) was presented to Americans via a printing press. After the first press arrived in America in 1638 from England, several colonies soon had presses. The first continuous news publication began in Boston in 1704, moving toward regular, and at times daily, publication. Today, it is a common belief that there are more than 1,200 daily newspapers in the United States, although it is difficult to locate specific, reliable sources.

Radio and television revolutionized America in turn. President Franklin D. Roosevelt gave his fireside chats on radio, and Radio Free Europe played a role in winning World

War II. Television then made its way into the news, and eventually, cable television seized sizable revenue shares from the news as it served as the intermediaries between the public and television.

Not long ago, many Americans trusted television figures like Johnny Carson and Walter Cronkite. They paved the way for how news could be delivered along with public station shows like The McLaughlin Group, which offered well-vetted stories. TV changed how we picked our political candidates, first noticed with the presidential debates between Nixon and Kennedy.

The internet arose in the 1970s and 1980s, beginning as a closed communication medium for government and academic researchers. As additional user-friendly tools were invented in the early 1990s, the internet opened its doors and windows to average Americans and other users.

The internet significantly changed the news-industrial complex. Today, virtually every media entity offers at least some news offerings via the internet, some requiring paid subscription agreements. But the move to the internet was a Faustian bargain for many media.

The internet created expectations that content would be free or almost free. Search engines like Google, social media sites like Facebook, video sites like YouTube, and direct communication sites like Twitter (now X) were provided mostly free of charge to the users (although often at the expense of other commercial solicitations like advertising or where users provided their data and utilization in return for free access). No longer did a large media company stand between the creators of content and readers/viewers.

There is also little doubt that today's mammoth social media companies face their own business declines unless their business models evolve. This is how the free press works, with free enterprise in a free society. The great upside is that we are facing an era where journalism is being democratized.

In authoritarian countries, governments meticulously design and control media to promote propaganda that aligns with the ruling regime's agenda. State-owned and state-controlled media outlets dominate the information landscape, ensuring a consistent and unified message that glorifies the government and its leaders while demonizing perceived enemies. Censorship is pervasive, with dissenting voices and opposing viewpoints suppressed or eliminated.

We understand the challenge of misinformation and fake news, which can undermine public trust in legitimate media sources and distort public perception. The algorithms that drive social media can create echo chambers, where users are only exposed to information that reinforces their existing beliefs. This can polarize societies and weaken democratic discourse. However, it also creates a fundamental check on government, a big advantage.

Yet, there is a dark side. Recent studies show that the public is increasingly tired of social media's negative and divisive language. A Pew Research Center survey found that most Americans (64 percent) believe social media platforms have a mostly negative effect on the country's current state.[11] This

---

11   Brooke Auxier, "64 Percent of Americans Say Social Media Have a Mostly Negative Effect on the Way Things Are Going in the US Today," *Pew Research Center*, October 15, 2020, https://www.pewresearch.org/short-reads/2020/10/15/64-of-americans-say-social-media-have-a-mostly-negative-effect-on-the-way-things-are-going-in-the-u-s-today/.

sentiment is shared across different demographics and political affiliations, with concerns particularly focused on spreading misinformation, hate speech, and the overall decline in respectful discourse.

What's the solution to this problem? We argue that market forces, rather than government, are better equipped. Several companies have launched initiatives focusing on creating culturally aware and positive content. They aim to foster stronger, more meaningful connections with audiences, a testament to the potential of market-driven solutions.[12]

However, to the critic, we say that history has repeatedly proven that your darkest predictions rarely come true. We have a long history of proving the skeptic wrong.

Thomas Malthus was an eighteenth-century British economist and religious leader. He published his philosophies in 1798 in a book titled, *An Essay on the Principle of Population*.[13] Fortunately, his philosophies had little influence on America's Founders. Malthus forecasted exponential population growth, yet he believed the resources needed to support such growth were linear due to disease, war, famine, or other calamities causing death. The evolutionary theorist Charles Darwin may have based his idea of natural selection theories on this concept.

Malthus was wrong, very wrong. He did not foresee the impact of the Industrial Revolution on humanity. Technologies and other automated activities transformed and

---

12    Dimitri Cologne, Catherine Sackville-Scott, and Awie Erasmus, "Social Media Trends 2024: A Culture-First Reset for Brands on Social," *Ogilvy*, January 22, 2024, https://www.ogilvy.com/ideas/social-media-trends-2024-culture-first-reset-brands-social.

13    Thomas Malthus, *An Essay on the Principle of Population*, 1st ed. (London: J. Johnson, 1798).

expanded the limitations of his day's agricultural and manual or animal labor practices.

Even now, we can't see how our future will be transformed. Yet, it is wise to be optimistic that our future is abundant and our progress will continue to move forward in good ways, even if the pace feels exponential. Many other writers and commentators, including those worried about the existential risks of climate change, see the future as limited, maybe even in decline, following these same standards of a Malthusian catastrophe.

In this new digital world, anyone can tackle almost any important problem. While there are exponential thinkers in government and big business today, they often run up against a "not invented here" syndrome that constrains the execution of new thinking. It is rare to find good examples of entrepreneurs who remain inside these cultures, cultures that are threatened by a democratization approach that diminishes existing power.

★ ★ ★

We certainly could not leave this story in this age without addressing climate change. We believe it is real; we believe it is man-made. We don't believe it is a greater threat to the world than nuclear war, as expressed by President Biden and other political leaders. Many doomers only want to focus on the fanatical and ignore the great improvements we have made and will continue to make. For example, humans reduced their reliance on coal as fuel. Solar, wind, and battery storage costs have declined substantially, down by 85 percent since 2010. The International Energy Agency predicted in 2020 that solar power would soon become the cheapest source of electricity in history.[14] And we are greatly encouraged by the technological advances and rising political support driving experiments with small nuclear power plants.

The future is not about disruptive stress but about disruptive opportunity. We have all been given the tools to change the future. Entrepreneurs engaging in exponential thinking, utilizing AI tools, increasing internet speed, and accessing amazing volumes of information are daily inventing a new and robust future.

Is there evidence of an abundant future? Sure! Some examples would be the declining cost of electrical power, the decline in the cost of airline travel, the power of computing, the rise of sensors enabled by the Internet of Things, lower poverty rates, higher life spans, major declines in auto and airline deaths, overall child and women and older adult mortality rates, and increases in literacy, among others.[15] As unbelievable as it seems, humans live in the most peaceful time in human history despite massive population growth, with deaths due to wars declining exponentially over the last 600 years.[16]

Today, even the poorest Americans have access to telephones, running water, television, and flush toilets, luxuries even the wealthy didn't have one hundred years ago. Through the system of higher education, America will continue to build even more talent to win the contests for whatever drives

---

14 See also "The Exponential Growth of Solar Power Will Change the World: An Energy-rich Future Is Within Reach," June 20, 2024, *The Economist*, https://www.economist.com/leaders/2024/06/20/the-exponential-growth-of-solar-power-will-change-the-world.
15 See, for example, Diamandis and Kotler, 2012.
16 Steven Pinker, *The Better Angels of Our Nature: Why Violence Has Declined* (New York: Viking, 2011).

future wealth, and we will continue to attract well-educated immigrants to build upon American success.

We believe America's future will be bright. As it becomes so, it will open the world to more opportunities for free expression and the free flow of information, powered by humans' overall freedoms to seek more individual liberties and opportunities.

The point is that our new way of communicating has dramatically increased the number of people who can confront our problems, and alas, it has also increased the number of people who can try and divide us. We see an upside to freedom-loving, economically incentivized, selfishly self-interested ideas that the system empowers. And we believe that the dividers who use incendiary language will be constrained because the customer wants something different. In America, the self-interested drivers of innovation—entrepreneurs (who know how to make oodles of money)—continue in place. America is the land of promise and continuing optimism in solving daunting and important problems. For the US, data and logic say we still have decades, if not centuries, of abundance in front of us.

# CONCLUSION
# THE CASE FOR OPTIMISM

THE INTERESTS REPRESENTED AT THE first Continental Congress resulted in a compromise that became the US Constitution. However, a more profound debate continues and often eludes us. There existed a clash between the values outlined in the Declaration. While it declared the equality of all men, it protected the economic interests advocated by Southern states, where all men were not considered equal.

It is inescapable that the Constitution was founded upon the moral principles espoused in the Declaration. The notion that all men are created equal and endowed with certain inalienable (or "unalienable" under the Declaration's language) rights was not solely intended to represent white male property owners. While the delegation remained divided on the issue of slavery, the original document did not contain the terms "slave" or "slavery."

This was no accident.

There were fifty-five delegates at the Constitutional Convention, of which twenty-five owned slaves. However, even among slave owners, figures like Washington and Jefferson acknowledged the inherent evil of slavery in various writings. Franklin, a former slave owner, and Hamilton became members of anti-slavery societies. A division existed at the Convention, and the most significant rift from our nation's inception was between those who sought to abolish slavery and those who viewed it as vital for their economic survival. Madison wrote, "It seems now to be pretty well understood that the real difference of interests lies, not between the large and small but between the Northern and Southern States. The institution of slavery and its consequences form the line of discrimination."[1]

A government was formed based on the premise that the individual is paramount. From this foundation sprang forth numerous marvels. It remains the greatest accomplishment of any government to empower the individual over itself. Consequently, it was inevitable that the Constitution would embrace capitalism and free markets, where individuals could rightly claim ownership over what they created. No other nation, in no other era, has contributed as much to human progress. This progress is on an exponential trajectory, offering the possibility of curing cancer, developing driverless vehicles, reducing poverty and illiteracy, and diminishing child mortality. We may even significantly extend human life, all thanks to the empowerment of the individual.

It was also inevitable that a nation dedicated to these principles would eventually champion civil rights, equal rights, and human rights. We view each of these advancements as milestones that have propelled our nation further along the path of recognizing all men and women as deserving of dignity and equal treatment by the government. These rights fostered more buyers and sellers who improved our economy, and they were necessary to fulfill the dream of our Founders—a dream

---

[1] James Madison, *Notes of Debates in the Federal Convention of 1787*, ed. Adrienne Koch (Ohio: Ohio University Press, 1966), 324.

that we believe was envisioned but could not be instantaneously realized.

We hold the heroes of this movement, dedicated to the individual, in high regard. These men and women, although imperfect, advanced the cause of liberty and equality. We did not create a flawless union; instead, we fostered a more perfect union than the one we inherited. Individuals such as Jefferson, Adams, Hamilton, and Washington made significant sacrifices for this cause. Later figures like Lincoln, Tubman, and Douglass sacrificed even more to propel this mission forward.

Certainly, the practice of slavery stained our country. There is no justification, but it proves that we are part of a great historical arc toward greater morality.

Alas, while our Creator endowed us with freedom, freedom is not a universal value. Values such as religion, party, class, and, most importantly, power are more universal than freedom. We believe in the endowment of inalienable rights through which we have been created, albeit with ups and downs, which led to the greatest economy in the history of humanity. Yet, some believe that short-term prosperity is more important than these values, and they promise that if we surrender them, they will deliver.

While many foreign enemies of liberty seek to overturn democracies, we also battle those at home who value the collective group over the individual, as they define it. We embrace the words of Martin Luther King, Jr., who taught us to love our enemies, to foster revolution through peaceful means at home, and to judge people by the content of their character rather than the color of their skin. This is based on the common narrative of America.

We view the alt-right and woke left as voices for a more authoritarian future. Yet, our values insist that they be granted the right to speak, even when they would deny us ours. We see ideologies that classify people by groups not only as immoral but also as unsustainable.

We believe the values of the United States, Western liberal democracy, and free markets are worth defending. Remember, there has been nothing like the United States in human history. Most criticisms compare us to utopia, but compared to other civilizations throughout history, we find no comparison that has propelled humanity forward faster and further. Countries that divided citizens into oppressors and the oppressed, as promoted by the alt-right and woke left in America today, witnessed incredible atrocities and spectacular failures.

The big questions concerning the US and Western liberal democracy revolve around our way forward. Critics ask how we can be optimistic with all the things going wrong—such as China's rise with a state-run economy, the economic disparity between groups, the fear of technology taking our jobs, and the concern that our children might not fare as well as we have.

The evidence triple underscores that these fears are fallacies.

China will not overcome the United States due to its insurmountable demographic problems, geography, and, most importantly, the repeated failures of its economic form of government.

The economic disparities across America are exaggerated, and technology will not take our jobs; it will dramatically improve our quality of life.

Moreover, it is pretty evident that our children will do better than we have. While we applaud efforts to address the inequities in our society, particularly in education, the problem of inequity is simply overblown. In his 2022 book, *The Myth of American Inequality: How Government Biases Policy*,[2] co-author Phil Gramm builds a case based on Census Bureau data proving inequity between classes is at an all-time low. Gramm examined current income levels and found that individuals in the top bracket earn fourteen times more than those in the bottom bracket. This marks a significant high over fifty years. However, a different narrative emerged when considering transfer payments directly made by the Internal Revenue Service to lower-income individuals and subtracting the tax amount paid by the wealthy, middle class, and poor. That comparison revealed that income inequality is at its lowest point in fifty years!

The best place to find reasons for optimism is in the data rather than the news. Logic and rationality provide the rationale for optimism. Over the past century, and even in the past fifty years, people in the United States and the world have made remarkable advancements in improving the human condition. Barring the destruction of American values, the evidence indicates that we will achieve even more significant progress in the next fifty years.

We keep making strides to reduce poverty, illiteracy, and hunger. As capital continues to flow toward us, we serve as a beacon to the rest of the world. People from other parts of the world are willing to give up everything to call America home, and those who don't still aspire to emulate our way of life.

Although it can seem that way, given media positioning, America is not irredeemably polarized. It is diverse. We encom-

---

[2] Gramm, Ekelund, and Early, 2022.

pass various demographics, including rural and urban dwellers, old and young individuals, employers and their employees, the rich and the poor, and racial and religious alignments. Americans are a multifaceted group with many opinions and perspectives, which has been the case throughout our history.

Certainly, there are some new factors at play. One such development is the ability to market opinions to millions of disgruntled listeners/viewers through various social media platforms. The news media is inclined to highlight polarization and focus on extreme viewpoints because it sells. More viewers prefer to consume controversy, to have discernment done for them, and to feel they have found a source that supports their fears. And, while the two-party political system has served as a crucible to support effective governance in the past, the bases of these political parties have become more extreme, leading more voters than ever to register as "other" or independent.

Today's most significant difference is the inclination toward demonizing the other side through extreme positions. We face an existential crisis where the victory of the opposing side in an election is seen as the end of the Republic. However, consider that Obama served as president for eight years, and the Republic survived. Trump was president for four years, and the Republic survived. Biden became president and served four years, and the Republic continued to endure again.

By constantly demonizing the other side in every decision and race, we perpetuate a perpetual crisis. With the media taking sides—leaning right or leaning left—a narrative of this existential crisis is disseminated. Winning becomes more important than free elections, freedom of speech, the rule of law, and the peaceful transfer of power.

We must understand how we arrived at this point to bring about positive change. We must understand the "alternatives" on the right and left and how they have come to dominate political parties. But if we desire to make positive change, we have options. There are new alternatives to explore.

We remain optimistic about Americans because the majority still believes in America. Most of us overwhelmingly support free markets and a society that does not categorize individuals based on oppressor-oppressed dynamics. We prefer to see and respect our fellow citizens as unique individuals with their voices. Most Americans support free speech, even though they acknowledge its messiness through the occasional expression of outrageous ideas. They believe better ideas arise from greater freedom of thought, and freedom of speech expands intellectual liberty.

Our optimism comes from a society based on the individual and evidence that it is not retreating from its commitment to this cause. Americans overwhelmingly desire a better life for themselves and their children. But Americans still believe in who they are and genuinely love who WE are. Even so, they recognize their imperfections and are dedicated to the idea that we are creating a more perfect union. All evidence says that Americans can count on precisely that.

We have never been prouder of our collective identity as Americans!

# ACKNOWLEDGMENTS

We, the co-authors, thank everyone who, over many years and in many settings (especially during our weekly jogging and hiking sessions) engaged with us on the issues we discuss and supported the development of the concepts underpinning *What's Right with America…And How We Can Keep It That Way!* We appreciate the insightful critiques, steadfast encouragement, invaluable guidance, and never-ending laughter.

We are grateful for our families and friends, whose belief in our work sustained us during long hours of research and writing. We acknowledge the contributions of our colleagues and mentors, who challenged our ideas and sharpened our arguments with thoughtful feedback and spirited debate.

We sincerely thank our first outside editor, Mary Holden, who took our work seriously and spent many uncompensated hours editing and supporting us. Mary introduced us to our great agent, Claire Gerus, who, after many dedicated hours, connected us with the team at Post Hill Press, which made this book possible; we specifically thank Anthony Ziccardi, Publisher; Debra Englander, Consulting Editor; Caitlin Burdette, Managing Editor; and Cody Corcoran, Cover Designer.

We value everyone who collaborated with us on publicity, especially the team at *The Optimistic American* podcast, which brings our book's themes to life daily.

## Special Recognitions by Paul Johnson

Countless individuals help shape our lives and the ideas we hold dear. In writing *What's Right with America*, I have been blessed to journey alongside brilliant minds, steadfast friends, and inspiring leaders. This book is not merely a collection of ideas; it's testament to a cause: the enduring promise of America, a nation built on empowering individual Americans.

I am deeply grateful to Larry Aldrich for joining me on this remarkable journey. I also want to thank dear friends Wayne Howard, Mike Lieb, David Berg, Steven Roman, my spouse Dr. Emily Bashah, my nine siblings, and my children. Our countless hours of debate and discussion about the American political system have been the crucible that forged many of these ideas.

I owe a special debt of gratitude to those whose insights and passion have inspired this book. I was honored to work with General Wesley K. Clark (Ret, U.S. Army) during his presidential campaign and subsequent efforts to improve civic discourse. His leadership has been a guiding light. Lawrence (Larry) H. Summers, economist, former Secretary of the Treasury, and former President of Harvard University, one of the most perceptive intellectuals in modern politics, has consistently offered an honest, unflinching analysis of our nation that has bolstered my confidence in its future.

The conversations I've enjoyed on my podcast, *The Optimistic American*, have been equally enriching. Engaging discussions with author Peter Zeihan, whose work, including *The Accidental Superpower: The Next Generation of American Preeminence and the Coming Global Disorder*, reshaped our views of global dynamics, and with Professor Steven Pinker, whose data-driven insights reveal how democracy, free markets, and the power of the individual have propelled human progress, have profoundly reinforced my belief in our national promise. I also thank Nobel Prize winner Professor James A. Robinson, co-author of *Why Nations Fail: The Origins of Power, Prosperity, and Poverty,* whose scholarship vividly demonstrates that only governments that protect individual rights can secure lasting prosperity.

I acknowledge the influence of those whose writings have reached me from afar. The forward-thinking visions of futurist Ray Kurzweil, whose predictions about technology have proven remarkably prescient, and the natural optimism of Matt Ridley, author of *The Rational Optimist: How Prosperity Evolves,* continue to illuminate the path ahead for America and the world.

A memorable dinner with Ronald Reagan and Pierre Salinger (former press secretary to President John F. Kennedy) reminded me that despite our differing political philosophies, our leaders' unwavering optimism truly matters. Their steadfast belief in America and its destiny has been a profound source of inspiration.

All these remarkable individuals have, in their unique ways, helped shape the central theme of this book: that governments that empower and safeguard individual rights – whether civil, equal, human, or property rights – are the only ones capable of driving long-term success and prosperity, saving humanity even! When a government gives its people the freedom to create, innovate, and flourish, it sets the stage for extraordinary progress. The evidence is clear, and America's future will amaze us all.

## Special Recognitions by Larry Aldrich

Many individuals throughout my business career shaped the themes in this book. After graduating from Georgia Tech, I planned a career designing and building airplanes or spaceships, only to decide one day – after listening to a litigation attorney in Atlanta, Georgia, teach a pre-law course – that I wanted to emulate him. I recall thinking, *"That man is a showman – I want to be just like that!"* I achieved that goal to some degree: I attended Tulane Law School and became an antitrust litigator at the U.S. Department of Justice, representing the "People of the United States," one of the highest honors of my life. Only in America ...

Serving the People shaped my views about the power of the federal government, the U.S. Constitution, and American laws that make everything possible. My subsequent career in the media honed that service and deepened my understanding of the powers and rights protected by the Constitution. Later, leading a newspaper organization in Tucson, Arizona, underscored the importance of independent media to American success. I honor the memories of many mentors, some no longer living, yet whose guidance endures.

During my eight years as newspaper CEO, our organization launched one of the first online newspapers in the country. Bob Cauthorn – the "rocket scientist" behind that effort (and a reminder that I remain enamored by rocketry) – helped me push the limits of my business thinking while staying true to our mission to protect and defend the First Amendment.

Running a business presents many challenges – some big, some small, some crises, and some minor annoyances that feel like crises. Every Saturday, I vented with my running group, the Slow Dawgs, as we trudged up the beautiful yet demanding Sabino Canyon trail. If you have never visited Sabino Canyon in Tucson, I urge you to go. Thank you, Slow Dawgs – where every Saturday, we tackled <u>every</u> business and community issue in Greater Tucson, even if we <u>forgot</u> those solutions by the time we finished our bagels and coffee.

As a newspaper CEO, I joined nearly every key business organization in the region – if not the state. I met many business leaders, especially Jim Click (to whom I dedicate this book), who cared deeply about everyday Americans as they built successful businesses. I particularly recall the leadership of the Southern Arizona Leadership Council, where I was honored to serve as the second chairman and drive both business and community progress. I cannot name every leader, but you know who you are.

After my time with newspapers, I worked in various capacities, including as CEO of the clinical arm of The University of Arizona College of Medicine. In that role, numerous doctors and university leaders helped me navigate the difficult choices required to serve our patients while running a successful business.

After medicine, I moved toward retirement and embraced the opportunity to follow my children and grandchildren to Greater Phoenix. There, Paul Johnson took me under his broad wing, helping me achieve better health through running and hiking and deepening my understanding of the key issues discussed in this book. Paul, you are fantastic, amazing!

I conclude by thanking my wife, Wendy, who has stood by me for over 50 years. More than anyone else, she kept me both sane and grounded. You might expect an aging, average-height, wiry, bald man to be humble. Possibly not! But

Wendy possesses the remarkable ability to point out my many flaws lovingly. Wendy always lets me "do my thing" and spend hours pontificating, as she tunes it all out. Without her, I am lost. Love you, Wen!

We recognize that this book results from collective effort and shared passion. We celebrate our successes and the challenges that enriched our work and remain committed to continuing the conversation about the ideals that make our nation remarkable. Thank you for joining us on this journey toward an even more significant, powerful, and generous America.

To everyone who has sacrificed, debated, and believed in the promise of America, this book is for you. Thank you for being part of this extraordinary journey toward a brighter future for our nation.

Finally, this acknowledgment expresses heartfelt thanks to all who have contributed and reinforces the central theme of *What's Right with America:* celebrating the ideals, institutions, and individual freedoms that have made our nation a beacon of hope and progress. And will continue to do so ...

# ABOUT THE AUTHORS

PAUL JOHNSON HAS BEEN ACTIVE in politics and policy for over forty years. Early in Johnson's career, he was chosen to be a delegate with the US State Department, first serving in Saudi Arabia where he studied its oil cartel business to understand a major Middle Eastern political issue better. After the fall of the Soviet Union, the State Department selected him to assist Poland in implementing new local governing systems as the new government in Poland was moving closer to democracy.

Over many years, Paul studied and visited almost every major site of genocide, including Cambodia, Rwanda, and Bosnia. He also went to China, studying the changes from the Great Leap Forward under Mao to the incredible economic progress after it liberalized it markets. He also visited Russia after the fall of the Soviet Union. As a result of his travels on behalf of the government, Paul received sobering insights into the dramatic differences between authoritarian governments and Western liberal democracies.

In 1990, Paul was elected mayor of Phoenix, Arizona, where he served until 1994. In 2016, he was selected among the "Top 16 People Most Likely to Watch in Arizona." In 2021, he was inducted into the Marquis Who's Who and received its Humanitarian Award. He has also managed the regional efforts of several presidential campaigns.

LARRY ALDRICH HAS A DEGREE in civil engineering from Georgia Tech and a law degree from Tulane Law School. He has been a federal antitrust prosecutor and a company lawyer for Gannett Co., Inc., as well as president and CEO of the two daily newspapers published in Tucson, Arizona (*The Arizona Daily Star* and *Tucson Citizen*).

Following his newspaper career, he launched Tucson Ventures, the first venture capital firm headquartered in Southern Arizona. He also co-founded and chaired the Southern Arizona Leadership Council, a key non-profit representing large and small private businesses.

He served as senior vice president and then chief executive officer of University Physicians Healthcare, which provided all clinical services for the over four hundred medical doctors at the University of Arizona College of Medicine.

He remains an active member of the District of Columbia Bar Association and a staunch defender of First Amendment rights.